No Parent
Left Behind

Lisa M. Calicchia

No Parent Left Behind
Copyright © 2020 by Lisa M. Calicchia

Library of Congress Control Number:	2020908354
ISBN-13: Paperback:	978-1-64749-113-0
Hardcover:	978-1-64749-115-4
ePub:	978-1-64749-114-7

Printed in the United States of America

 GoTo Publish

GoToPublish LLC
1-888-337-1724
www.gotopublish.com
info@gotopublish.com

No Parent Left Behind

By Lisa M. Calicchia

Dedication

Dearest Nichele, Niana and Nila,

You can do anything as long as you try!

Love always,
Mommy

Preface

We must put the village back together again!
—Lisa M. Calicchia
August 21, 2006

There is an African proverb that says, "It takes a village to raise a child." But how can a village raise a child when the village itself is messed up, in crisis and completely in disarray? As parents, we are supposed to rely on the village. Unlike African villages where the immediate and extended families make up the village, the American village has changed to consist of many different entities. Society is raising our village. Some television and radio networks are raising our children. The churches, community groups, business partners, caseworkers, social workers, non-profit organizations, children organizations, juvenile systems, PAL centers, group homes, foster care, kinship care, and sadly the streets are raising our children.

Our children are getting information from society in the most disturbing places. What is on some of the radio, reality shows, and videos? Most programs have topics or television shows that have all kinds of sexual content, violence, and profanity. All kinds of inappropriate foolishness that our children are not supposed to be watching. Our young children shouldn't come into the classroom and be able to give a better summary of what went on while watching television at all hours of the night instead of recalling time spent with their parents. Our children today can tell you the lyrics of any song and give you a summary of any show without skipping a beat. Students can clarify misunderstandings in television episodes, compare characters between the programs, shows and the radio personalities they listen to. But as soon as we ask them to summarize a paragraph, compare characters within a story,

3

or conjugate verbs, the students can't. They look at us as if we asked them to speak backward in a foreign language or to build spaceship by themselves.

We now have a different generation of parents than the one that most people grew up with. The current generation of parents drops their children off at school and ceases all other responsibility. We have a generation of parents who believe that since they dropped out of school and are illiterate, then it is all right for the third and fourth generations to continue the downward spiral. I have actually heard parents and grandparents say this, "Well, I dropped out of school, and I's be fine." Coming from the ghetto, the bottom, the hood, or the trailer park is now glorified instead of being a daily inspiration for graduating from high school and going on to college or taking up a trade. They don't want to be disturbed until June when it's time for their children to get out of school. We must find a way to change this generation one parent at a time. Changing one parent will change many children, teachers, classrooms, schools, districts, states, and countries one at a time.

Teachers and staff must deal with a multitude of dynamics to navigate through daily. We must work with decisions:

- made by many powers that be such as governors, superintendents, CEOs, area executive officers (AEOs), board members, principals and politicians, some of whom have never worked in a classroom or have been so significantly removed by time;
- legislations, at times, to create bureaucratic red tape, hold or defer funds from various districts for many reasons and such as politics, lawsuits, consent decrees, etc;
- testing legislations at the federal, state and local level, which to them, defines the effectiveness of instruction
- that still do not deal with the issues of equity for ALL children, families and communities.

4

We repeatedly go to workshop after workshop after workshop to meet the professional standards that are required of us. We continually take classes to be knowledgeable of new and important information pertaining to our area of experience.

There are the few bad apples that make the rest of the profession look bad. Society sensationalizes the few teachers who cross that professional line. There are teachers who get away with so much because they have a close relationship with the administration, or they scheme their way through the system. We call them the principal's pets: resource teachers who don't teach their assigned subject, staff who get to come and go as they please, and personnel who act inappropriately with other staff and children. Some of the bad apples just cruise through the system getting a paycheck. Like other professions, teaching is not composed of perfect people. There is much we must deal with. We take most of it in stride.

The overall lack of parental involvement is a common theme of concern voiced among teachers and schools. It truly has become an epidemic. Too many parents are not taking care of their children or behaving in a manner that suggests that they aren't interested in the welfare of their children. Too many grandparents and other family members are slowly killing themselves trying to take care of children and themselves. Our grandparents need to be back on the porch watching our neighborhoods as they did when I was little. I couldn't walk from block to block without seeing a senior outside on the porch talking to a neighbor or working in the yard. Many grandparents and family members are so heavily burdened with caring for their children's children that they cannot look forward to the golden years of their lives. Other parents are just indifferent.

The question for myself and other professional educators isn't, what can I do? The question now is, can anything be done? No matter how unbelievably chaotic and crazy the world may seem today, the answer is, yes, something can be done! We must encourage all parents to take responsibility and accountability for the lives we have brought into this world. To all who read this journal, I challenge you to reach out to a parent or guardian. I challenge you to softly whisper a better way of time management for a stressed family or to model to parents a better way of disciplining and speaking to their children. Teachers are no longer just teaching children but have become surrogate parents and advocates for multiple lost generation.

Names have been changed to protect the privacy and identity of the children, families, and staff members that I work with daily. I commend all who take this journey with me.

Table of Contents

Teachers' First Official Days
Wednesday, Friday August 23-25,

Here We Go Again

Well, summer is officially over. I started work today. Every year we must go to a meeting, or as the bigwigs call it, professional development. We meet all day to introduce ourselves to our new staff members, go over the goals, objectives, expectations, and any new procedures for the year. Each principal does their own thing as far as where they have their first day. We get treated to breakfast and a good lunch. I love the cookie tray at two o'clock. Our school happens to meet in a conference room at a nice hotel that's about ten minutes from the school. Anyway, today was a good day. It was nice to see some faces I haven't seen all summer. A lot of teachers had to work summer jobs to survive over the summer. Some teachers enjoyed their summer.

After the meeting, the real work begins. Now I hope some person down at the school board or headquarters is reading this part. After the meeting, we, the teachers, must go to our school to set up our classrooms. I do want to let you know that some of us did try to come into the building while we were still on vacation to get started in our room. Depending on the school district, some teachers are allotted a couple of days to get their rooms done. I am in a district that allots for one paid day to work in your classroom uninterrupted. I still haven't been able to figure out why we must come in after-hours during the week and on the weekends to work tirelessly like a slave trying to get our classroom set up for the school year. We don't expect to have everything up that we took down at the end of the year. But we do expect our classrooms to be functional and welcoming for the first day of school. I applaud the principals, area executive officers, and school systems that allot time for us to set up our rooms. That week before school starts, we are running around like a chicken with its head cut off. Someone once asked me, don't we have people to set up our rooms? No, indeed, we do not have anyone to help us get our room together. We get on our family and friends' nerves every year with the packing and unpacking and the moving and removing of our instructional materials. That doesn't include the other things that we bring into our rooms that makes them more bearable to be in. Things such as microwaves, little refrigerators, plants, etc. What about the teachers' lounge, you ask? Are you serious? Most of the time, we don't even get to make it to the lounge. If we do, we must wait in line to use the microwave. There's not enough room, or someone has eaten your lunch that you were looking forward to eating.

Sunday. I am excited about tomorrow. Yeah, I miss my summer break and really needed it, but I miss my paycheck too! The Lord knows I'm always behind in September and must catch up with my bills as soon as I can. All teachers have some excitement and anxiousness on the first day of school. You don't know who your students are going to be. You wonder if you've had one of their siblings. If you've been in the system long enough, you may have taught a parent or two. I came into the building again today to do some more work in my classroom. I needed to hide and shove some stuff somewhere. I don't have storage or space in my room, so I need to make them magically disappear. I don't have everything I would like out such as my calendar, which I can't find, but it's enough for me to get started on the first day. I'm quite sure I'll find needed materials as I go through my boxes. There were a lot of teachers in the building today trying to get as much as they could do before the building closed. They usually keep the building open until eight o'clock at night for us to work in our classrooms. The first quarter of the new school year is about to start. I really am excited and anxious about the new school year. I don't care how many years you've been teaching, there is always some excitement and anticipation about the new school year. You want to know if some of the names on the list are boys or girls because you're not sure. There is such a curiosity about what your class is going to be like.

I Am A Gift

By Lisa Calicchia

I am a gift

As you can see,

But do you really know

What's inside of me?

Love, kindness, peace and joy

Not a child who wants to annoy!

Greatness, determination and dedication,

I am a child of God's creation

Mom, dad and family

Please do all you can to encourage me!

I'm a king a queen and so much more!

A surgeon a pilot and one to adore.

A spirit, a soul, a brain and a heart,

Just wait, I'll show you I'm smart

So, don't just look and judge what you see

You have to open me up to see my destiny!

Help me be great, your love uplifts!

Children are precious, priceless, irreplaceable gifts!

Quarter 1

Teacher Objective: Teacher will set the tone for classroom management by teaching classroom rules, procedures, routines, behavior consequences/rewards and instructional goals.

Let me give you a little background knowledge. On the first day of school, teachers must set their high expectations from the very first moment the students encounter you. Now seasoned teachers who have been teaching for a long time usually have a little easier time with transitioning the children into a classroom routine. We know what we are going to expect and what we will and won't tolerate. A lot of teachers know their students' names by the end of the day, if not by the end of the week. We can also identify if we had a sibling of the student in the previous year. Seasoned teachers within the first week of school, within a month's time, pinpoint the characteristics and behaviors of each student. We know which one the talker is, whiner, troublemaker, studious, sarcastic, aggressor, shy, overachiever, class clown, etc. The list of individual and multiple personalities goes on and on. We are constantly changing desks around to have the most compatible chemistry between the students. For example, students who were in the same class the previous year usually need to sit away from each other because they will talk all day. A child who is easily agitated needs to sit by himself, but not totally isolated from the remaining students. The class clown needs to have a limited number of children around, so he/she doesn't have a consistent audience for his/her foolishness. Sometimes we strategically place a lower-performing student next to a higher-performing student. I could go on and on. On the first day, we seasoned teachers are usually ready to go at the sound of the bell. Now don't get me wrong, all teachers must be ready that first day, as well as every day.

On that first day, we must show the students that we are in control. It's just that new teachers are a little more anxious and nervous because they've never had the experience of starting the first day on their own. The very new teacher has a much more stressful first day because they lack all the above-mentioned experiences and more. For the new teacher they must start from scratch to get their up and running.

I remember my first year as if it was yesterday. I wanted all the students and parents and staff to like me. I wanted to please everybody all the time. I worked every day until seven o'clock at night. Some nights, I even made it until eight o'clock. I lie to you not. Now things are very different. Eight years later, I'm out the door after I get the materials I need for the next day's or week's lesson. I leave around five, two hours after school lets out. I tidy my room, and I'm out. Eight years ago, it was just my oldest daughter, Whitney, and I at the time, so we were together all the time. She went to the school where I taught, so it worked out well. Now I have two more beautiful girls and I need to be there for them.

We do the best we can with what we have. What I'm trying to say is there is a lot of work that goes on before the first day of school. We've never just shown up for the first day and just start teaching. Never!

> *Parent/Guardian Objective:* The parent will have child ready for school by sending child to school with needed materials and on time daily.

One of the parents' responsibilities is to send their child to school with the needed materials. I've never understood why some students are not prepared for the first day of school. They have new clothes and shoes but don't have the required materials to work with. Any person with a child in their house should have the basic materials always. Those items are pencils, crayons, glue, notebook, notebook paper, composition book, and a ruler. Students do work, and teachers do teach within the very first hour of school. We do start our lessons on the first day of school.

Day 1
Monday, August 28
You Have to Start from Scratch

On the first day of school, as well as the first month of school, I'm really focused on getting to know my students and establishing the classroom rules and procedures. I don't assume anything. I don't need to know what they did last year because today is the day that matters. Today I went over everything, and I'll go over a hundred times more before the school year is over. I went over how to sit at the desk, where to put their things, and how to raise their hand if they need me. I'll go over how to line up for the hall, the bathroom. I went over all the procedures for everything there is to do in school. I talked about their behavior expectations. You name it, I talked about it. I assigned seats, which I guarantee will change at least six times this year. I had to be ready from the first moment they were with me, or they were going to think that they could run the classroom.

As far as the population of children that came today, I had only six out of twelve children show up. That's half the class that didn't show up! I was surprised. When you've been teaching a few years, nothing tends to surprise you. Usually, the first day of school is overflowing with children and parents full of excitement. And for the children that did come, the parents dropped them off and left. In most Pre-K and K classes, the parents stay around for at least ten or fifteen minutes to make sure that they are okay as students transition and settle in their new classes. Not this year. It's more like "YAY! School's open, I have a babysitter, now I gotta drop this kid off and go!" Oh, and let me explain for those of you who say, "Only twelve children? That's great!" To the naked eye, twelve to fourteen students are great. But

14

to the trained professional, when you have children with some of the backgrounds that they have, it really means that I still have twenty-five to thirty children in the class. You'll understand in a few minutes. Anyway, one of the children that showed up was a precious child named Jaron. Jaron was a challenge as soon as he walked in the door. And the family knew he was something else, that's why they left. By the end of the first day of school, Jaron, a five-year-old, had told me several times, I don't want to do this, I don't want to do that, I don't want to color. What do I got to do this for? I want something to eat. And on and on and on. And for that day, he was right. He did not do any work, he did not color, he didn't attempt to do anything. He had tantrums and outbursts and yelling spells. He wasn't going to do any work. He was standing firmly in what he believed in his mind. He wasn't going to back down either. I think this is the first time that I had an extremely rough time with a student on the first day of school.

So my day with my remaining new students was overshadowed by this one child who has obviously never been to school before. The rest of my new friends seemed sweet. Four of them had been to school before, and two of them had never had any formal in class training. As I've told you, my wild-child Jaron has never set foot inside a structured class. So, I came home exhausted. My body had to get used to standing up on my feet all day long. My throat is sore from talking. My legs and back are in so much pain. Then I still had to get my three girls situated with dinner and homework and the normal nighttime-routine. What a first day. I didn't even get to go see my mom for her birthday today. I did call her, though.

Day 2
Tuesday, August 29

Today the children were able to go to their resource, music. My students have resource at eight in the morning. I always try to sit in on their resource class at the beginning of the year so they can have a smooth transition. I want them to know and to understand that wherever they go, they still must display the same expected behavior no matter what adult they have before them. They must model appropriate behavior at all times to all people. As soon as we returned to the classroom from music, I started the diagnostic testing in reading to find a baseline of where the children's level is in reading. Ms. Brown and I worked cooperatively to get it done. We couldn't spend the whole day testing. Her students came to my class while I taught, she tested and vice versa. Outside of the testing, it was like the first day all over again. I went over all the classroom procedures. I had the students practice them as well. I read stories to the children and gave them academic related coloring activities as well. I already started into the curriculum which incorporates multiple learning songs and games that I will to teach my students. Most of the songs have rhyming words for children to gain understanding of a specific skill. The day went by pretty quick and was uneventful.

Day 3
Wednesday, August 30

Today I continued the testing for reading. Overall, the children were well behaved for the most part because they don't know anything about me. But I'm sure they are ready to try me. I was able to complete the testing for the students to get a basic assessment of where they are academically. Most of the children do not know any of their letters, sounds, and high-frequency words. There are only ten words that we test them on at the beginning of the year.

We also had our first of many fire drills. We must have so many in the school year. That wasn't too bad. The children followed my direction very well, considering it was the very first time for them. The exit door is right next to mine, and we just walk out of that door and straight to the chain-link fence that surrounds the school grounds.

Day 4
Thursday, August 31

Today I started the diagnostic testing for math. Once again, a lot of the children are unable to recognize their numbers, shapes, and colors. Some can't count either. Some did know how to count to ten, but that is not impressive at all. By the time children are five they should at least be able to up to twenty. There isn't anything new or out of the ordinary done for today. I'll just be glad when these assessments are done so I can really get into a normal routine and teach even more. The first few days are all basically the same. I'm working on establishing the routines and procedure for academics and behavior expectations for the year. There is so much that I have to do already. I really don't have any time to write today which has been therapeutic for me.

Day 5
Friday, September 1

It is the end of my second week working and I am exhausted. The children seem to be having a difficult time adjusting to school. I have three students who've been to school before. The remaining children are having an even more difficult time. They are whining about being hungry, tired, and having to go to the bathroom all day long. They don't know how to hold pencils, write their name, or any other skill needed to be successful from day one of their academic career. They can't even color on the level that a five-year-old should be coloring or drawing. When I ask the children to draw me a picture half of the children yell out

17

they can't draw. The other half scribble scrabbles an unidentifiable picture. After the week's assessments and conferring with the other teachers, we all realized that we will have a long school year. The consensus after the first week of school is that the students are terribly behind.

Saturday. I was still thinking about all that needed to be done into this new school year. I was thinking about all the school supplies and materials I wanted to buy but didn't have the money to. I need to but some Clorox wipes to sanitize the desks daily. I need to go but some containers of sticky letters and numbers for the children to reinforce letters and numbers I've introduced already. I was thinking about all the activities and lessons and just everything there is to think about pertaining to school. Sometimes I think that I think too much. This weekend I need to get their work folders ready. I started today but haven't had a chance to finish. My two youngest daughters, Faith and Trinity needed their head done. I also had laundry and other house work to do. I'll get the work folders completed before the month is over. I've already collected work samples from the students. I always collect and keep work from the beginning of the year. I used to compare the students' growth and progress or lack of it throughout the year.

Sunday. The girls and I went to church, then went over to my pop's house and napped. I am so exhausted. In between my nap and dinner, I was thinking about my goals, hopes, and expectations for this school year. I'm hopeful that I'll have a good school year this year. Last year wasn't too bad. I was really shocked as to how unprepared and how low performing children are entering into the school system.

You'll find that most of the Sundays, if not all, are basically the same. I get to relax and sit around or get downtime only when I go visit my family's and friends' homes. Those are the only places where I can't keep busy with housework and laundry. After we ate dinner, we went home. Then I gave the girls their bath so they could go to bed.

Monday, Labor Day

No school! I rested today. I needed a break already. Working for all those days in a row takes a toll on your body, when your body has become used to having the time off. My feet, legs and back hurt. I need to go to the gym to build my puny muscles and gain endurance for standing on my feet all day long.

Day 6
Tuesday, September 5

Well, today was like the first day all over again. The students had three days off, so I really had to exaggerate the importance of the classroom rules. The children's behaviors are always off if they are out of school for more than three days. So just imagine more redirection of behavior after every three-day weekend or winter and spring breaks. Today was like the first day of school. The lessons are different, but the implementation of classroom management is in full force. The first couple of weeks of school seems redundant because we must keep going over the classroom rules, routines and procedures. In addition to that, every time a new skill or concept is introduce, we must spend time on that skill in addition to review all that was previously taught. It is like a constant flow of the old with the new.

Day 7
Wednesday, September 6

We all had to go to the parking lot today after dismissal. That's what we were told for the afternoon announcements. We were supposed to have a staff meeting, but it was cancelled. I thought it was weird that every staff person had to be outside. Usually, only those staff members without a homeroom class are supposed to do outside and hallway duty before and after school. Well, news always gets around school fast. Apparently, a parent wrote a formal letter to the principal and headquarters complaining that we don't do enough to watch the children after school. The letter allegedly quoted one of the teachers that said she can't police the children every second of the day. If the parent is upset that something will happen to her child after school, then she should be up here when the bell rings to get her child. I don't understand how parents have the audacity to continually complain about the school systems, and yet they don't see how they contribute to the problem or don't help to solve any problems. Like I said usually, teachers who don't have an assigned classroom have outside duty. But that wasn't good enough. Her child got into some argument or fight after school before she got there, and the school gets reprimanded for it. I think the teacher is right in one aspect of it all. The teacher is right, we are not the police, and we should not be policing children's behavior all day long. we are supposed to be teaching all day long. that is what we are supposed to do. It is their responsibility to ensure that their children know what to do before, during, and after school. Not too long after dismissal, a parent calls my colleague who teaches second grade, infuriated because her child didn't get off the bus where she was waiting for him. They didn't know where he was. He dismissed him to get on the bus. The parent called the police, the police came up to the school, and everything. The teacher worried about her student all night long. To make a long story short, I found out the next day when he came in that he didn't get on the bus because, he said, he stopped to tie his shoe. Some children ride the bus every day, some don't. There is no communication to us or the bus driver, most times, when there is a change of schedule, so a bus driver wouldn't know who is supposed to get on the bus that day. Things happen, and we must train our children what to do if things don't go the way that they were planned. To make sure he didn't miss the bus any more the teacher told him to tie his shoes if needed before he left the classroom. I wonder if the mother told him that as well. I wonder if she told him about his responsibility of going to the bus stop from class and straight to the bus stopping for nothing. I was wondering why he didn't go to an adult in the school instead of taking it upon himself to walk home. Did his parent tell him he could walk home? I don't know but, children must be taught and shown as much as possible before the parents just let them go in life and then we get the blame when they didn't train their child accordingly.

Day 8
Thursday, September 7

I don't even remember what happened in class today because of what I overheard after school. While I was in my room cleaning up and preparing for tomorrow, a parent yelled at her child, "YOU DON'T DO ANYTHING RIGHT! I HATE YOU!" I don't know what he did to warrant such a strong statement but, I was I was speechless as my heart just sank. Tears swelled up in my eyes. She went on cussing at him while she walked pass my classroom. I went out into the hallway to see and possibly talk to her to see if there was anything I could do. But the young mother was already next door talking to the teacher, who was giving after-school tutorial for today.

An adult should never ever tell a child that. Never, under any circumstances, should you blurt out hurtful statements that can ruin a child's self-esteem forever. Parents forget that their children will eventually grow up, and how they are raised has an impact on their perceptions of life. Not one child in this world asked to be here. So, if you have misguided anger, then it should be directed at yourself if you're that angry. You created them. I don't care how angry you are with a child. Some things you just don't say out loud. We all have negative thoughts about different situations. I myself have been working on thinking about what I want to say before I respond immediately to the things that my children do. I have to especially do that with my teenager. For example, I'll tell her I'm disappointed in her choices of behavior, not in her. If my oldest daughter Whitney doesn't clean up the kitchen before she goes to bed, I tell her my feelings about not getting the dishes done. I don't go on and on about her being a no good lazy child that isn't getting her chores done. She knows that if she doesn't get her chores done then there is going to be something that she wants to do but can't because she doesn't get the dishes done. I don't attack who she is as a person. We all make stupid mistakes. But would we rather be called stupid or that the choice we made wasn't a good one. The bad choices that children all make, doesn't have to dictate who they are because of the negative choice. There is a huge difference. If you concentrate on the actual behavior that you want to change, then the focus is the behavior and not the child. You don't tell children that they are stupid and no damn good like their mommy or daddy. If that's the case, then as I said earlier, you should take it out on yourself and not on the child. I want to choose my words carefully because words are damaging. I still remember things that were damaging to my self-esteem as a child. It doesn't matter if it was meant or not. It was said, and the damage is done. You can't take words back.

Anyway, from what I overheard, the second grader apparently made some bad choices in behavior. Nothing that I heard called for his mother to go off on like she did.

Day 9
Friday, September 8

I'm happy that today is Friday, and it's a payday. I get my first paycheck for the new school year, and I'm happy because I can start playing catch-up for the first two months of pay that I earn. I'm usually only a month or two, at the most, behind in bills. I try to save enough money for my mortgage and food for July and August. The money definitely doesn't include family trips or vacation. I'm looking forward to the years when I can take my girls on vacations somewhere at least twice a year. Well I'm striving for once a year. I want to take them to Disney World, Hawaii, and on a cruise one day. But for today, I need to sit down and see what I can pay for right now. I say one.

Today a new student hid himself in a locker, so no one could find him. It wasn't funny at the time, but I did laugh later. The principal and other staff members were all over the school in a panic, looking for this little first grader. I couldn't leave my class, but I did step into the hallway from time to time to see if there was a child wandering around out there. Apparently, he got upset that his teacher wouldn't let him eat lunch with her, so he ran out of the room. When she came to the door, he was gone already. So, what we usually do is call up the office to let them know a student has run out of the room. The office will make an announcement, asking the child to return to his classroom The child usually returns or shows up with another staff member.

Saturday. We were stuck in traffic all day long on my way to my uncle's wedding in Philly. We missed the actual wedding ceremony but got there in enough time to get something to eat at their reception. It's days like this that I dread because I know I'm going to be behind in the work I brought home. I still haven't been able to get the children's work folders labeled. As a result, I have a pile of class work and assessments that need to be organized and filed away.

Sunday. Normal day. I went to church. I went home, took a nap. Got up and did hair, clothes, dinner, and got ready for tomorrow. I bring a bag of work home every day to get done, but it seems as if I just don't get a chance to get to it. There is always something to do and always the unexpected looming in the atmosphere.

Day 10
Monday, September 11

My morning didn't get off to a good start. On this day and around this time are ceremonies that remember the victims of the 911 tragedy. My heart goes out to the victims and the survivors of that awful day. I remember that I was in the middle of teaching on that morning, when parents starting to come get their children out of school. Obviously, we were unaware of the attack while we were instructing in our classes. By eleven o clock, schools were dismissed early. So, I was a little somber this morning from watching the news coverage on all the ceremonies that were going to take place today. For the morning announcements at our school we usually have a moment of silence to remember the victims and their families.

My oldest daughter, Whitney, didn't help either by not getting her morning chore done. Her chore in the morning is to make lunches. Sometimes I need her to help me with her younger sisters depending on the time. So, I was rushing and running late, which made me leave my lunch. It was a good lunch, too. I arrived at my school at about seven thirty. That was good, but all I did was get my jury summons from off my desk, signed in at the office and left right back out.

9:30 I'm at jury duty! So, while I'm down here waiting for whatever it is I'm going to do, I'm worried about what's going on in my classroom. I wonder who the substitute is. I wonder if they are following the lesson plans or if they are just doing whatever. I hate taking days off from work. I'll go to work terribly sick before I take off. I've never served on a jury, so I don't know the process to talk about it. I am happy that I found a nice leather sofa to sit on. Anyway, I don't like taking off from work because if my class gets a substitute, then anything can happen. If they split my class, then the students will be taught by three different teachers. Well another teacher is out also because of death in the family. The beginning of the school year is the worst time to be off. The students have just a little idea of how I am. They have a little idea of what to do and what not to do. I don't want any of my materials messed with or destroyed, lost, or stolen.

Day 11
Wednesday, September 13

I am more exhausted than usual today. When I'm having a bad day, I tell my students that I'm not feeling well. They usually have mercy on me when I say I don't feel too good. Even little children have compassion and want to show you that they care by behaving a little better than they usually would. I had a rough day today because I had a rough night. It's the bad days and nights we have in our personal lives that sometimes make our already-stressful day more hectic. I must put my needs on the back burner to teach my students. Faith isn't in school today because she is sick. It isn't gravely serious, but I still feel bad that she is feeling miserable. I can say my students were more cooperative today. I was able to get some lessons completely taught. Usually I must spend a lot of time getting the children focused after not being with me for a couple of days. But that wasn't the case today. They had mercy on me I guess.

I think all families should have an emergency plan for various situations. I'm not even going to go there right now. I just speak for myself. I have somewhat of an emergency plan. When I think I'm getting ready to have an emergency, I call all the family and friends I can to let them know I may be asking for help with a potential situation. For example, yesterday schools were closed for elections. I didn't write about it last night because I was exhausted. My plan was to get up and go vote, do my marketing and other errands. But of course, my plan was nothing like it. The only thing I did get done on my lists was voting. My four-year-old, Faith, was sick overnight. I was up all night long with her. In the morning, I took my other two girls to my girlfriend Trianne. She was supposed to watch them anyway while I went to the market that day. I took Faith to the clinic, and after two hours, they told me I had to take her to the hospital because she had blood in her urine. Well, I was shocked because I didn't see any blood in her urine, and that was new to me. I called my other girlfriends and my family to let them know what was going on, just in case. I picked up my other two girls from Trianne and took them to my girlfriend Melissa because Trianne had an important appointment. I dropped the other two off, and I went to the emergency room with Faith. I did call her father, and he was aware of what was going on. I just knew that he was going to say that he would meet me at the hospital. Instead, he said that he was going to get on the Internet and find out some information. If I'm already at the hospital with his daughter, why would he think getting on the computer would be of any help? He didn't say he would meet me at the hospital. He didn't say he could watch the other two girls. He said he would get on the Internet. What kind of foolishness is that?

26

I would have shown some other support other than getting on the computer. He never showed up at the hospital. And I'll leave it at that. I don't have anything nice to say right now, so I won't say anything at all. To make my very long Tuesday short, Faith had strep throat that she probably caught from this dirty school, and she needed IV bags. I spent my whole day in the hospital instead of getting my errand done and resting. Even though her father didn't help any as usual, I'm thankful I have friends and family who can help me in an emergency. It's what villages are supposed to do.

Yesterday reminded me of one of my good friends, Evan. He's in my village too. He never watches the girls, but if I need him to fix something at my house, he's there getting it done. I really must really commend him because he is a single dad who takes care of his kids. He doesn't start all kinds of confusion with his children's mother either. He completes side jobs to make sure he makes ends meet. He goes to work every day, and he is going to electrician school. I watch his oldest daughter after she gets out of school. He is legally doing what he needs to do to take care of his children and make a better life for himself. I commend all the parents who are doing their part.

Day 12
Thursday, September 14

I know it's time for me to make a career change. My patience is very short. I used to have a lot of patience for a lot of things. But now my spirit has changed. I spend more time on behavior management than I do teaching. Yesterday was too good to be true. I guess they have no more mercy. The children want to argue, fuss, talk, play, and tease each other. They tattle all day on the simplest things. And it's not

27

just kindergartens. The same things happen in all the grades. All day long, teachers must spend their time on things the children should have been taught at home. That's why so many of our children around the country are behind now. The child's behavior isn't a major factor or concern to the parent until they are getting into trouble at school or within the community. The parents just assume that "they know better" and will do great in school. If you haven't taught your child how to solve problems at home, then how are they going to solve them at school? If you let your child suck their teeth, huff and puff, roll their eyes at you, what makes you think they won't do it at school? All day long, throughout the year, all my days are filled with "Oooooo, she did this"; "Oooo, he touched that"; "Leave me alone"; "Get out of my face"; "Why you lookin' at me?"; "Mind your business"; "I'm going to tell"; and so on. I wish someone could do a study on how many times a teacher's name is called in one day for foolishness. It's early in the year, I know. But guess what, experienced teachers know it will be the same in January and the same in June. I can't train them to behaviors that they should have been learning for the first five years of their life. The children don't even know how to speak to each other. They don't even know how to talk. They scream or yell loudly and seem to think that is a normal tone to speak. And the way they solve their problems is with violence. The first thing they want to do is hit, push, punch, and kick. In case I haven't said it already, please don't tell your child, "If somebody hits you, hit them back." These are the days of my school life!

Day 13
Friday, September 15

Ms. Brown came and told me today that one of her kindergarten students told her that her eight-year-old second-grade brother wants to have sex with Ms. Brown. I wish someone could tell me why an eight-year-old is even talking about having sex with anyone. When he was asked where he got that idea, he said he was watching it on television. I won't mention the name of the cartoon, but the cartoon is for adults. I tell you, we have to hear, see, and go through so much foolishness through the year. Personally, especially when I taught third grade, I received two letters from my male students expressing their feelings for me. I thank God I've never had one that was out of the ordinary for a typical boy going through puberty. No student was ever that bold enough to say that they wanted to do anything with me. One little boy wrote me a letter to say that he liked me like a girlfriend. I did call his mom to see if she could talk to him about his feelings being inappropriate. I also talked to him and let him know that he couldn't like his teachers like a girlfriend. I told him he could like his teachers because teachers do a good job teaching him and make learning fun. I don't know if he understood or not, but I had to let him know just in case he didn't.

Day 14
Monday, September 18, 2006

It's the third week of school, and already I feel overwhelmed, burnt out, depressed, and disgusted. I love teaching children. I love facilitating learning for children eager to learn about anything. When I taught first grade, I loved teaching the children and watching their brains flourish right before my eyes. When I taught third grade, I loved exposing children to different aspects of learning and life that extended past their neighborhood. I had problems here and there with administration, the school system, and other things. But the point here is that I was able to teach much more when I taught those grades. Last year, my principal "asked" me to teach kindergarten. He didn't have to ask, but he was courteous anyway. There are some great principals. And then there are those who are not. That's for another book. Principals can move a teacher to whatever grade that a teacher is needed, if the teacher is certified to teach that grade or content area. I know I can be a great teacher at any grade. I just chose to be certified in early childhood because I couldn't decide on one subject that I would want to teach all day long. In elementary school, I get to teach all subjects. I just didn't know eight years ago that elementary school is the hardest. So, I am in the beginning of my second-year teaching kindergarten. Over the last three weeks, I've concluded that I'm not teaching anymore. I'm raising other people's children. I know a lot of people are going to have a problem with that statement, but it's true. And as we all know, sometimes the truth hurts. With that conclusion, I just want to teach and not raise other people's children.

Days 15–23
Tuesday, September 19- Friday, September 29

I'd be lying if I tried to keep up with the daily confusion that has been going on in the last nine school days. Yep, another school year is here. Already I want to know, where are all the parents? It's been just sixteen school days, and I'm ready for the summer break already. In the first fifteen days, I have had enough stress to last me the entire school year. My face has broken out with pimples and bumps twice. I got physically sick already with a bronchitis attack and strep throat. It's from this dirty school with poor-quality air. What is going on with these children at home? They come to school knowing nothing. They don't know their name. I take that back. Most don't know their birth name. They can tell you their nickname and their parents' nicknames, but not the ones on the birth certificate. And they don't know how to spell it. They don't know colors, shapes, numbers, or letters. I feel like a broken record so maybe people will get tired of hearing this and do something about it. They don't know what I mean when I say draw a picture. It is very frustrating. But they can tell you their nickname and everything else that doesn't have to do with school. They can sing every song on the radio. They can tell you every grown-person conversation verbatim. Every year, teachers have so many more responsibilities added to our already-overloaded plates. Thanks to *No Child Left Behind*, so many wonderful teachers are being let go because of tests that really don't prove anything. So what about no parent left behind? Where are the federal laws that mandate that high-risk parents are held accountable for their own children? Where are the tests that some parents need to take to be rated as highly qualified parents? They don't even have to prove that they're highly qualified. There isn't anything at all for that matter that qualifies someone to be a parent in the first place Just have them prove that they can take care of their own child. Where are the laws to govern parents' behavior in public schools and just govern their behavior, period? Where are the federal laws that mandate parenting classes for first-time parents?

The school systems are raising children more than teaching them. I didn't go to school for eight years to raise other people's children. I want to teach children. Yeah, I said it. I'm not afraid to go out on a limb and tell the truth that no one seems to be dealing with. What's the difference, you ask? When children come to me, I am supposed to be teaching grammar, sounds, letters, writing, forming letters, and so on. What are we teaching the first part of the year? We are teaching the basic skills that they should have been trained to do at home. I'm teaching them how to sit in a chair, how to actively listen to a story. I'm teaching children how to write their name. Most of our students can't even recognize their names on the desks and lockers. I'm

31

teaching children manners and etiquette skills. I'm teaching them how to greet people when entering a room. I'm teaching them how to say yes, no, good morning, please, and thank you. I'm teaching them the appropriate way to solve problems without cussing, hitting, and calling each other nigga, dog, or yo. These children haven't been trained to sit down, write, draw, color. They don't have ADHD, ADD, or any other problem. They have an undocumented case of NHT. You've never heard of it. It has been around for the last couple of years. It's becoming an epidemic. No home training! They can't sit still unless there is some type of rapid movement, as in television or video game. So, when they get in front of a teacher, the teacher is not captivating enough to sustain the child's attention.

How old are they? Well, I'm glad you asked that question. They are four- and five-years-old. Yes! I said four- and five-years-old, who come into school telling you what they want to do and don't want to do. Children who openly defy any authority figure in the classroom. Some of the children want to climb on tables and chairs. Some of the children always try to run around the building, cafeteria, and classrooms. They haven't been trained to sit still for any significant amount of time. A lot of the children haven't been trained to sit down and eat. They want to walk around eating in the cafeteria. Then they tell me that they want some Kool-Aid. They are not at home. The list goes on and on.

Day 24
Monday, October 2

In case you didn't notice, there is no entry for this weekend. I was too distraught. I thought I had a terrible weekend. I cried all weekend long. I had a few moments where I didn't. But for the most part, I cried all weekend long. Teachers have feelings too. We have a life of roller-coaster emotions that we put aside for seven hours as a part of our professional responsibilities. The government just continues to add more on us as if we don't have anything else to do. That's not even including staying after-hours to work in our rooms, coming in early, or taking work home. Things we don't get compensated for. Anyway, I myself had some undocumented issues this entire weekend. I was in a place where I felt as if I'm always there for everybody and nobody is there for me. It all started with my soon-to-be ex-husband, because he doesn't want to come to my house to pick up the girls there. He wants to meet somewhere else in the neighborhood. I wanted them to go from our home to his home. I don't want them to associate going with their dad to a landmark. Then every time we pass that designated meeting area, the girls are going to think that they are going to go with him. People just don't understand the unnecessary hardships and confusion they put on their children. It's still near the house. He says he has bad memories. I wanted to say, "You caused most of the bad memories." I didn't. Just the thought of him is a bad memory for me. I don't even have to see him to have a bad memory. So, who is he to say anything at all? My soon-to-be ex-husband gets under my skin. I must really work on regaining my control over my feelings. I must do better with my outlook and perspective when it concerns him because he really isn't worth any of my tears. I can let this divorce process uproot me like this. It's easier said than done, but I know I will be healed one day.

In addition to this terrible divorce process, my twelve-and-a-half-year-old daughter, refuses to take any initiative at home, my riding lawn mower is broke, and the people went from a $40 assessment fee just to look at it to a $470 bill, and I can just keep going on about this crazy weekend.

All of that got pushed right to the side this morning when thirteen-year-old Ramon told me he slept outside last

33

night. This child is an older sibling of a little girl I had in my class last year. He included me in his circle of trust and just started opening up to me when he picked up his sister. Even though his sister isn't in my class anymore, he comes by my class to talk to me from time to time. When you think you've got it bad, there is always worse for someone else. It's eight, and my school day is just starting. Once a child tells you that he slept outside last night on the school steps because his mother told him to leave, it makes all my problems seem insignificant. I know I only heard one side of the story. But he looked like and smelled like he slept outside. It's just horrible when it is a child that is going through worse times than you are. I asked if there was anything I could do to help, and he told me no. He looked so hopeless and weary. He looked as if life had already gotten the best of him. He already has a social worker, and he said that he was going to call his social worker later on that day. After he left, I immediately started to think to myself, *Can I take on a fourth mouth to feed? What can I do to help? How can I be another positive person in his life? What can I do besides pray? How can I enroll him into school? Where is his mother?* Countless thoughts were running through my mind, just adding stress on top of stress.

Today, a colleague is upset because she had to make the choice of pressing charges against a child for biting her. To take it to another level, obviously, the parents were livid about the decision the teacher made. I don't know all the exact details, so I won't comment too much. It's just another example of the things we go through, and this is on the elementary level.

Day 25
Tuesday, October 3
Little Things Make a Big Difference

Parents are turning in field trip money late. The organizations and businesses that host our schools are very kind, understanding people. However, business is business. They have bills to pay like everyone else. So if a school can't come up with a deposit, then they will usually accept the next school that can send it. Field trips are usually on a first-come first-serve basis. A lot of indoor trips have a capacity limit for fire safety and other code regulations. For every one school that was able to lock in a reservation for a trip, there were many others who didn't get one. I don't know how to explain to parents and the families year after year, that if they don't turn in the money, then we will have to cancel the trip. I've seen parents pay for video games, name-brand shoes, but not for an educational field trip. There are many education trips that come to the school, and then there are the traditional ones that take the children out of their immediate neighborhood. Not only do we have to pay for tickets in advance. We must arrange for busses as well. We must count all the students, plus possible chaperones and the teachers that are going. We must call the bus companies and make reservations with them as well. Then we must notify the cafeteria staff in advance for them to prepare bag lunches for all the children. It takes a lot of work to plan a trip for over one hundred children. Parents, please pay the field trip money on time.

A parent came up here to ask me about why another child hit her child but hasn't been up here one time to volunteer or ask what she can do to help her son. I wanted to say "Lady, give me a break. Not one time have you asked me anything about the progress for you child. You don't even speak to me, but you have the audacity to come up here because of what your son said. Lady go back home!" That is what I wanted to say but didn't. I came to find out that he was lying about somebody hitting him. So, she walked up here for nothing looking real crazy. And even though she doesn't ask how her son is doing, I tell her anyway. Like she did any other time, she just looked at me, said o.k. and walked away.

I appreciated the parent who came in to check on her son, knowing he has some behavior issues. One of my grandparents sent in a container of wipes today. I was so happy and touched. It was as if I received a lottery prize or something. I typed a nice note and had all of my students sign it.

While I was in the post office after work today, a grandmother was complaining that she had to go pick her grandchild because all he would do is sleep and wouldn't wake up in his pre-K class. The grandmother said that his mother let him stay up all night last night until one in the morning. She said that she has told her daughter time and time again about not letting the child stay up all hours of the night. Of course, the mother doesn't listen, which causes the student, teacher, and grandparent to be affected. I think it messes up the universe, and the equilibrium is off in the world. There is no balance. There are too many children and adults out of control. For all of you who are reading this saying, "I do what I am supposed to do as far as my child's education!" So why should it matter to you? The reason it should matter is because your child goes to school with other people's children, and you don't know how they were raised. And furthermore, your child may be smart, but how do they behave? How does your child act out of school? How does he behave in the malls and in the supermarkets? How does he act in the church, synagogues, and other sacred places? Is he having tantrums at home or in the middle of the store? Is he screaming at the top of his lungs agitating other shoppers? Is your teenager huffing and puffing and rolling his eyes while talking underneath his breath? Does your child outsmart you, telling you all the reasons why he wants or "need" a cell phone and other expensive electronic gadgets?

Day 26
Wednesday, October 4

First thing this morning, I saw some previous students that I taught over five years ago. They remembered my name and were happy to see me and I was happy to see them. They are still in school and doing well. That makes me smile as I headed into my school. It does a heart good. A parent came in and helped me with a stack of papers to color, grade, cut, or file. I was so appreciative and grateful that she was here helping me today. The work never ends.

So far, one of my students has missed nine days out of twenty-six days of school. That's almost 50 percent of absences already. The kindergarten and pre-K teams had to meet with the principal on our lunch break about more paperwork crap. We must discuss the assessments and related data to determine where we need to step up instruction and so forth. I am so frustrated today. I am sick and tired of the same foolishness. Teachers must be highly qualified, certified, and must jump through hoops to do everything under the sun to prove that we are worthy of teaching. It is time for a massive change with the parents of today's children. Some of our parents must be mandated to prove that they are highly qualified and certified. Make some parents take classes and tests. We can make all the provisions for teachers and students all we want. We mandate that for everyone in the world, but where are the parenting classes and assessments for parents? Parents don't get assessed for anything until social services or the law has gotten into the picture. When those two agencies get involved, then sometimes it's too late. A tragedy has usually happened.

I saw a young lady breast-feeding her child right in front of the entrance/exit door at dismissal time. There isn't anything wrong with breast-feeding in public. I think that some moms could be a little bit more discreet and selective about where to breast-feed. Breast-feeding your baby right at dismissal time with your boob hanging out for all the children to see—really, that wasn't the best place to nurse. I understand that when the baby needs to eat, he must eat. If there are better options to use, then they should be used. She could have gone into the teachers' lounge. She could have had a blanket or a nursing shirt to cover up her exposed breast. A lot of children haven't been exposed to that part of life. We just got to love our parents.

Day 27
Thursday, October 5

Today was okay. I must turn in progress reports that I just received yesterday. I'm tired of all this paperwork. Some of it is needed, some of it is not and are just redundant like all the behaviors I encounter daily. My wild child didn't come to school today, so my day was a little less stressful. Having eight boys and only three girls is just an injustice, if you ask me. Now I know if you are reading this, you are saying, "You only have eleven children in your class, what could you possibly be complaining about?" Well, sugar, let me tell you something: When you have a class of children who have limited to no skills at all, and behavior problems too, it's really like having twice as many children in the classroom. With low-performing children compounded by negative behaviors, it could possibly be classified as a special-education class. Oh, don't get me wrong, I had my fair share of twenty-seven to thirty different personalities in the classroom. However, with kindergarten and pre-K, you have to literally do *everything* for almost all of them, and I mean everything. And that's where the parents come in. I should not be teaching a four- or five-year-old how to write his first and last names for the first four months of school. They should have exposure to or knowledge of colors, shapes, and numbers. How can children in America live in here for the first five years of their lives and not know anything? These poor babies have little to no vocabulary development. There are so many things within their lives and in their daily activities that would expose them to the terms that they need to develop a rich vocabulary of basic words. Everywhere we go and everywhere that we turn, there is math, reading, and science all around. There is no excuse for every child in America not to know certain skills and basic vocabulary before they formally go to school. For example, children should have some concept of transportation, fruit, vegetables, farm animals, zoo animals, city animals, and family members, and those are just some categories that children should have exposure to before they ever get to school. If a child doesn't have the exposure to pictures and objects in the world, then their vocabulary is limited. Then if their vocabulary is limited, once they enter school, then they have a difficult time associating with pictures and words. They are unable to follow directions because they can't pick up red crayon and color the chair. They can't draw a line from the left side of the page to match something on the right. Too many of our children have very poor language development. They are unable to communicate because no one talks with them to develop their language. A lot of children are yelled at or talked to, but they are not talking with anyone.

Every day I ask my girls how their day went, and did they learn anything new or interesting. When I ask my toddler what she did, I usually know the answers, but I ask her anyway. I want them to know that I really care about their day in school. I ask all three of my girls in the three different stages that they're in. For my toddler I ask did she

39

do anything special today? Did she go anywhere? How was her day? Whether or not she can answer the entire question isn't important. What is important is that she has opportunities to express herself and be listened to. What is important is that she's learning to have a conversation and dialogue. So as time progresses, by the time she turns three, she will have a very extensive vocabulary for a three-year-old. I tell her the names of all objects, whether she can say them or not. I talk with her and not just to her. She will get to a point where she will ask questions, and I will not shut her up because I'm tired or don't feel like it. And will I have those days? Do I have some bad days now? Yes, I do! When I do have my little funky days or moments, I just kindly direct her to my oldest daughter, and she still would have fun asking many questions or just talking away. A lot of times I just must get my attitude together and put my personal feelings aside and just deal with it. Sometimes, I find another activity or put on children's songs to refocus and gain her attention.

In my class, I want to teach my lessons that consist of letters, sounds, basic vocabulary words, and sorting and classifying different groups. I haven't been able to do that because the children don't even know their colors. There is precious time that is taken away from the limited amount that we already have. Lunchtime, bathroom breaks, tardiness, behavior problems, intercom announcements, assemblies, interruptions, and everything else to mention take away from the little bit of time that we have. We don't even get to have recess. When the children do not know their basic skills, it just complicates our jobs a serious amount. My heart goes out to my colleagues who have twenty to thirty pre-K and kindergarten students in the classroom with no aid. It may get a little better depending on the grade, but not much. For example, in the middle school and high school levels, a teacher may not waste time on teaching students to write their names. We also have overcrowded classrooms, with inclusion students, some with IEPs (Individual Education Plan), and children with undocumented but obvious issues. We will spend hours teaching conflict resolution, self-esteem repair, how to take care of yourself when your family doesn't, how to wash your clothes, wash yourselves, or fix something to eat for dinner. Teachers will spend time encouraging students to come back every day, walking past the drugs, alcohol, fussing, cussing, and arguing in their house or on the street. A lot of problems carry over into the school. They will spend hours teaching children how to talk to each other without yelling and how to have a conversation. It's a never-ending job with endless job descriptions.

I've introduced lessons. We've sang songs and played games incorporated into the curriculum. It's not how it should be, though. I should be able to get through most of my lessons, if not all. Right now, it seems as if it's just bits and pieces of the curriculum that I'm able to get to. I don't expect for my students to sit like little soldiers. I do expect them to have manners, I do expect them to listen when someone is talking, and I do expect them treat each other with respect. I can't complete a full lesson because of their behaviors. When I try to teach a song, some children start singing popular songs you hear on the radio. When I try to teach about a certain letter, the children are so busy worrying about what their neighbor is doing. When it's time to practice writing lines and letters, then I must repeatedly walk around the room to show the students how to hold and control the pencil and paper at the same time. What? Did you just say that's my job, so what am I doing? Of course, it is now. How much farther along would the children be if they had experience at home coloring, drawing, and just being familiar with the process? It's very difficult to ask children questions that have no answers. They don't know how to dream and imagine. They don't know how to draw. I mean, I will tell the children to draw what their favorite thing is to do or to draw their favorite animal. First, they look at me stumped, as if to say, "What do you mean *draw*?" Then they will immediately start complaining about how they don't know how to draw. Then come all of the questions: how do you draw this animal? or that animal? By the age of five, a child should just know what it means to draw a picture without problems. I'm not talking about anything to sell in an art gallery, but it should not be a problem for children to draw. The one child who is well prepared is going on and on to the other students about how he knows everything. The children have very little to no social skills at all. They just don't know how to get along with each other.

Have you read anything about where I have been able to successfully teach a complete lesson yet? No, because we are raising the children. I'm teaching them how to take turns, how to wait patiently for their turn, how to speak without yelling, how to so on and so on and so on. The children will get taught. We have to ensure the school system doesn't waste the little time it has to teach the children skills needed for them to compete in the world. By no means can we give them the initial foundation back, ever. Their foundation started at home, and it's maintained at home. We can try to build on what exists in their lives. However, it seems as if everything that we build at school is torn down as soon as they set foot out of the school's doors. The children are broken as they walk to get home past the crime, drugs, and violence. They are broken when they go home to an empty house. They are broken when they have no one to ask how their day went. They are broken when they have no real, good, nourishing meal to eat. They are broken when they have no guidelines and boundaries to follow. For the next day, it's the same process all over again. Then they get up in the morning to go to school to get a little built again for seven hours, all to be broken again at dismissal.

We hear the children's cries! Do you? Are you even listening for them? Some system will teach the children one way or the other. Which system will teach your child or the children in your family or your friend's? The legal system? The juvenile system? The educational system? The streets? We do the best we can with what we have and how the children come to us. We just need help stopping the cycle, so we can be more effective in doing our job. My prayer is that it is at least the staff of the school system will help and not the juvenile, social service, law enforcement, or street system. I must go now to pick up my eldest from school.

Day 28
Friday, October 6

I feel much better today. I woke up my usual self. I was in a slump for a whole week, but the Lord decided to wake me up, I'm content. Not because it's payday either, because I'm going to pay bills with the money anyway. I feel content because I feel at peace right now. With all that is going on, I have my peace back. Even if it doesn't last long, for the moment, this peace is priceless. Every day I tell my students that every day is a new day to start over.

Today was our chance to get out of the building. The trip is rescheduled due to the rain. We'll go to the Orange Meadows Farm next Friday. Fridays are great days to take field trips if you can. Obviously, we stayed in school and carried on with our next lesson. The children were understandably upset that we couldn't go on the trip. They didn't care that it was raining outside. I had five children absent. On rainy days and snow days, attendance is very poor. I can understand the grandparents and senior citizens not going out in the elements. For everyone else, I guess some people think they will melt if they get wet, or maybe their child's brain will shrink on the way to school because of the weather. Who knows? That's another thing that gets thrown on our shoulder. We are supposed to have 94 percent attendance. Now you tell me, why am I responsible for the child showing up to school on time? Soon they are going to make teachers go pick up the child from home and bring them to school. (Now I will say that I think that the high school curriculum needs to be more hands-on and not lecture type all the time.) But how can I get a negative evaluation in my record because children don't show up for school? It is not a five-year-old's responsibility to get himself up and ready for school and then transport himself to the school. A lot of teachers offer incentives for attendance. I tried a dollar in a jar for each day of perfect attendance. I told the children we could have a party at the end of the year or split it. I don't think I made it past $10. There are all kinds of crazy reasons as to why parents don't send their child to school. A child isn't sick every Friday. The car didn't break down every other Tuesday. The babysitter isn't missing every other day. Most times it is just plain laziness or lack of care. Yeah, I said it. So not only do we have to make parents take care of their children, we have to make them bring them to school. Yea, right! We can't make parents do anything they don't want to do. Sometimes we pull parents to the side and let them know in a professional manner that their child had miss school too many days and that missing needed work. No matter how much we encourage parents, the final outcome is up to them. There are a lot of cases when the school is just used as a babysitting service. They don't want the children sitting at home with them all day ruining their sleep, sex, drug, alcohol, or lazy life. And don't think I'm just referring to parents in the projects, ghettos, or slums. I am speaking of any parent who is ignorant to the knowledge that is needed to help their child educationally, physically, emotionally, spiritually, and so forth.

We, parents, are the children's walking advertisement. Parents are the billboards and the magazine ads. Parents are the television and radio commercials. Parents are the unpaid endorsers of the lifestyles that their children see every single day and night. We must be especially careful in their formative years when they get to that age of asking all those questions. Who? What? When? Why? Where? And how?

And yes, the children do come to school the next day telling all their family's business. You can't tell them not to tell because if a parent's lifestyle is affecting the child in a negative manner, they are going to get it off their chest. Most times, the children don't even know that they aren't supposed to know that information in the first place. They just talk about their night as if explaining something that they saw on television. If the children don't tell all their family's business, then their neighbors or other family members do. We are the role models that they should be looking at. It's not the people on television that should be capturing their minds. I'm also speaking to the parents who ship their child off to a friend's house every other day or off to boarding school because they are busy or have other things to do. I'm not talking about just the working parents. You can sit down and tell a child that you have to go to work to pay bills and make a better life. I'm talking about the parents who go to the club more than they go speak to their child's teacher. I'm talking about the parents who give their child the world but not themselves. I'm talking about the parents who spend more time on the Internet shopping, sending e-mails, and looking at porno than spending the little bit of time they have with their child. I know being a parent is hard. It doesn't matter if it's being a single parent, married, guardian, or if it's kinship care, foster care, group home care. It is a hard job. But guess what, our children didn't ask for the job of being a child. I know it's hard being a child trying to grow up when it seems as if your own parents are against you. You don't want to hear my story right now. That would take another book entirely. For right now, especially while I'm going through my divorce, I don't have any gentleman callers coming to my house or calling me on the phone. I do have male associates and male friends in my life. However, my daughters have never seen me affectionate with another man other than their father. They don't see me kissing, hugging, or having some man all in my face. I don't go out all hours of the night. I don't, but that's just me. I'm talking to the parent who reads more gossip than check their child's homework. And you don't have to know everything on the paper. Just take the time to make sure that it is neat, clean, presentable, and complete. I'm a teacher, and sometimes I don't know everything on my daughter's seventh-grade homework. But I go through it from time to time to make sure it looks presentable and not written in any odd way. I don't have to check it every night now because she has already been trained to get her homework done. When I go up to the school or check her progress report and find out she didn't do an assignment, then she suffers the consequences of her actions. I usually know what I'm looking at when I look at her homework. If I don't, then I just make her think I know what I'm looking at most of the time. Ha! Some parents drop their children off an hour early and pick them up an hour late, as if we don't have a family to go to. It happened today. These children have been in school for a month; they know what the hours of school are.

A coworker came in on my lunch break needing a hug, a smile, and words of encouragement. He's going through something traumatic time in his life. I just tried to encourage him as much as I could. His is another story of how his wife's choices affected his entire family, including four children. I listened more than I talked. He asked me how long the pain would last, and I said I didn't know. I don't know. Families just aren't made the way they used to be. It's a good thing for the families who have broken, terrible family cycles. Then on the other side, it isn't good at all. For the most part, it isn't. The family structure and foundation in too many homes are totally unstable these days.

Today we had to turn in our emergency lesson plans as a part of our "professional responsibilities." I don't know why we must turn these plans in. They usually don't get used for many different reasons. In my experiences, when I have been absent unexpectedly, the work has never been used, and I've never seen any of the emergency plans and copies that I had to turn in to the office. It's a whole bunch of wasted paper that probably gets thrown in the trash at the end of the year. Anyway, it's a bunch of unnecessary paperwork, if you ask me. We have to make all the copies for three days' worth of work. Sometimes the substitutes are given the copies and sometimes not. I've never come back to work to see any of the emergency plans. We must turn the plans in at the beginning of the year. The plans are usually generic, not pertaining to any given scripted lesson because no one knows when the plans are going to be implemented.

Day 29
Monday, October 9

Over the weekend, I graded some tests. I was also able to glue homework in on yesterday. I didn't do anything on Friday evening and Saturday. I just played with my kids and hung out with my family. Today was a hectic day. Usually, the first returning day after the weekend is a hectic day. I call myself getting an early start this weekend by taking the students' homework home with me. Our paid time at work doesn't include checking massive amounts of homework, classwork, assessments, and other documentation. I don't have that much time at school to check work. We are given three planning periods a week. However, sometimes our planning periods turn into meetings with administration to go over data, or meeting other staff such as reading coaches, support personnel, or the representatives from the math and reading specialists of our school's program. Or we must solve a problem or get needed materials during our so-called planning time. In all honesty, we don't get to use our planning time effectively for its intended purposes. From the second day of school, we are already trying to play catch-up. I was able to check two weeks' worth of homework. As usual, some children didn't do their homework, and some children had their homework done by someone else. We can tell immediately when a child has not done his own homework. I wish someone could explain to me how in school the child can barely hold the pencil the correct way. And at home they have completed homework with perfect penmanship.

Overall, the day was pretty good until I dropped the desk on my feet. I was showing students how to keep their desks organized. Since I am six feet tall, and significantly taller than these little desks, it is easier to lean over the desk from behind. It's too much stress on my knees to squat down so far repeatedly and daily. Well, I leaned over the desk and tilted the desk a little too much, and the desk fell onto both of my feet. The pain was so intense that I fell to the floor and instantly curled into the fetal position without my feet touching the floor. The pain was so excruciating. It hurt so bad I couldn't cry. It was crazy to me because the pain that shot throughout my entire body made me feel like crying, but I didn't. I think it was my students in the classroom that prevented me from going into a full-blown crying spell. I felt as if a tingling sensation ran through my entire body. While I was on the floor, in the background, I could hear my students starting to ask me, was I okay? I was in so much pain that I couldn't talk. I could hear my students, but I couldn't talk. It took everything to hold back the tears. I already felt as if I lost my professional composure because I was just lying on our reading carpet, curled up. I thanked God they understood. One of my students came over and started patting my back. I don't know who it was because I was waiting for the initial pain to go away. I needed that pat on the back. After about five minutes, the initial tingling pain started to diminish but was being replaced by a painful throb. I slowly got up from the floor to a standing position. I took my work shoes off. My left foot took most of the impact, in which I was able to see the beginning of bruises immediately.

A parent came in almost right after the incident and asked me how I was doing. I told him I was glad he wasn't here five minutes ago. I wouldn't have wanted him seeing me on the floor like a little baby. Mr. Evans is a helpful parent. It doesn't take much to help teachers and help in the classroom. He started straightening up my room while I was getting myself together. I like it when he comes in because he always asks if I need help with something. He never comes in just to be noisy or just to come in and sit down or stare. A little help can make a big difference. He is very attentive to his son's needs and shows a true interest in his educational career. Some parents look at me as if I'm crazy when I try to let them know their child's abilities or lack of skills.

It is four ten in the afternoon. The accident happened at the end of the day, which was almost two hours ago. Even as I sit here, my foot is throbbing with pain. I was able to put ice on it, but the ice melted away very quickly. I'll see how I feel tomorrow. I still need to go to the gym tonight because my knees are in some major pain. I need to maintain my muscle mass to take the strain off my joints. But now I won't be able to work out because of this crazy accident. Oh well, as usual, I must suck it up and go on.

Day 30
Tuesday, October 10

I didn't experience any parental drama today. I did see a mother walking slowly today with her one-year-old. It made me smile. I hate it when people drag little children to make them keep up with them. If they are not going the speed you want them to, then you need to get a stroller or pick them up. Their little legs can't keep up with an adult.

Outside of that, there was no parent drama because I spent my day at the city clinic. I didn't sleep well last night, and I didn't expect to either. I kept putting ice on my foot. I was also taking a thousand milligrams of over-the-counter pain reliever. This morning, I limped around the house in agonizing pain. Whitney was of major help this morning. After I dropped Trinity off at Trianne's house and the older off at school, I headed downtown to the infamous clinic for city employees. I don't ever want to go there again. I would have been better off going to my own doctor and getting a referral for an X-ray instead of spending the entire school day downtown at a clinic. I did have a great time listening to all city workers tell of their reasons for being in the city clinic. They all shared other life stories that were very interesting. The greatest conversation was the one that four of us were having about parents. I did not start the conversation either. I was sitting there minding my business. I had my teacher's guide, writing my math lesson plans, minding my business. I don't know who started, but I considered it research for me, so I was obligated to put my professional two cents in it. One lady was a parking-patrol worker, the other lady was her sister, and then there was a gentleman who was also engrossed in these conversations. He said he used to drive the school bus, and he hated it. He said that the children were so disrespectful, it didn't make any sense. The children cussed, argued, fought, vandalized, and everything else they could and wanted to do on the bus. He said the children were out of control and got worse every year. Then the conversation went from the children's behavior on the bus to the children's behavior everywhere else. We were all in agreement. The final, unanimous decision: it's the parents' fault, the home life or from whom or wherever they come from. It's not just the school staff within the school that encounters those badly behaving children who lag in class. From the time the children leave their house until the time they get back home, they are encountering someone in the public. They pass the corner stores, crossing guards, public transportation, people walking on the street, people sitting on their front porch, and everyone else in between. No one lives in this world alone. We are all interwoven into one fabric. Our fabric is ripped apart and we need to repair the part that is torn.

Day 31
Wednesday, October 11

I'm back! Although I'm still limping around, the day started off pretty good. In math, we were working on numerals 1 through 5. I decided that I wanted to do an activity working with those numbers. Last night while I was at home, I prepared the construction paper for the activity that they were going to be completing. I also went to the store and bought rice, pasta, and split peas to glue on the construction paper to make the numbers. They also used cotton balls. By the time the children were finished with their math activity, they had tactile numbers. Not only would the students be able to look at the numbers to review, they would be able to feel the shape of the numbers as well. It would reinforce the numbers for the students who don't know them yet.

Two children didn't show up for school today, which made them miss that lesson's activity, among others. They won't get to complete the activity at all since I don't have time to go back and complete it with them. If I had someone in my room to assist me, then it would be possible. I try to tell the parents that the kindergarten curriculum is so structured that we don't have time to go back. If a child misses a skill, letter, sound, then that's it. If the parents don't take the work home and help them to complete, then they missed the instruction for the whole day. We are given a vigorous schedule for the school year, down to every minute that we are to instruct. Our pacing guides, as they are called, are supposed to be followed to the exact time. We can explain being off by a day or two, but no more. The pacing guide doesn't account for all the other parts of the school day. There are no lunch periods, no bathroom breaks, no recess, and no travel time allotted to get to the designated places within the school. So you know if we are given a schedule with no lunch included, then you don't have any time to go back. "You must follow the program and schedule with fidelity." Ha! That was a teacher joke. I'm sorry if you didn't get that one. We are often told that we must follow the curriculum with fidelity and there are no exceptions or excuses not to.

A student came late, of course. Here I go again. Prayerfully, by the time you finish reading this book, you will be tired of reading about the foolishness that goes on every single day. Hopefully, the repetitiveness in these daily behaviors will cause you to join me in causing a paradigm shift in education and in the lack of parental responsibilities. Once time has passed, you cannot get it back, people! Children miss breakfast and sometimes resource classes when they are late. They know that they aren't feeding the children before they send them off to school. Many older siblings are trying to get to school themselves so they that they can eat something. Even if our school breakfast is nothing but sugar, it's the most satisfying thing to a hungry child and it makes all our days here easier.

Back to the parent who brought in her child late. She dropped off the child in her pajamas. Now I am no fashion expert at all. If my clothes are neat, clean, ironed, and look like a match, it's all right with me. I'm wearing it, and I'm on my way to work. My sister hates the way I dress. I don't have an eye for fashion at all, but I do know not to go to a public place in my pajamas. I especially wouldn't go to my child's school like that, so all her friends have another reason or opportunity to mess with her. I would not dare wear a pair of pajama pants that I can see through. And if I was ghetto enough to do it, I would not wear underwear under my pajamas that say *"Kiss This, Kiss That, Have Some?"* Or any other phrases written on my underwear that people can see through my pajamas. That's all I'm saying. The children get what they get from the parents, the home, the relatives, the friends, and whoever else impresses them. Their minds absorb everything like a sponge. They can't blame everything on teachers...

Today eventually turned out to be a challenging day for me. My foot continued to be in an intense amount of pain. I was able to rest last night, so I though my foot was better. I felt as if I could handle going to work, and that's how I ended up here today. I hate missing work, and it's not because I love my job so much. I used to be able to say that. It's a shame, but that's how I feel. I come to work because I don't like substitutes in my classroom. Sometimes I'm blessed to get a good, no-nonsense substitute who can handle the children as well as teach. Some substitutes let the children tear your room up, use all the things the children aren't supposed to, and use supplies and materials they aren't supposed to as well. I lock up all my markers and chalk. Otherwise, I won't have any when I come back, or they will be destroyed. I can't find paperwork and other things that I left a certain way. A lot of times, it is more of a hassle to take off. It isn't even worth the aftermath. I like being here because I know that the students are getting the instruction that they need. So, I'm present and accounted for today, and all my students' behaviors are off. I don't know if it is because I was out yesterday, or if it's because this is another long week for them. My half-day child was back to his old behavior. He had his usual loud, disruptive outbursts, yelling, and carrying on. He is like adding fuel to a fire. Once the remaining students see that Jaron is getting off track, they see it as an opportunity to join in the madness. All the boys wanted to keep playing and wrestling when they thought they had a chance too. The little girls thought that everything was funny today. The children would not calm down on the carpet. They drove me crazy.

Day 32
Thursday, October 12

Today was a nice day. It was beautiful outside. It wasn't too cold and not too hot. It was a nice autumn day. My children were making good choices all day. They had some moments where they were getting a little antsy. But for the most part, they had a good day too. Even my half-day child was able to stay all day. The day got started slowly. When I was ready for instruction, I had only five children in class. I'm not going to give another speech about the parents sending the children late to school every day. I'm just tired of it. Now I feel like, why even say anything? No one is going to listen to me anyway. So, I tried to prolong breakfast a little to give more students time to get to school and have a chance to eat breakfast. That didn't work because I still had only five children by the time I was ready to begin instruction. I went to my colleague across the hall and asked if I should continue with so little children. She said yeah. I was thinking the same thing, but it's a no-win situation. If I don't teach the lessons for the day, I fall behind, and the children that are present don't get the instruction that is needed. If I do teach as I did today, then the children that are not here are again behind. I have two students that show up only two to three times a week. It should be a crime punishable by law. No, seriously though, something needs to be done. Absences aren't brought to anyone's attention until I think they have missed like thirty days or something. Then they get a letter and must go to court. It's some long, drawn-out process. Anyway, today was a good day.

A grandmother came up to me while I was standing in the lobby for dismissal. She just started talking to me. I had to ask her to start over because I couldn't hear with all the children in the hall. She was disgusted with what she saw in the hallway every day. She said that the children have no respect for themselves or the school property, and that's while the parents are standing right there. So, we got into a whole conversation about parents these days. And once again, I found another person who is in total agreement. Parents need to step up to the plate. The parents who are missing in action need to find themselves back on track. And whatever track that may be for them, for their child's sake and future, they need to find the track that will lead them back to the village. I don't know if it's a treatment or rehab center. I don't know if it is counseling for some unresolved issues. They could just need a swift kick in the tail. Whatever it is that they need, it is vital that they get it, so they can get their life and their children's life back on the road to their destiny.

Day 33
Friday, October 13

The morning started slowly again. There were only three students when breakfast came. Jaron came late and thought he was going on the trip. His uncle, who is fourteen, sat in my rocking chair, which is in the reading area in the back of the room. I proceeded to leave to go find a first-grade class that he could stay in while we went on the trip. His uncle then asked me if they, Jaron and he, could go on the trip. I explained to him that the money had already been sent off and that the buses were full. I would have to wait to see if there was room. So, I talked with my colleague about the situation. I really wanted Jaron to go because over the last week, he really has tried to do much better with his behavior. So, I said that I would try to squeeze them in. I asked him for

55

the money, but he didn't have enough. He said that no one in the family knew anything about how much the trip costs. Now the grandmother had to sit with him every day when his behavior was out of control. She knew how much it was because she kept telling me that she was going to pay for the trip. She never paid. Ms. Brown also had a parent who sent the child to school with his lunch and bag for the pumpkin patch and didn't pay for the trip. This whole time, she said she would pay and didn't. She was trying to get over on us and the parent asked if she could pay when we came back. Ms. Brown told her that the trip had to be paid for, or he could not go. Not only that, we really didn't have any more room.

We finally went on the field trip to Orange Meadows Farm. The buses were snuggly packed, and we could hear the parents complaining about why we had to ride on those yellow busses. One parent went with my class, and that was Mr. Evans. Outside of the bus complaints, everything was going all right until we arrived at the farm. All the teachers gave out the stickers to gain entrance into the farm. One parent got upset at the gate because she lost her sticker as soon as it was given to her. The people were not letting her in. Of course, she immediately came to us while we were trying to get the remaining stickers out. She got upset with us because we told her that we only had the exact number of the stickers for parents, students, and teachers. I don't know how she lost it in that short amount a time. There were about five of us backtracking from the bus to the gate to find this parent's sticker. It is a big bright, colorful, very sticky three-inch circle sticker. All you have to do is stick it on your coat when we peel it off and give it to you. We were already off the buses and lined up, ready to go. She was carrying on about the farm employees to better let her in "cause I paid for dis trip, and I'm not payin' again. Dey bette let me in, or we gonna have problems." *Here we go,* is what I was thinking at the time. Here we go with some unnecessary drama. She paid for the trip, and she isn't paying again to get in. The other teachers and I who were left outside even walked her up to the entrance just, so she could see that we would try to vouch for her, but we knew that wasn't going to work. We just didn't want her to talk about us not even trying to help her. After hearing another polite rejection, she had that look as if she was going to go off. I couldn't afford another $12. She finally got in because someone took their sticker out to her and snuck back inside after another group went in. So, after a couple of classes went in the farm, someone took their sticker off and sent it out to her, so she could get in. Why do some parents have to carry on and embarrass us out on these trips? Those people don't have any problems calling back to the school and telling the principal that we can't come back. Calling the principal and telling them that the school is welcome back to their establishment has been done numerous times. There's always one in a group holding everybody else up.

After all that got worked out, everything went well. There were so many schools, day cares, and families at the farm. It's a beautiful thing for me to see moms and dads positively interacting with their children. My children, whom I knew needed a chaperone, were the very ones I had to talk to all day. It didn't help any that my nephews went on the trip. I asked my sister to help me chaperone since Faith was with me in my class. My nephews had my students pumped up even more than usual. They weren't bad, they just wanted to be all over the farm instead of staying with my class. Cotez kept wandering off as usual, as he does in the classroom. Kevmani and the other boys just wanted to keep moving to the next area without spending time at the one we had just arrived at. I had to stop several times, tell them how we act in public and how we walk and not run off all around the place. When it was time to get back on the buses and head back to school, the children had gone on a hayride, milked cows, run around with chickens, patted baby sheep, and seen a big nine-hundred-pound hog with cute little piglets. There were many animals out for them to see. I enjoyed watching the children point at so many different things they didn't get to experience before this. I enjoyed answering all their questions and just talking about what they were experiencing. Watching the little faces of children light up is a good feeling. I really enjoyed milking the cows with them today. The children were making all kinds of comments, and they were so excited about the experience. I took a picture of each one of my students milking a cow, so they could have a memory of it. The last thing the children were able to do was to walk around piles of pumpkins and pick their own pumpkin. The only rule they had was to pick a pumpkin that they could carry by themselves.

Earlier I had to get off the bus to get the tickets, so no one told me that I had to be back at the bus at twelve forty-five, and I forgot to ask. I arrived at the parking lot at one, thinking I was the first one on time. It wasn't until I saw that everyone was on the bus that we were the last class with a few lingering parents with us. Things happen. It was a good learning day, after all. The bus ride on the way back was fun. Mr. Evans and the children were telling jokes. They were cute, child-appropriate jokes. I don't know if it was me just having a concerned parent on the trip or if I'm a pretty good judge of character, but Mr. Evans seems to really love his son and would do anything he could for him to be successful.

Day 34
Monday, October 16

I got a new student today. (Currently, as I type, it's my lunchtime, but I just had to write this.) How do you send a child to school with nothing? I know that when a parent has a child, they must know that somewhere down the line, their child is going to have to go to school. This could probably sum up what we deal with daily. The children come as they are, and that sometimes means nothing. They have nothing mentally, spiritually, educationally, or morally. My new student is another boy. He had no materials at all. Sometimes students come with an empty book bag, in hopes of having something go into it by the end of the day. He had no crayons, no pencils, no notebook, and no glue. Structured prekindergarten and kindergarten programs are serious business. Playing games and singing songs is just a small part of the students' academic program. I think that people are truly misinformed or not informed at all, about the first six years of a child's life. Later, I will share my proposals and all my bright ideas that I think will change when America starts to implement them.

Anyway, the parent came and dropped him off in the middle of my reading instruction. We were on the letter *u,* which means he has missed formal instructions from *a* through *u.* I had to let my children practice writing the letter *u,* so I could get a quick assessment of the student. All I really needed to know was if he had any formal school training. I quickly talked to the mother and asked her a few questions that would help me for the moment. Has he ever been to any kind of preschool? No, this is his first time in school. After all my little interview-style questions, I reintroduced myself and reassured her that he was going to be just fine. I also let her know that I would have his name on a desk and locker by the end of the day. (I'm eating my plain tuna fish for lunch. I got a little off my healthy-eating lifestyle, so I need to get back on it. I must stay healthy for myself, my girls, and my destiny.) Anyway, I'll get his name situated later. After his mother leaves, she comes back five minutes later to bring me his lunch money. I told her that she can give it to him from now on because I want the children to have some responsibility and accountability for themselves in the classroom. She said that she's giving me the money because he's slow. So, I asked her what she meant. She told me that I will see once I start talking to him. I asked her if he was diagnosed with something, or did he have an IEP (paperwork that basically states the problem for a child and the child's modifications for instruction)? She said no. My question again is, what has the child been doing for the last five years of his life? If he is slow, then he is probably slow because no significant learning has been taking place. In all reality, children could learn to read by grade 1. The federal law No Child Left Behind Act mandated that children read by grade 3, but that's too late. It should be that children read by grade 1. How and why? Think about it as this: Pre-K, K, first, second, and third grades together make five years. If children are exposed to everyday learning experiences at home from birth to age five, then they will be reading by grade 1 and not grade 3. And I'm not talking about making children stressed out to become child geniuses and brainiacs. I'm just talking about a good foundation of learning. A parent is the first teacher a child ever has. I'm getting ahead of myself. (I'm sorry! I was almost in another zone again.)

As for the rest of the day, it was nerve-wracking. My new boy that came today makes nine boys. And they drove me crazy. They were all over the place. My throat hurt a lot today because I had to stay on the students all day about paying attention, following directions, and not playing and jumping around before someone gets hurt. It's Monday, and I'm exhausted as usual. I am so glad that Thursday and Friday are professional days. On Thursday, I have to go to another unnecessary workshop again on how to fill out paperwork. I think that the people at headquarters should ask us if we need to go to a workshop in the first place. They would save us and them a lot of time and a lot of money if they would just specify the teacher who has never filled out this required paperwork, which would probably be a first-year teacher. Then they can go to the workshop for that information. On Friday, I am coming right back to my room to do some work. It was highly suggested that we go to a workshop. But why should I have to pay to go to work? That's really what it is. I have to pay $20 to $45 to go to a workshop. I have just two more days this week with my students. Thank God.

Day 35
Tuesday, October 17

Today is a gloomy day, and it's cold in the building. The rain is pouring down outside. My class is in the portable, so you can hear the rain coming down on the roof. My heating unit did come on earlier today, but now it isn't coming at all, and I really need it to. Whitney doesn't get out of school until five, so I'll stay in my classroom until quarter of. It's three now, so I have a significant amount of time to sit in this cold room. The rain is really coming down now. The rain appears to affect the children's behavior also. If it's not the rain, then it's a full moon. Once again, my boys were off, and Jaron was back to his true self again. I thought I would be able to recommend to the principal and to his grandmother that he can come to school all day. But he really isn't ready. He didn't want to do any work. I thought he was going to have a good day because he came in to class on time to eat breakfast. Sometimes his excuse for making bad choices is because he hasn't eaten breakfast. I can understand that excuse. It is very difficult to function if you are hungry. Jaron eating breakfast didn't make a difference. He just had more energy to magnify his typical behaviors. As so many previous days, my day was full of his outbursts, getting out of his seat, messing with the little girl sitting next to him. He is supposed to be picked up every day at eleven thirty. Different people come pick him up, so he's been getting picked up late at different times, way past eleven thirty. I really want him to stay all day because he is missing math instruction and other learning activities and skills that we do in the classroom. Staying in the classroom is supposed to help him socialize with other children and adults as well. But his behavior is so disruptive that it interferes with the learning of others.

Here is another major point in this book. Many years ago, it just used to be minor interruptions in the classroom. Minor interruptions used to be someone eating gum or a child who was a little chatty. And those interruptions were dealt with in the classroom with that look that says *Don't even think about it*. If it was a more serious problem with a student, back then, if you even threaten to call his parent, the child immediately got back on track. Not these children. They will tell you to go ahead and call their house. I've been told that there is no one home anyway, the phone is cut off, or their parents aren't going to answer the phone. They fear no consequences at all. Sending them to the principal at our school is a joke. The principal's office, as well as all other entities of the school system, is on overload with what seems like a series of endless daunting problems. Every discipline problem that is sent to the office has to have a paper trail. If the bigwigs at headquarters feel as though there are too many paper trails, then someone is going to go talk to the principal. But the principal doesn't want to hear it. What goes up must come down. If the problems are sent to office and come down on the principal, then the principal comes down on us. We get it from all ends of the system. We have to handle it as we handle everything else that comes our way. The principals have so many interruptions to deal with because of lack of home training and discipline. It's a big domino effect that starts at home and ends in death, destruction, incarceration, or somewhere in between. It interferes with the learning of others and the continuity of the school day.

Around eleven forty-five, I was ready to send him home. No one had shown up yet to pick up Jaron. I kept looking out my classroom door. No one ever showed up. I told him that if he wasn't going to let me help him complete his math work, I'd just send him to the office again. I had to do that yesterday. As usual, I told him that he could make the good choices to listen, follow directions, and do his work. I was trying hard to coax him into believing that he could do great things if he tried. He wasn't trying to hear anything I had to say. He kept going on about what he was not going to do. So, I said, "Come on, let's go to the office." He sat down for another half hour. When it was time to do the next activity, he got up and ran out of the room. I already told you, I was not running after him. At least he didn't go out of the building this time. He knows where the office is, so he figured that he could go on his own. I walked across the hall, tell Ms. Brown that I was going to walk him up to the office, and so she could watch my class. He saw me coming down the hall to catch up with him. He made a pit stop at his locker to get his belongings. At this point, he was trying to hurry up, so I didn't catch up with him. I couldn't run even if I wanted to because of the accident with my foot. My foot was still in pain while I was trying to walk briskly to catch up with him. By now, he was all the way at the top of the hall. I was about fifty feet behind him. He stopped at the top and started to shake his behind as if he was doing the chicken dance without the arms. I wish I had a retractable belt that could reach his tail from where I was. I got to the top, and he ran into the office right past the principal. I don't know if the principal saw him or not because he was talking to a parent. I go into the office to let them know that Jaron needed to stay until someone picked him up. That quick while I was talking, he ran out into the hall. The music teacher saw him and said that he would go get him. When the principal freed up, I told him that Jaron was running in the hall. Jaron was down the other end of the hall. Our school is on one level, and we have very long halls. The longest hall may be about as long as one city block. The principal and I saw him from up by the office. He was all the way down the other end, but we could still see him. I started to walk back to my class. By the time I got about twenty feet away, the music teacher had him. When the music teacher caught up with him, he fussed at Jaron for running out of the office. I looked back and saw that the principal was behind me about fifty feet. I just turned around and kept on walking to my class.

As far as the rest of the children, I was very frustrated that my new student who came yesterday is totally behind. He can't write his name. My students, who have been here since the start of school a couple of weeks ago, have already learned how to write different kinds of lines. I taught them about slant, circle, vertical, horizontal, and curve lines. I taught them how all these lines would eventually form the letters of the alphabet. While the rest of the students were working on the current letter, I had to give my new student a mini lesson on the basics of drawing lines.

Day 36
Wednesday, October 18

I had an uneventful day. It was another rainy day, so I had only seven children to show for school today. Five stayed home and missed another day's worth of explicit instruction. I did get to smile today, though. My new student had to write the letter *W* since that's what I taught. While the other children knew what to do since they've been here since day one, I sat right beside him. Even though he was struggling, I was happy that he was putting forth great effort. He made me smile when he had an "aha" moment. He saw that he could do anything as long as he tried. He looked up at me, smiled and said *I did it*. The only good thing about so many children being absent is that I have more time and attention to give to the remaining students. I was able to work with each of the seven children on a given skill that each needed. We were able to work on some other educational manipulatives and activities that I normally don't get to implement into the day on a regular basis.

Professional Day- No Students
Thursday, October 19

For professional development today, I sat in a meeting and listened to various presenters tell us about more paperwork and added professional responsibilities we have to do. I will spare you all the details and professional vocabulary and terminology. All the talk about implementing this strategy and this technique really doesn't make a difference to some children because many of our students and their parents need to be healed from the inside out. It's those social and emotional skills and strategies that they need from other professionals. For these meetings, I usually take a bag of schoolwork that I need to complete. I'll sit, listen, and work quietly while the presenters present their information. Every year there's more and more we have to do. It is crazy. It does not matter how many programs, curriculums, and training sessions they provide for teachers. Until parents are mandated to take routine workshops and training, then things are just going to get worse. I'm not talking about getting worse just in the school system either. Too many of our children are quickly going nowhere. Some will end up right along with the rest of the people struggling in America and around the world if something doesn't change soon.

Professional Day- No Students
Friday, October 20

For my professional development today, I was in my classroom professionally developing my classroom environment. That sounded so good. I cleaned up and threw junk out, filed papers, checked more papers, and then filed those as well. I was so exhausted that I woke up late, which means I got to work a little later than I wanted to, but still on time. On professional development days, we don't have to get to work until a half hour later of our regular time. At my school, it's eight. I say I was late because I wanted to get there at seven thirty. On my lunch break, I went to go drop off the three rolls of film for one-hour developing. Two of them were from the Orange Meadows Farm. My coworkers were able to display their field trip pictures right away. I guess they had digital or phone cameras. I'm used to the old-fashioned way of getting a hard copy from the photo lab. I guess I'll have to get a digital camera soon. I didn't take my Polaroid instant camera on the trip with me because it seems as if I'm the only one in my circle that still uses the Polaroid. My friends and family always make fun of me when I pull it out. An hour later, I was able to hang those field trip pictures with their drawings about their experience at the farm. I was surprised that no one drew a picture about milking a cow. It's not every day in the city that you get to milk a cow. I was also able to grade and hang up papers that were piling.

Mr. B and I had a great conversation today. Mr. B is one of the custodians at our school. He came into my room to clean up, and we started talking about how the building is going to go to a K-8 school next school year. Some people like it, some people don't. The rumor going around is that the city is trying to save money by shutting down eleven schools and moving the students into other schools in other neighborhoods. When, and if, that happens, then you open a can of worms with those older children who are territorial. I've never been in a K-8 school, so I don't have any experiences to compare it to. I do know that if our fifth graders look like eighth graders now and are a handful already, I don't know if I want to be here. The rumor also includes the idea of all this extra space in the schools due to low enrollment. The city decides to make money with that extra space that is allegedly in some of our schools. The powers that be close the schools down and let businesses, companies, and other organizations rent or lease the extra space for revenue. Does the money get reinvested or redistributed back into the schools? I say no, but I really don't know. The schools that used to be occupied by a learning community of teachers and students are then occupied by people making their own money. I think that they should fill some of the spaces with classes for parents. They can put all the resources parents need right now to be successful parents. The community can come together to develop GED (General Education Development) classes, rehabilitation services, counseling services, AA (Alcoholics Anonymous) and Narcotic Anonymous meetings, childcare classes, and whatever else is needed. Whatever they need to do, whatever it takes. That is what should be done with all this so-called extra space in the schools. After the parents drop their children off, they can go right to their parent institute. We can give it a fancy name to take the stigma off needing some parental guidance. Parental help and guidance should not mean that you are a terrible parent. It means that you just want to be a better one. It should be used as a means of empowering the parents with knowledge to empower their own children. Some parents need to hear their children's cry?

Saturday. Last night I was so enraged that I know that I'm going to have to start sharing my personal testimonies, so you can see that teachers have to go through storms outside of school as well. It's just a matter of how we choose to come out of them and behave in a professional manner once we get to work. On Friday evening, I had to go to my primary care doctor to see about my left foot. It still hurts and is still in pain. Right in between my big toe and the next one to it, I can't feel anything. I tried pricking myself with a safety pin, but my skin still doesn't pick up any sensation.

Anyway, you should have seen me with my three girls and my seven-year-old nephew at the doctor's office. I was able to order them pizza and drinks from Pizza Hut next door. (I just love their ham and pineapple pan pizza.) The food had them calmed down for about twenty minutes while they ate in my truck. I was limping back and forth between the truck and the waiting room, waiting for my turn to see the doctor. Of course, they couldn't bring the food in, and there was nowhere for them to sit. So, I figured the truck was the best place to eat. I didn't have a jacket, so the fall air was causing me to shiver. I was limping to go eat a slice of pizza in the truck with the children, and then I was limping back to the waiting room. The good thing is that the waiting room door was five feet away from where my truck was parked. I was able to stand in the doorway to watch them and hear my name called. Once I was called to be examined, I limped to the truck one more time, and they were finishing up and almost ready to come in. Whitney does a good job with them, and I knew she would be all right getting them situated into the doctor's office. Well, I knew when they were done. I'm about fifty feet back from the front door in my exam room, and I heard them all enter, loud and clear. The entertainment begins. The kids weren't making bad choices. They just seemed to be very loud in a very quiet office. I came out of the exam room to walk to the lobby to find out why they were so loud. By the time I got to the front, my eldest, Whitney, had the youngest, Trinity, underneath her arms asking me to take her. They were fussing over the two massage chairs in the lobby. There were four of them and two chairs. My little one is kind of feisty, so she was demanding to sit in a chair. Of course, the older two, my daughter and my nephew, found it hard to share with the younger two. I ended up taking my two little ones into the room with me. Now we all know that those rooms are small, with thin walls, and not soundproof at all. Trinity and Faith were even louder because of the amplification of the room.

One was on the table, and the other was in the chair. I sat on the table with Trinity, and she was climbing on my back. My younger two seemed to have super energy after dark. It was almost seven, and I was ready to go.

I finally got my turn to see my doctor. After she looked at my foot, she told me that after two weeks, my foot was still swollen. The lack of sensation on the top of my foot, near my big toe, is probably because my nerves were crushed. I still have a few bruises on my foot too. And I'm so disgusted about forgetting to take a picture of my injury. Anyway, she wrote me a whole bunch of prescriptions. One to see a foot doctor, one for an X-ray, and one for a shoe boot. I told the people at the city clinic that there was something more seriously wrong with my foot than a bruise.

After I finished with the doctor, I was anxious to finally get home just to relax, or at least try to. I was driving south down Route One to get home. Out of the blue, Whitney told me, "Speed up." I was like, "Girl, I'm tired, and I cannot afford to get a speeding ticket." I didn't understand what she was rushing me for anyway. Then she was like, "Slow down." I was like, "Girl, I'm not in the mood for your playing around tonight!" Whitney then tells me not to let the kids see the movie in the car that was immediately to our right in the next lane. I'm thinking that if they saw the movie that's playing, then they would want to go home and want to watch the movie that was playing. There are many people fortunate enough or make sacrifices to be able to play children's movies for their children while traveling across town. I've seen it, you've seen it. I'm not mad at you either. Instantly, I was trying to think of all the possible movies that the children shouldn't see in the car next to us. Whitney then asked, "You don't care if they see the movie?" I said, "I don't care if they can see the movie because we're almost home. If it's not a dirty movie, I don't care. They will be all right." She said, "It is a dirty movie." So, I tried to focus on what my daughter was talking about without crashing. Sure enough, it was an XXX-rated movie. I could see it clear as day. I don't need to be descriptive right now, do I? Just imagine body parts humping and slapping and smacking all over the place. It wasn't that regular little five-inch screen either. They had the nerve to have a bigger screen too. Those actors were just going at it as if there was no tomorrow. I slowed down so they could go on. It was only eight thirty in the evening. The guys in that car had no class, no dignity, no pride, and definitely no concern that children were able to see what they were watching. They obviously only cared about themselves. I wished I was a police officer. I would have given them a ticket for something. It should be against the law to watch porno in public. I don't even know if there is a law such as that. I'm going to ask and let you know if I find the answer. It's an embarrassment to the ancestors who have come before us to make this America a better place.

I spent last night at my pop's, so he could watch the girls for me. Whitney and I needed to get our hair done.

Getting to today, I spent four hours in the hair shop. I was tired from taking out all those braids from Whitney's and my hair this week. I was dozing off almost the entire time under the dryer and with my stylist. The two of us went to the shop to let someone else do what I'm too tired to do right now.

My sister and I went to the SRI Shoe Warehouse, and I bought myself two pairs of sneakers and two pairs of shoes. I've been wearing the same beat-up sneakers for two years. We went back to Pop's house and finished reading my book, *The Pursuit of Happyness* by Chris Gardner. In addition to wanting to read what the book was about, I also wanted to know why the day care center had *happiness* spelled with a *y* and not with an *i*. The misspelled word really disturbed me. I didn't find an exact answer, but I found his story very encouraging and inspirational. It's a teacher's pet peeve to see things spelled incorrectly, I guess.

Finally, I went home and gave my little ones a bath and went to sleep. I didn't get any schoolwork done today. Every weekend I have work to do, and rarely do I get it done.

Sunday- I went to church, of course. I went over to Pop's for about two hours. I wanted to kill time before I went back to church for a last-minute baby shower and to have a meeting with Whitney's dance ministry. We ate, went home, and took a nap. I was only supposed to just nap for about a half hour, but I ended up napping for two hours. I was refreshed, but now I was off schedule. The girls had to eat microwave meals because I woke up too late, near the time they are ready to eat dinner. I keep a few of those from time to time for emergency purposes only. I rushed to Sam's Club because they needed lunch for the week, but they were closed. I went back home and did four loads of laundry. We all went to bed kind of later than usual because we all overslept on our naps. I didn't get any schoolwork done.

Day 37
Monday, October 23

Instead of going to work today, most of my morning was spent downtown. I had to go to court since I'm going through this whole divorce thing. I did well today seeing him for the first time in almost four weeks. Seeing him the last time was what helped trigger me into going over the edge and crying all weekend long.

Things didn't go the way I would have wanted them to go. I want to be divorced from him right now and forever. It is so easy to get in and terribly difficult to get out. I hate this process, and the sad part about it is that it didn't even have to go this way. We're down here today for child support and visitation. I don't even feel like going into the details. I'm just tired of this.

When we left the courthouse, I wasn't even upset when I saw that he bought a new-money–green Mercedes Benz. It didn't bother me one bit. I just smiled to myself and thought that every dog has its day. I may not see that day, but he'll have it. For the life of me, I can't understand why people claim they don't have money for the full child support, but they can buy cars, two plasma wall televisions, a new house, new clothes for themselves, and $300 cell phones. Of course, I'm not talking about anyone specifically either, ha! I'm talking about all men and women who make that claim but seem to be living large at the expense of their children.

Later in the day, when I talked to my girl Melissa about the latest court adventures, she had a different perspective about the situation. She basically said that some noncustodial parents just want to pay what is comfortable for them to pay. I never even looked at it like that. She said that after I told her of the following conversation that he and I had. My soon-to-be ex told me that he was doing the best that he could with child support. I said okay and left him alone. But in the same conversation, he said that he was living comfortably. I raised an eyebrow when he said that. That automatically told me that something wasn't right. I don't think that either party should have to struggle after a divorce. Statistics show that most men suffer financially because of divorce. Well, in my case, I feel it's the total opposite. Here I am, not eating much or not eating at all when I fix dinner, so my girls can have a full stomach. I haven't been able to afford to take them to the movies and do other things because of my finances. When he left about three years ago, I had gone to the child support office and picked up the paperwork, but never filed the papers. I was thinking about him and his welfare, can you believe it? Me neither. I didn't want them to take so much that he would then be struggling to do things with the girls. Eventually, I realized that he is just giving me what he wants to give so he can maintain a cozy lifestyle.

On the flip side, parents who receive child support are supposed to be supporting the child. Their child's food, clothing, and shelter come first! It isn't the manicures, pedicures, hairstyle, haircuts, and other stuff that doesn't have to do with the child. Some people have all that stuff, that bling, that ice, and those rims. When you look closer, they really don't have anything because they barely have a relationship with their own flesh and blood. As long as I have my girls in my life and their beautiful spirits in my soul, I'm the wealthiest woman in the world. Thanks to the grace of God. Anyway, that's enough about my personal issues. We all have a few of those, right? You know you got some undocumented issues too!

I saw Jamon today after school. He was picking up his little sister Jestinie, whom I taught last year. I asked him how his day was. He said it wasn't a good one because his mother was beating him. Then he took off his hood and showed me his lip. He said that she was already mad about something, so she just took it out on him because of the misplacement of a radio cord. She called his probation officer; however, once Jamon proceeded to tell the probation officer his story, he told Jamon that it sounded as if she was being abusive and neglectful. She was trying to get him sent to a group home. It just breaks my heart to see so many of our youth stressed out, overwhelmed, and heavily burdened. Parents are a major factor when it comes to major influences in a child's life.

Day 38
Tuesday, October 24

Today was an interesting day. I was running late today. I got here at seven forty-five instead of seven thirty. I was hoping that I didn't get a red circle around my square where I sign in on the sign-in sheet. That red circle says that you are late. I called one of the teachers and told her I would be running late and to look out for my students. Rarely do any of my students get here on time anyway, but that's no excuse for me to not be there on time. I couldn't even get my class listed as having good attendance for the month of September. I guess being on time and in attendance on a regular basis is too much to ask. Whitney and Faith got to school on time, though. Yuan was the only one that was here when I arrived. Kevmani's mom came in and brought me a box of school supplies. The supplies were donated from a local neighborhood bank that she works at. She also dropped Twan off, but Kevmani didn't stay because he was on his way to the hospital with a 102-degree temperature. What is going on first thing in the morning? I was sorry that Kevmani didn't feel well, but I was so happy to see all those materials. It was as if I won the lottery. It felt as if I had a new-money–green Mercedes Benz. She said I just had to write a thank-you letter on our school's letterhead, so her job would be able to account for the money they spent. I gladly obliged, and it was fine with me. No problem.

I had a parent volunteer in my room today. I think that she has to for some program, but I haven't pried and asked why. I was just happy to have her, and she was very helpful too. She was supposed to start yesterday but didn't. That's okay. Teachers always have stuff to do. Today Ms. Denia greatly helped by listening to the children read their decodable books, putting up my high-frequency words, filing classwork and test papers and helped me clean off my massive amount of junk and papers on my worktable. I don't really get to do any work there because I don't have time.

Jaron cussed at the grandmother who comes to volunteer in the cafeteria every day. I felt terrible for him as if he was my own child. She was enraged, and I let her vent. She was just going on and on about how her own children and grandchildren would have never even thought about disrespecting an adult. She said she had never seen anything like it. She had had children being disrespectful around her but never directly to her, and at such a young age. Ms. Anna really doesn't deserve to receive any abuse from any children. Every day she brings her grandchildren to school. Then she goes downstairs in the basement and volunteers in the cafeteria. She discards the food trays and wipes the tables. She does it almost every day too. She took him to the office from the cafeteria, but he ran as usual, twice. He was found hiding in the music teacher's room. He said that it's the best place in the school because that's where the movies are. The usual happened with him. A phone call was made home, and someone had to come get him, if they weren't already on their way to do so in the first place.

Jamon showed up after school to see me. He said he wants to start school on Thursday, but his mother won't buy him any school clothes. I'm speechless right now. I really would like to hear both sides of the story, but I don't want to make things worse. I know he has a cases worker that helps him. As I said, it was another interesting day.

Day 39
Wednesday, October, 25

Today seemed to be like that children's book *Alexander and the Terrible, Horrible, No Good, Very Bad Day.* Go to the library and read it if you haven't done so already. My students got on my everlasting nerves today. I don't know what it is about these Wednesdays, because the children just seem to have a bad day. First, I think it's because on Wednesdays, they don't have a resource class, and they are with me all day in the same small class. Second, I think that these children really aren't totally adjusted to even be in school all day anyway. I try to have an art activity, so they can start the day with something fun and not so strictly academic. The activities are always educational.

Jaron came back to school today with no adult that was supposed to sit in there with him. I was told that he was going to have to be sent to an alternative school because he is not ready for a social school environment of learning. But no! I don't believe that lie either. The only way children are transferred from our school is if they stab somebody or something. I really don't fall for what I call the "pacify technique." I used to believe everything that I was told. I used to believe that I would always have teacher support, supplies, unlimited amount of resources, and a whole bunch of other broken, empty promises. I know he isn't going anywhere. They'll just keep sending him to school, and the school will keep letting him come until he seriously hurts a child or an adult.

People are going to act as if they are shocked when we must start having alternative schools for elementary children. I won't be. Our school is not too far from it now. We don't have a perfect staff and a perfect building. What I can tell you is that most of the staff here is dedicated to the children and this community. We all have our personal dilemmas to fight. Every day as I walk through the hall, I see my coworkers struggling on the same journey. We have a lot of investment in our school. They also give their heart, soul, time, money, tears, and sweat to the children here. It just seems as if we are fighting a winless battle. I don't even bother trying to call some of the parents anymore. Sometimes, we do call to give good reports, and we can't even do that. The numbers that the parents give don't even work, or it's the wrong number. Then some see the caller ID and don't answer the phone. That's why I stopped calling from school because they know that number. When I call from my cell phone, they answer that because they don't know who it is. Once they know my cell phone number, then they don't answer the call again.

As I was saying earlier, their behavior is out of control today. Ponto whines and cries like a one-year-old whenever things don't go the way he wants them to go. As I said earlier on in the year, they have no home training. They want to call each other names. They think everything is funny. They had to take their first trimester tests today, which consisted of identifying twenty uppercase letters, twenty lowercase letters, ten high-frequency words: *and, I, a, an, the, here, we, see, he,* and *is.* They also had to give me five words that rhyme with a word that I gave them. Must I remind you that I've been teaching my tail off every day, all day? I teach, model; they practice and review every day with every skill. *Every day!* We have sung a different version of the alphabet song; we have practiced writing every letter that was taught. We have learned an alphabet cheer. We have practiced every single day except for our field trip day. Did they do well on the assessment? Thanks for asking. *No!* One student, Kevmani, was able to identify all his uppercase and lowercase letters. He was also able to fluently read seven out of ten high-frequency words. The rest of the students either looked at me stumped when I pointed to the random letters, or they just shrugged their shoulder and didn't even try. Getting an early start makes all the difference in the world. And then once they have that initial foundation started, it's the parental support that sees them through to success. Their education should have started when they came out of the womb.

One of my students took the "drainage" from his nose and smeared it all on his desk. I made him get up and go get a tissue to finish wiping his nose. I had to explain to him that whenever he needs to wipe his nose, he needs a

77

tissue to do it. Disgusting, that is so nasty. I put on my rubber gloves and used a disposable cleaning wipe to clean his desk. That is why I'm so hesitant about touching the desks, books, and hands. I have caught pinkeye and strep throat so many times from contact with children. They dig, pick, scratch, and wipe all day. I have no idea what is on them.

I wish I had a close relationship with all the parents, so I could just blatantly ask them, why are they coming up here picking up children smelling like weed? We don't need to come in contact with anything else. We already have enough chemicals and substances we have to inhale daily. What happens to people doing their dirt after dark when the kids are asleep? I also want to tell the parents to pull up their pants. No one wants to see their drawers. It is not sexy at all. Obviously, it's my opinion. Seriously though, we have so many grandmothers up here, I think it is very disrespectful to carry on that way. Parents have cusswords on their shirts too big for everyone to see.

Day 40
Thursday, October 26

My baby turns two today. I haven't even seen her today because I had to drop her off at my sister's last night, so she could take her to the doctors for me. She had to get shots on her birthday. Poor baby. I wish I was there with her, but duty calls. We must choose our days off wisely. I'm glad that she will feel better before her birthday party on Sunday.

I had a good, productive day in the classroom. I had fun teaching my students. In today's lesson, the students learned about the formation of the letter *Y*. I haven't formally taught the sounds yet, just the introduction of what the letter is and the way to write it. After the last letter is taught, then I will formally teach each sound. I was able to read the new story. I love reading children's stories. I get to be over animated and silly. I change my voice, move around, and do

78

whatever else that I need to do to captivate the children's attention. I want them to see and feel that reading is fun too and not just hard work. I want them to know that once they get past the work, they can have so much fun reading too. Temporarily, while I'm on this natural high of reading, all my problems and concerns disappear like magic, and I implement one of the gifts of life. Using one's imagination is so awesome because no one can steal the visions that are imagined in the mind.

For whatever reason, the gym teacher's schedule had to be adjusted, so they had gym later in the morning. When the schedule is thrown off for various reasons, sometimes it starts a domino effect that throws off the rest of the day. So, we didn't get to finish language arts. We were able to complete our lessons this morning with fun and excitement. It's just hard to get them to calm down when the fun part of learning is over, and they must do more concrete work.

While I was at a gas station, directly in my front view, I saw a beautiful sight. A young man was carrying a sleeping toddler. The toddler was about two years old. I don't know if the young man was the father or not. These days, we can't just assume so. There are so many siblings who must take care of their family members. During all the confusion of this busy intersection, that man was holding that child as if no one could come near him without going through him first, and that is how it should be. Our village should be so strong and tight that the outer elements, wolves, have no chance of going through us to get to our children. Today, the village is handing the children right over to the wolves.

Day 41
Friday, October 27

I'm sitting in this parenting class, thinking how this one parent, my almost ex, is screwing the day up for everyone connected to me. I must take the day off from work. So, a whole class isn't getting the best instruction for the day because I'm not there teaching. I must make arrangements for my children to be picked up from their different child care and school locations.

While I'm in there, I'm thinking he just might be the scum of the earth. I'm not going to start any name-calling, but there are some words that are not nice that pop in my mind when he is the subject. I had to take the day off from work to go to a parenting class. How ironic is that? I can teach the class! I'm in here because he isn't man enough to be one. While he's trying to hurt me for calling it quits, not only do I miss a day from work, I must get someone to watch Faith so I can get downtown early enough to get a parking space. Then my thirteen students must be split among five teachers because there is no substitute. So, because of him, twenty-one people's lives had to be altered for the day. I'm not teaching today. Instead, I'm downtown hearing what I've been trained to do. People fail to realize that the decisions that they make do affect others. I guess that's why they call it the domino or butterfly effect. I will just continue to pray and continue to believe that God will have the final say when this divorce is all said and done.

I've learned from my mistakes. If I were to ever get married again or have any more children, I will follow my heart and be careful with whom I have children with. I don't even see myself getting married or having any more children. You spend your time trying to show someone that you truly do love them, and it just seems that nothing that you do is good enough. Mothers and fathers who go home to their families choose to do so. Life isn't peaches and cream, but they choose to love each other and work on it daily. Then those mothers and fathers that run the streets while everybody else is at home obviously choose not to be home and work it out. I'm tired, and my patience is very short and intolerant of stupidity in a relationship. I can do badly all by myself.

I have a girlfriend who is going through a divorce also. She said that the things her husband does don't affect anyone on his side because he has no one. In her opinion, he is an old lonely, mean-spirited soul. He's one of those miserable people that love for everybody else to be miserable too. Their spirits weren't compatible as time went on, and that's why it didn't work. He wanted to be out in the streets, having his cake and eating it too. She and her kids are going through it with that man. He left them six times. What kind of foolishness is that for a mother or father to be moving in and out of the children's life? They don't know the negative impact it has on their impressionable minds. Her soon-to-be ex is trying to get out of his true amount of child support; he is contesting everything important. He denies cheating. And now he has allegedly stopped going to the reserves, so they don't count that income. He bought the new car, so he can say he has a car payment, and now he's trying to take full custody from me, the only parent that has been there since the day our children were born. One day in about ten years or so, I know I will have to apologize to my girls when they get older for the poor selection I made in choosing a husband and father.

Saturday. I got to clean my room, ate lunch, and went to Walmart. I had to buy Trinity a shirt and some earrings because her ear piercings was closing. I bought a fun children's CD. Whitney pointed it out to me while I was in the aisle trying to get picture frames for my half-ruined degrees certificates that got wet in my flooded basement. The next thing I know, we were dancing in the aisle to the different songs on the display board. Then we went over to my mom's house to pick up the two little ones. They spent the night over there last night. Once Whitney and I got over there, we ended up staying in her house for a little while and watched *X-Men 3* with my sister and my mom.

Sunday. I went to church, Sam's Club, had Trinity's birthday party, came home to prepare for Monday. The kids were hungry again. I warmed up the stove, so I thought. While the stove warmed, I figured I would make the cookie dough that was given to us as a gift. But of course, this would be the day that the oven doesn't work.

Day 42
Monday, October 30

8:30 a.m. It's a manic Monday, all right. This is the first time I had to type first thing in the morning. My students are in resource right now. Anyway, my oldest daughter would not get up this morning. I had Trinity's clothes for the week packed last night. I didn't get to do Faith's hair, so first thing this morning, I did her hair before I signed in. Faith was able to complete her homework from last night, in about two minutes.

Ms. Brown came into my classroom. We do that sometimes. We walk across the hall or next door to another colleague to exchange professional expertise on given situations. Once in a while, we also vent for thirty seconds. It's not good for us to keep the frustration inside. Teachers would teach for their entire life if we had the parental support from every parent. Anyway, Ms. Brown was upset at seven fifty-five this morning because she had several parents that asked her if she can pay for their child's field trip. We don't have money to pay for the children's field trips. Obviously, they do not understand how much money we spend on their children throughout the school year. They say they are going to pay it back, but then there is an excuse for the rest of the year as to why we are never paid back the money. One of my students, a boy, came in with a ponytail, looking like a girl.

Automatically, students said what I was thinking, "You look like a girl!" And the students started laughing at him. I had to immediately diffuse the comments and focus off Ponto. I knew I had to prevent him from having a tantrum from the children teasing him. I had to redirect their attention to waiting patiently for breakfast to arrive. While we waited for breakfast, we reviewed the letters and sound cards. I don't need anything throwing me off my schedule of all the things that I have to get done. I have to always be prepared for the unknown, or the children will go crazy. I have paperwork I have to fill out for each student, homework to grade, and new homework to put in their book. A container of what seems like a million letters and numbers fell last Thursday. I keep forgetting to get them up. There is so much stuff to do that if you don't do it while you see it, then you forget about it until you see it again. The container fell behind my desk that is in the back of the room. I only go back there to get things that are in the closet. I have to leave early today because of my foot. As usual, I feel overwhelmed, and it's still early in the morning. My professional responsibilities are supposed to take precedence over everything else. Well, that is what is drilled in our heads. On that note, I'm going to have to use some credit to purchase a laptop so I can type at home and get more classroom work done here. I'm not obligated to stay here after school, but I do because I don't want to waste gas driving all the way home on the other side of town, then I would have to come back on another twenty-five minute drive back on this side of town. I really want to get this typing done because it has been a form of therapy for me. I don't use credit cards at all anymore. I only have a home-depot card for household emergencies that need repair. Now I need to buy a stove, and it will have to definitely go on credit. The laptop will definitely have to wait after the stove.

A parent texts me a message say, "Hi, sexy." I don't think that's sexy at all. A man being concerned and taking care of his children is sexy. Treating the other parent with respect despite your differences, that's sexy. Volunteering in the school is sexy. Sending a text message flirting with me first thing in the morning doesn't make me feel sexy but insulted. I hate using my cell phone to call parents. As you can see, they don't have any problems calling me. One of my parents called on my phone almost two hours after school started, asking me to let her and her daughter in the side door. I told her that she had to go to the front door so she can sign in and not have her child marked absent for the day. When I call the parent, I don't get a response. But they sure don't have a problem contacting us when they want something. I wish they would put a phone for teachers to use down here in this darn portable so we don't have to have this foolishness going on. I ignored the message.. I don't have the patience because it takes me too long to text a message anyway. Don't send me a message. Come in the classroom and help me glue this homework in. Come check your child.

10:05 a.m. I'm on my lunch break in the morning. Another thing I can't change but just have to deal with. I am not having a good day. I've misplaced the $72 my daughter's teacher gave me to take up to the office for her. I only went to the bathroom. If I can't find it, it's gone. Stuff get stolen from our classrooms every day. And I misplace things just about every day. There's a 50 percent chance it's misplaced or stolen. My checkbook was stolen from me by one of my parent volunteers last year. So if I can't find it by the end of the day, I'm going to be even more distraught. (I'll be back. I'm going to look for it again.)

10:45 a.m. I found it! I left it on the chalkboard ledge when I went to go write the date. In the middle of looking for the money, a grandmother came to my room and told me something that was a little unnerving. She said that if Nerimiah didn't show up on Tuesday, then they had to go into hiding because of what a nephew got into. She stated that his actions resulted in his entire family getting threats. One of the children goes to Whitney's school. What if they come up here or to the other school to get revenge? One person affects the lives of many. Now I'm worried about that. I get to praying on that unfortunate situation too.

As you can tell, it's another one of those crazy, packed days. I had a half day at work today since I have to get my foot checked again. I rushed downtown after running late from trying to get my students situated into all of the different classes. I stayed at the clinic for four long hours, waiting. No one comes and says anything to you. There is no television, no radio, and no vending machine. They make it that way so you don't want to come back. Even if someone was trying to rip off the city by getting off of work and collecting workman comp, it wouldn't even be worth it to sit here all day and having to come back for all of the follow appointments they give you. They don't let you know what's going on with updating where you are on the list. Then they get an attitude when you walk up to see how much longer you have until it's your turn. I did have a bag of schoolwork with me. I get tired of doing schoolwork to pass the time. I wish I had more time during the school year to have a life. Our job just doesn't allow for it. Any way you look at it, some area of our life, if not more than one, gets neglected during the school year. At two, I called Melissa to pick up Faith since she is working right in the school. Then at four, I had to call her back to ask her if she could get Whitney picked up. Then around four forty-five, I had to call to make arrangements—the same arrangements for Trinity. I know she was sick of me this afternoon. I'm glad she has my back, though. It's that village thing.

I was finally able to see the doctor at almost five. I lost my composure with the physician's intern because she was talking to me like a dog. I'm the kind of person that asks questions. I like to know "useless information," as my sister calls it. I just like to ask questions about whatever is going on. I've never looked at it as one of my occupational nuisances, but maybe it is. I don't know, and I don't care. I think people should ask more questions from their doctors. That is what they are there for. Over time, I have learned to ask questions instead of just accepting what is said to me. I truly felt that she didn't like my questioning her. I just wanted to know why I had no feeling in my foot, and how come I didn't get a boot or crutches. Then she basically got smart with me, telling me that I didn't come back two days later for the follow-up. I tried explaining to her that when I was down here for my initial visit, there were no accommodations made for me and my foot. The clinic didn't have a wheelchair for me to go across the street to get X-rays. No one was available to go with me, so I was on my own doing the best that I could. I explained to her how I almost got hit leaving the clinic while trying to cross the street into the main hospital to get X-rays. For the past three weeks, I've been walking on the side and heel of my foot. Every single time I asked a question, instead of answering my questions, she came back quicker with a question. I was in total disbelief that this day was the way it was, and it is only Monday. At this point, I was so angry at myself for even coming to this city clinic in the first place. I should have gone right around the corner to Sinai Hospital. But no, I just had to follow the given protocol for hurting myself at work. I ended up having to speak to the manager of the facility because I don't care who you are and what position you have, you just don't talk to people any old kind of way. After I spoke to the supervisor, I left. But I had to go back because I had forgotten to get my ticket validated. I got that done and then proceeded to go back up to the eighth floor of the parking garage.

This morning, I was thinking about whether or not I should go to the KIPP (Knowledge Is Power Program) Parent Association meeting at Whitney's school tonight. I said that I would go, so I would be a liar if I didn't. Believe

86

it or not, I've never been to a PTA (Parent-Teacher Association) meeting before. Whitney was always with me at the school that I worked in, so I already knew the information that was going to be disseminated in the meeting. I would just go ask the staff members conducting the meeting. This year is different because she is in a new charter school here in the city. They are in the process of developing a PTA, and I was requested as one of the parents to be a member of their committee. I'm thinking that I may or may not be needed there. My perspective would be different because I am a teacher. I would see concerns from three perspectives instead of two. I view aspects that represent a teacher, a parent, and a student. I really don't need anything else on my plate right now. I feel honored that I was one of thirty-five parents even asked, but at the same time, I like to be able to be really committed when I am doing something. However, after the day that I had, I wasn't even able to go because I got out of the clinic so late.

Day 43
Tuesday, October 31

Today had a little better start. I had a parent helping me in the morning because we had a field trip today. She didn't get to stay for the entire trip because she couldn't get the whole day off. I was grateful for the time she was able to help. A parent wrote a note saying that her son did not have permission to go on the trip because they didn't celebrate Halloween. I called her, but she wasn't there. I did leave a message with the grandmother, letting her know that this trip to the skating rink wasn't to celebrate Halloween. It just so happens that this field trip fell on this day. Two of the students who weren't able to go went to a pre-K class while we went on the trip. What parents don't understand is that children need to come out of their neighborhoods and experience life outside of their box. This was an outing to reward the students who did exceptionally well academically in the first quarter. We don't just have educational trips for form or fashion. We have trips to educate as well as reward and commend our students for doing great things in school. Parents are selective when they pay for trips. They pick and choose which trips their child goes on, if any. But the parents still don't pay. They can pay for the movies and fun centers but won't support their child to participate in educational and rewarding trips. The trips are affordable. This trip was only $5. I know $5 is a lot if you don't have it. However, I do believe that anyone could gather five bucks from family members. Sometimes the trips that reward the honor roll and perfect-attendance students are free.

Anyway, Lemonte cried because I told his stepfather that he would have to go to another class because I wasn't going to be here. He called the child's mother, and she said that he could go if it wasn't too late to pay. Before he could pay, I had to go see how many buses we had and to make sure there would be a seat for him. The stepfather paid for the trip, and Lemonte stopped crying, of course.

The trip was hectic, as usual, for little children. They are so excited that they just want to go and don't care about waiting patiently in line to get in and to get their skates. I went to an attendant at the rink and asked for a trash bag to put my students' shoes in. Otherwise, it would take me forever to look through all of those shoes. I always gather the students' belongings in a big bag. That ensures that no one's coats and shoes will get lost or misplaced or even mixed up with someone else's shoes. My volunteer parent and I also get the lovely task of putting on the skates of all the wonderfully scented feet. When I went with my third-grade classes, they were able to fend for themselves. They could stand in-line to get their own skates and put them on too. Sometimes I would have to tighten them up for them, but that was about it. With my little gems this year, I had to make sure that each skate was the correct size and was tied properly. That's the extent of my responsibility on the skating trips. I make sure they are safe and accounted for at all times. But by no means do I skate anymore. I also let the students and parents know in advance that I do not skate. The parents can respond accordingly with that information. If they want to go or send someone with them, then they can do that. Even if I wanted to, I couldn't skate anyway because of my left foot. I have just been able to bend my big toe completely over the last couple of days. I was on my feet the whole time at the trip. I didn't get to sit down for five minutes. When it was time for lunch, most of the teachers helped to distribute the pizza and drinks.

I did get to take a picture with my daughter, and our picture was adorable. I just love her and the rare opportunity to spend time with her on her trip. After that, I went back to rounding my troops so we could go back to the school. Actually, I was able to sit on the way to and from the school during the trip. The children had fun. They were all well-mannered. There was no hitting, arguing, fussing, or fighting. I was very pleased with all the students that came with our school. I didn't even have to talk to most of them until it was time to go. And that was to gather them all and help them get their skates turned in and the coats and shoes back on. Near the very end, after they got their shoes on, some of the children went back onto the skating rink. Some of my boys, of course, were running around the skating rink floor. The man on the microphone was telling them not to run and to get off the floor. I had to go chase them off the floor. When it was time to go at one, a parent didn't show up to pick up her child as she said she would, so we left. I can't hold up over 150 people because you are whenever you are. I just don't understand. Oh, I did have to talk to Cotez about staying in the right areas. He kept trying to go off into areas no one else was in. He didn't seem too interested in skating. They had video games they could play, but he didn't seem interested in that either. He just walked around almost the entire time. I told Cotez's mom that she would have to go with him on the next trip because he walks off too much. I appear to have three children that need their own assistants right now. It's never going to happen because they aren't that severely offbeat. It would be nice to have an assistant, though. Oh well.

Now to top the day off, why did one of my students get an early dismissal because they had to get ready for a Halloween party? It was around one thirty. It's not even a holiday. You're getting dressed to go to a party to get more candy than what they already eat on a daily basis. I wanted to ask, "Are you serious!" Who takes their child out of school early to get ready for a party? I almost became unprofessional. I wanted to scream, "Hell no, he can't go!" He gets out of school at two twenty-five and goes home early to get ready for a Halloween party. We aren't finished with our day. They can wait another hour for them to get out of school to go put on a costume. What is the world coming to?

When I got off work at two thirty-five, I went to go pick up Trinity and my goddaughter Chantel. At five o'clock, I picked up Whitney from school. We went over to my pop's house. I fixed them plates of leftover Hamburger Helper. At six fifteen, I took Chantel and Whitney to go see *One Night with the King*. The teenagers were from my church. Since we don't celebrate Halloween anymore, I wanted her to do something in place of that. The rest of us went down to our Family Life Center. The church had an alternative for those who didn't celebrate Halloween. The little ones and I had fun. My sister and her boys came also.

Day 44
Wednesday, November 1

Early this morning, one of my best friends and coworkers called me, crying. I felt bad because I didn't know what she was saying. This was my first time I have ever heard her cry. So at one point, I had to ask, was she laughing or crying? I tried to get her to calm down so she could get to tell me what was going on. All I could get out was that her car was stolen. She had just got her car from the shop yesterday and had to pay the $500 deductible for that. I would have been upset also. Anyway, I said all that to say that I was running late again this morning. I stopped over at her house to see if she was okay. She had stopped crying. Her neighbor was there with her. So I gave her a hug, and I called the Magic Man. The Magic Man is another good friend of mine, whom I call for just about everything. He's like my personal handyman and one of the ultimate fix-it guys. She was asking me questions about car insurance and towing. That's not my area of expertise, so I called the Magic Man. By the end of the school day, she had her car back from the pound. It still needs some work.

After I got to work, I had to redo Faith's hair. Her hair is so soft that I literally have to do it right in school so it won't look as if I didn't do it in the first place. Jaron comes in on time with a bagful of candies for the students. That was nice of him and his grandmother. It looked as if it was all of the candies he must have collected last night from trick-or-treating. It was a huge bag. He asked me if he could give the candies out before he had even made it to his seat. I told him that if he and the others made good choices, then he could pass some out for lunch. I thought that would have given him a goal to work toward for the morning. After the children ate breakfast, Jaron started picking on the children. He won't sit on his assigned space on the carpet, which was right in front of me. So I told the children that we would try to ignore his behavior. Early in the morning, around eight thirty-five, I noticed that all the boys were wired. They must have been allowed to have a lot of candies last night or this morning. Now I've mentioned earlier that Wednesdays are not very good days for our class. I have not yet been able to figure that out. I'm quite sure there is a study somewhere about it. Anyway, I already have to ask the boys to try to sit like kings and gentlemen, keeping their hands in their personal space, and so on. They are wrestling, fussing, bickering, tattling, and playing. Cortez was up, walking around as he usually does. Ms. Nixon was a God-sent angel today. It was as if as soon as I was getting unnerved by Jaron, Mrs. Scott showed up at my door with Ms. Nixon. She said that she would come every Wednesday. I was just elated that she was there. Apparently, Mrs. Scott shared with her that I had some friends in my class who needed some special attention. You see, sometimes riches and wealth doesn't add up to someone in your classroom to help you. All the money in the world can't help a school if there aren't parents, family friends, and sometimes complete strangers to come in and say, "I got you. Go on and teach, and I'll sit with him or her."

The rest of the time until lunch was much more bearable. Jaron and my special friend Leandre were sitting beside Ms. Nixon while she sat in a chair. Even still, Jaron was reaching under the chair to hit Leandre. Leandre didn't have to say anything because I saw what he was doing the whole time. The students and I were able to continue working on their syllables and introduction to the new unit of "Finding Friends." Before the students went to lunch, I allowed Jaron to hand out one piece of candy to all of the students. He was worrying for about five minutes when he knew that it was time to go to lunch. After Ms. Nixon and I walked the children to the cafeteria, she stayed down there with them in the cafeteria. Bless her heart. I was able to go back to my classroom, sit down for about fifteen minutes, and eat my lunch too. The remainder of the time, I was rereading what I needed to do for the lessons after lunch. I went to pick my students from the cafeteria, and everyone was good. Jaron got his first good report in the cafeteria because Ms. Nixon was with him. That's a good sign, and hopefully, he will be able to make some positive strides in his behavior.

On our way back up to the classroom, we stopped at the bathroom. I noticed that there was a young lady waiting at the front lobby diagonally from the bathrooms. She said that she was there to pick Jaron up early. Now the boy already had to leave early at eleven thirty because of his behavior. What made today even worse was that he was being picked up on a day when I had someone to assist me with him in my class. He still had another forty-five minutes to go. I didn't know who she was because she hasn't been one of the many people picking him up on a day-to-day basis. Anyway, I told Jaron to go get his stuff. Before I could ask her who she was, she told me that she was his mother. I was thinking that she was an aunt, cousin, or maybe a sister. She looked awfully young to be a mother of a five-year-old. I think she was a little upset that I didn't remember her from the two minutes that she dropped him off on his first day of school. I think we both had the same feeling of being awkward. After she told me who she was, I played it off as if I had remembered her face when I really didn't. I asked her what her name was again, and she said Maytoria. She asked me how he was today, and I told her that he had a good day today. I did tell her that he got off to a shaky start and didn't want to participate this morning. She said that she has heard of his behavior over the last two months and that the behavior would be changing immediately. I said okay, and that if she needed anything, to just let me know.

The remainder of the day was much more bearable. Ms. Nixon stayed the rest of the day. She helped to take them to their lockers and to the bathroom. She counted the smiley faces in their behavior journals so I could award prizes for the month of October. I needed her today. I had a migraine headache that brought tears to my eyes from all of the early-morning stress.

Near dismissal time, Twan's mother showed up, and I had to ask her if he was supposed to go to the recreation center attached to the school. Today I was told that he was supposed to go, and here she was to pick him up. She's been coming to get him since she's been out of rehab. I came to the conclusion that there's no communication between the two parents because she told me that she didn't know what was going on either. She proceeded to tell me that Twan was staying with Kevmani's mother. She was just up there because someone told her he needed to be picked up. She further added that since Kevmani's mother and Twan's father broke up, she doesn't know what's going on. Well, I don't know either, and I have no intentions of trying to get myself webbed into their drama. As his teacher, I just wanted to ensure that he arrives safely to where he is supposed to be after school.

Day 45
Thursday, November 2

At 8:05 a.m., I had five out of seventeen children present and accounted for. Nerimiah still wasn't there. I wondered if everything was okay. I think that if people could understand beforehand how a situation touches so many lives, then people would be more conscientious about the choices they make. Ms. Street came in to do her volunteer hours. She helped me separate the foam letters, numbers, and shapes. She hung up my November decorations for me. She also took down the old work from our last reading unit, which was "Shadows." I tell you, a parent just doesn't know how powerful they are, just by hanging some stuff. It moves the world! Well, it at least moves mine and helps me.

When I went to go pick my children up from lunch, Ms. Fields was brining Jaron out of the cafeteria, holding him by his left hand. She told me that Jaron walked up to her and tapped her on her arm. When she acknowledged him and asked him what he needed, he told her that she was, "the ugliest thing I'd ever seen." For the record, Ms. Fields is not ugly. She is a nice, attractive-looking young lady. So of course, she was a little upset; I was almost embarrassed. She wasn't getting ready to cry or anything. She was in shock that he even said that. Usually, when a child comes to you, you expect a hug or a request of some sort. You don't expect to get insulted by a five-year-old. If he was my child, I would definitely be embarrassed. However, I would have probably plucked him in his lips and made him apologize. I immediately asked him why he said that, and he immediately became enraged. I was just going to explain to him that some things aren't nice to say and that we shouldn't say them. He was angry that we were disappointed in his comment, so he threw a full-blown tantrum. After about ten minutes of trying to calm him down from his tantrum, she took him up to the office. I took both of our classes back up to my room. I didn't know what was going to happen on their way to the office. I could only imagine.

Ms. Fields came to my room and began to give me an update about taking Jaron to the office. The students needed to go to the bathroom, so we all walked down the hall. We had to wait because there were other classes utilizing the bathrooms. Ms. Fields was telling me the continuing adventure on the way to the office. While we were waiting to take a bathroom break, Jaron and his mother came around the other hallway. I don't know if she just happened to be on her way up here or if she got a ride up here after someone from the school contacted her. She stopped to tell me that she was going to take care of him when he got home. She explained to me that she has just come home from being incarcerated, and Jaron has to get used to her all over again. Apparently, Jaron has been in the care of his grandmother, and she said he's been taking advantage of her. By the end of the conversation, my students were finished using the bathroom, so we proceeded to walk back to the classroom. On the way up the hall to our class, Maytoria stopped in front of Jaron's lockers for him to get his belongings. The next thing I heard was him telling his mother to get her hands the f—— off him. He was also scratching on her skin, trying to make her bleed. She acted as if his behavior toward her was normal and didn't seem to faze her at all. I was speechless! I've never heard a little child cuss at their mother before. I've heard teenagers cuss their parents out, not that it's excusable. He wouldn't stop giving her a fit until she told him that if he didn't calm down, she was going to have to call the police. A mother telling her five-year-old she's going to call the police on him is what we have to look forward to? If the children are our future, then we're in trouble if this terrible cycle continues like this.

Ms. Mookie came up to me this afternoon. She told me that she saw Twan today. She just happened to go over to their house, and he answered the door. Ms. Mookie asked him why he wasn't in school, and he said school was closed. She told him that it wasn't and told him to go get his mother. The mother said that she overslept. Ms. Mookie reminded her that he could have come to school late. I have a student who comes in late every single day. They live right across the street. I mean literally right across the street. Anyway, Ms. Mookie said that Twan was back at the house where his mother is. She is supposed to be in rehab. I thought that she had come back kind of early. I don't know the exact time she needed to stay, if any. Each person is different, and their time spent in recovery varies. There are so many programs that have different times for completing the initial stage. The movies portray the withdrawal process in a matter of hours. I did think that a week was kind of short. The program that we have in our school's neighborhood is a couple of months long. As I said, I don't know what program she is supposed to be in. Anyway, I agreed with Ms. Mookie when she said that she needed to go back and get herself together. I would take him under my care if I could. I know that I have a lot on my plate right now with just this divorce process alone. That's not including all of my professional responsibilities, personal, health, and family problems. And sometimes this writing seems addictive. I feel as if I'm relieving some of my stress, as if I am actually talking with someone. I think this is a good therapy for me right now. I sure can't afford a $30 co-pay to talk to a counselor right now every week. I'm stressed out because of the severity of the behavior problems and lack of educational experiences of my students. Behavior problems and low academics should never be combined in a class with appropriate and readily available resources. One student maybe, but to have the majority of the class with problems and issues is a problem.

Day 46
Friday, November 3

It is weeks like this that make me say to myself that I'm ready to come out of the classroom. With my eight years of experience and level of education, I assume I can do many things in education. I've never checked. I definitely wouldn't be good sitting behind a desk, pushing paper. I did choose to be on the front line and fight this war head-on, but it's days and weeks like this that just make me say enough is enough. What I signed up for is not what it is now.

Children came to school late, of course. Nerimiah didn't come back today. Mr. Shiller told Jaron's mother that he couldn't come to school today. So I wonder if he is on punishment for his behavior or he just gets hit upside the head, cussed out, and then allowed to watch television or play games. Ponto came in again with his hair "looking like a girl," as the students so honestly and frankly say. I have wanted to do his hair all week. People who don't know him think he's a girl. A lot of children don't have distinct boy or girl features. It seems as if these days, if you were to put a dress on the boys or a suit on the girls, you would never know the difference if no one didn't tell you. The girls were off today. The behavior of the boys is now influencing the girls; there was only one student I didn't have to talk to today. That's my new little girl, Shamira.

And where do some of these names come from? I know I'm going to get a lot of feedback about the following comments, but let the truth be told. I was walking in the hallway and actually read the names on the lockers. Parents just don't understand that there are some rules to the English language. Now I'm not talking about ethnic names or names that come from any particular heritage or culture. I am now talking about the super ghettoized names that people create from somewhere in their imagination. Sometimes they take a known name and spell it or pronounce it differently. Imani pronounced as Emani, or vice versa. I think I'm pronouncing the child's name correctly, but I'm dead wrong. Then they have the nerve to get upset with us because we don't get it correct on the first try, or it takes a while to learn the name because the composition of the name goes against a set rule. For example, Tarje. I am told to pronounce it as Tarjae, but it is spelled Tarje. There are names such as Destine, Eternity, Poetry, Future, Mercedes, Lexus, Rashina, Tramaine, or Quatraine. If the person can tell me a reason or justification that I can understand a little better other than, "I just made it up 'cause it sounds cute." It never occurred to me that one day my own children, among others, would curiously ask why their name is what it is. I think that some valid reasoning should go into a name. That's not even including the nicknames that the children believe are their real names. Most of them begin with *little*. Little man, Little L., Li'l something. Now I can work with Destiny, but a lot of names sound like an object or an idea and not a person. This was not a great week as far as the rest of the day outside of my class; it just wasn't a good day. It could have been worse. I lost the keys to my classroom. It fell off my lanyard that I wear around my neck. Today was also picture day. I gave

Faith's teacher $25 cash in an envelope sealed with thick brown tape. In the envelope, there was a $20 bill, three $1 bills, and $2 in quarters. When the time came to have Faith's picture taken, Ms. Ellis couldn't find the envelope. I was trying to watch my class and help her find the money. To make a very long part of the day short, Ms. Ellis had to write a check to pay for the pictures. Faith had to have her picture with my class taken again because the picture people didn't have the envelope. I wasn't happy with the picture either. Faith was upset that she had to come out of her classroom to pose again for the picture. She also had to have her picture taken with me there. We all know kids act funny when their parents come around. On the computer screen, her face looked as if she was constipated. It's her very first school picture, and it would be my daughter whose picture was jacked up.

After school when I went to go pick up Faith, her teacher told me that one of the twin boys took the envelope off Ms. Ellis's desk and threw it in the trash. I wasn't surprised either when she told me it was one of the twins. I had to say something earlier this year to the little boys about putting their hands on my daughter and other students in the class. I had to scrape up that money last night. I've had to nickel-and-dime it as everybody else. And I know Ms. Ellis didn't have money to waste. Children should be taught by the time they go to school not to touch things that aren't theirs. Everyone will say that it is her fault. I do disagree. When you raise your child with rules, manners, morals, and principles, children will most likely not steal or touch things that don't belong to them. Will Ms. Ellis get her money back? Probably not. I know the parents will think it is Ms. Ellis's fault for leaving it on the desk with a whole bunch of four-year old's.

After school, around four o'clock, Twan was still in the building. I usually walk all the way up to the office to clean out my mailbox. When I clear it out in the middle of the day, I usually have to go all the way back up there anyway. It is too far of a walk to take just to walk for no reason at all. The poor child was sitting in the office. No one had picked him up yet. He looked like a sad little puppy. I asked him, was he okay? And he told me that he was. I reluctantly walked back down to my room.

Saturday. I worked on report cards until eleven at night. I don't have a nice work area to get paperwork completed. I have to sit on the couch or the floor, which is very uncomfortable for me. I'm almost done. I'm always telling myself I'm almost done, and then it usually takes me two more days to get them done. I also cut out pictures for the students to do a Thanksgiving activity next week.

Sunday. I went to church, came home, and worked on report cards. I've stayed up until the wee hours of the morning. I believe it's around one o'clock, and I should be getting to bed now.

Have you ever wondered what *a.m.* and *p.m.* means? Well, I'm glad you asked. *A.m.* is the abbreviation for the Latin *ante meridiem*, which means "before noon" in English. *P.m.* is the abbreviation for *post meridiem*, which means "after noon." My sister would say it's another piece of useless information I have learned over the years. Hey, you never know when you might want to be on a game show.

Quarter 2

Unity
Author Unknown

I dreamed I stood in a studio
And watched two sculptors there.

The clay they used was a young child's mind,
And they fashioned it with care.

One was a teacher; the tools he used
Were books, and music and art;

One was a parent with a guiding hand,
And a gentle, loving heart.

Day after day the teacher toiled,
With touch that was deft and sure

While the parents labored by his side
And polished and smoothed it o'er.

And when at last their task was done,
They were proud of what they had wrought.

For this thing they had molded in the child
Could be neither sold nor bought.

And each agreed he would have failed
If he had worked alone,

For behind the parent stood the school
And behind the teacher, the home.

Teacher Objective: The teacher will enhance and support students' skills by further implementing small-group instruction, workshop, and other academic activities to support student learning.

In case I haven't mentioned earlier, we teachers have hundreds of objectives and goals for the year. (Actually, I just stopped to calculate. For elementary school, we have about 1,600 objectives for a school year. Why? Well, every subject has a specific outcome or goal that we are trying to teach to the children for them to learn. The students have a specific targeted skill that they need to learn for that particular lesson. For example, if we teach character education, phonics, phonemic awareness, vocabulary, language, reading comprehension, math, science, and social studies, then those are nine different objectives a day times 180 days, which equals at least 1,600 objectives.) Anyway, in quarter 1, we are teaching with a lot of focus on classroom and behavior management. By the time we get to quarter 2, the classroom environment should be established as one that promotes learning. We can now spend more time on teaching the academic skills that the children need. There's no actual day to transition into this phase. Every day is a building block for the next. If you have a good group of students who are focused on learning and don't have a lot of behavior problems within the class, then you can move on earlier. A teacher can fly full speed ahead a week after school starts. That would be ideal. However, in my nine years of experience, it usually kicks in around the seventh to eighth week of school. I want to focus on getting into the skills that the students need. My time now definitely should be spent on classroom instruction and not on negative behaviors, and disciplining and reprimanding students.

Parents' Objective: The parents will continue to support their child by continuing implemented routines at home.

It's all about unity and being on one accord. The school system cannot function to the fullest capabilities without the support of the parents and family. The two go hand in hand. We really need parents to help their children with their homework, feed them dinner, and get them to bed at a reasonable time. Children need a good night's sleep in order to function well at school all day long. We need parents to keep the family drama away from the children as much as possible. There are so many students who come to school with the weight of the world on their shoulders because of grown folks' business. Before the child even gets out of the house on the way to school, They need to be told something positive and encouraging, even if you yourself don't belief it. Get them up on time and before they get out that door, they should be at least told that they are loved. Tell them to have a great day learning or to make you proud. Our children's encouragement shouldn't be predicated on how we feel. We all have bills, responsibilities and other things going on. That's not our children's problem unite with the school by supporting your child in every way possible, so that they will be open to learn and have a great day at school.

Day 47
Monday, November 6

Today was a good day even though I woke up with a headache. Thirty minutes into the school day, and I only had two students. Jaron didn't show up for school today. I get more done when I don't have to attend to him and other students with behavior problems that interfere with instruction and the learning of others. Three other children didn't come either. The most interesting part of the day happened right after school.

While I was standing in the lobby area, making sure that students were leaving and not playing in the hall, six older students came up to me. I assumed that they were coming into the portable to come pick up a sibling. Their grades ranged from third up to fifth. The third grader said, "Here, Ms. Calicchia!" And he held out his hand to give me something. I didn't immediately grab what he was giving me because I was just trying to see what it was that seemed so exciting to him and the others. He put the object so close to my face that I wasn't able to focus on it right away. At the time, I was just thinking that it was some toy or something his teacher gave him for being good today. Once I focused on what it was, I was momentarily speechless. And oh! Was it something! It was a small, one-inch pink plastic pencil–topper in the shape of a penis. Yes, I actually but reluctantly mustered the courage to write this one. It's not a misprint. I did say a little pink penis with the little testicles and precise details of a real one. (I'm cracking up as I write this.) It appears to be an eraser. When I looked on the inside of it, I could see the metal part of where the pencil used to be. It's not that it's funny that children have X-rated party favors in their possession. It's just that every time I think I've seen and heard it all, it isn't actually the case. I didn't think that this is something that I would be writing about. It's just another example of the direction that our future is going toward. I think I was grown, in my mid-twenties, before I saw such a thing.

Anyway, I immediately asked the children where they got it. The fifth grader said she found it on the floor in their classroom today. Instead of throwing it in the trash or giving it to her teacher, it becomes the center of amusement for the remainder of the day. I feel honored that they felt comfortable enough to bypass everyone else and give it to me. However, I just so desperately wish our children could

104

keep their innocence. There was no shame, no embarrassment, no hesitation, and no bashfulness in just openly passing the little plastic penis to me. It was as if they just handed me a piece of candy. It's all insane. I don't know if I should keep it in a little container, just in case people think I'm making up this stuff. I have no such imagination. I can admit that I'm naïve to believe in true love for me, no more wars for any country, and that the future of our children will be greater than it is now. However, I could never make up the experience I've witnessed and heard of all these years. I wonder who was the original student who had it, and where did they get it from? How did they feel about it? Do they really know what it represents? I wonder if they went to a party and got it themselves or if they got it from their parents or other family members. I don't know. It's just a shame that children so young are into things so grown.

Damon came by to see me after school, and I gave him $7 since that seems to be the holdup from getting registered for school. He didn't stay long because we both had things to do.

Voting Day- No School
Tuesday, November 7

I voted today. While I was waiting in line to vote, I took a really good look at the school. It was so depressing. I can't understand for the life of me why schools are built like prisons and not as institutions for learning. The same cinder blocks you see in the prisons walls are the same blocks you see in schools. I hope the candidates for presidency have a plan to overhaul the entire United States school system. I will be listening to any future debates to see where the candidates say they are going to put their focus as the next president. America is the wealthiest nation in the world but appears to be the dumbest, if you ask me. We are as rich as our poorest people. We are as bright as our most illiterate

105

adults. I'm talking about some of the choices that are made on our behalf by government officials. The way things are now is just too antiquated. The buildings are old, dusty, dark, and depressing. There is only a small population of schools that are very technology equipped. Throwing one computer in every class is not considered technologically rich either. Some schools have a lot more, and some have significantly less. There should be a mandated standard across the board. There shouldn't have to be vouchers for parents to send their child to another school because that school is safer and, overall, equipped with better materials and supplies. All schools should have the same level of excellence to ensure that students receive an equal playing field of possibilities. Who wants to learn in a gloomy place? Going into a lot of these schools is like going into a cold, damp, moldy basement. We need to make sure all schools look like miniature colleges and universities that are full of life. It should be a place that staff and students are eager to get to every day.

Every day, my students and I, along with millions of more students and teachers, recite the Pledge of Allegiance. And that pledge states, "Indivisible, with liberty and justice for all." By no means am I a high-strung, far-out political person. I'm just a mom and a teacher who wants to see all children, regardless of their demographics, have an equal opportunity to learn to the best of their abilities. I believe that every day, we become more divided and that there is less justice for all. I've never seen so many senior citizens working in my life before. I don't think they retire and say, "I think I'll go spend my supposed retirement working as a cashier, security guard, or flipping burgers until I actually pass away." There is nothing wrong with those positions. But there is something wrong when the elders of a great country have to work to eat and get or buy medicine. It used to be a choice after retirement, and now it's not an option. The list goes on and on of all the inequalities from school district to school district, from state to state. I just hope that education and parental responsibility is taken seriously by our government in the near future, or our children will continue not to have a great one.

All right, I'm finished standing on my imaginary little soapbox. I did get the truck checked. I thought I was hearing something. It turned out to be nothing. I also went to the market today. It is such a tedious task. When you go from shopping for two to shopping for four, and for the entire month, it can be exhausting. After Whitney and I put the food away, I took a nap, and she watched her sisters for me. After I woke up from my nap, I started to prepare for tomorrow.

Day 48
Wednesday, November 8

Jaron and Dimani showed up late. Three children absent, one withdrawn. Cotez and Reshae left early. Jaron didn't leave until one thirty. I didn't even mind him staying either. He did a pretty good job completing all of his activities to the best of his abilities. I think he really tried to do his best for me today by listening and paying attention. His true character was still present, but I think he may have been tired, and that's why he was a little more calm today.

Jamon showed up to tell me he starts school next Monday. It rained today. It was a gloomy, rainy day. I don't have the energy to even talk about the day. It just seems pointless for me to even come in here anymore. I feel like an overpaid babysitter. I don't need any awards, I don't need to be Teacher of the Year, I don't need to be validated as a teacher by anyone. I just want to know that I'm making a difference in the life of the students. I don't feel like I used to do. Every day, despite my own feelings, I am encouraging, pushing, and giving high expectations. I tell them to try their best. Why would they believe anything I say if they don't even believe in themselves? I can believe with all my heart that they are going to soar high into the sky, but I can't send the rocket up all by myself. It takes a team.

Day 49
Thursday, November 9

After school yesterday, I started making sight-word flash cards for my class. I took them home last night with every intention of working on them. I didn't. I don't get home until six every night. Then I have to make dinner and make sure Whitney does her homework. Faith always gets her homework done in about five minutes, unless it's some kind of project. By the time I get the younger two settled, I'm ready to go to bed myself. I was in bed at eight fifteen last night, just exhausted.

Today was a successful, good day. I almost had perfect attendance. Jaron didn't come to school today. I thought he would have come back since he had a good day yesterday. He really needs to come every day. It's a catch-22 with him. He is not ready to be in school, but he needs to be in school to learn. He has already missed the first quarter of math. The rest of my students got here close to the correct time. Even Dimani came in earlier today. I was elated. I was able to teach the children their lesson on compound words and read a new story, and they practiced writing numbers *6* to *10*. We were also able to go over twenty high-frequency words in great detail and practice. I had an overall good day. One of my parents who said they were going to come in didn't. I saw her in the office yesterday when I had to make a request to get some copies run off. She said that her third son, four months old, had an ear infection. I'm quite sure that's why she wasn't able to make it in today. It is totally understandable.

Somewhere along the day, I was just thinking how disappointed I am with the parental involvement over the last several years. And all my colleagues and coworkers have also noticed. Last year, I had two parents who volunteered at least once a week or once every other week. That was my best year, having the help of parents. They would cut, glue, paste, and color. They would help me do the little things that make a big difference. A lot of parents think they will have to actually work with a child to volunteer, but that's generally not the case. There are so many things that need to be done that we cannot possibly do in the seven hours that we get paid for. A lot of behind-the-scenes preparation and paperwork are what takes a lot of our time away from ourselves and our own children throughout the school year. The lower grades such as nursery school to third grade need a lot more volunteers, but the remaining grades need volunteers as well. Parents make a difference sitting in the back of the classroom, making copies at their own job, or taking a stack of papers home to file or grade. They can grade papers, organize, file papers, or display work on the bulletin board or on the wall outside of the classroom. There are many things that help. For the parents, guardians, grandparents, and extended family members who couldn't come in, they would just send snacks or a couple of dollars once in a while to help. I had a grandparent last year whose legs weren't cooperating with her, so she would send in snacks and money throughout the year. Every time I sent notes home asking for help, only the same four people would help. And I try to make it convenient for the volunteers. I never overload them with an impossible task or massive amount of work. Just a little at a time does a classroom good.

This year, most of my students haven't even had the basic supplies such as crayons, glue, and pencils. I have spent so much money on these items. And since the children do not know how to use the materials, the crayons and pencils get all broken. I have run out of the three most important materials that little children need in school. Pencils, crayons, and glue sticks. I had to use liquid glue for the past two weeks. When I teach and model for them how to use glue, I softly squeeze one little drop of glue out onto the paper. When they do it, do you really think that's what comes out on their paper? No! There is glue all over the paper, hands, and clothes. Sometimes the glue makes it into their mouth and hair.

My contractor and friend Big G came here after school today to discuss some work that is being done on my house. He saw me sitting here in the corner and asked me what I was doing, and when I told him I was documenting some of the craziness that goes on with the parents, students, and my job daily, he got fired up on another whole topic. Then he and I went on and on for another half hour or so. He and I did have an interesting discussion. He further questioned me as to why I am writing this book. He thinks that I should be writing a book about the war between black men and black women. First, I told him that all ethnicities have their own wars within. Some are more than others and take on different forms. I told him that it isn't just black parents fighting against each other. There are too many parents period that have let their hatred for one another cancel out their love for their child and disillusioned them. I don't know everything that makes it to the national news every day. There are documented cases of parents of various backgrounds who have let an argument, dispute, or disagreement snowball into a full-fledged war in their family. All because of the love they think they have lost or that they once felt for each other. There are so many reported cases and many more unreported cases of violence that trickle down to the children. I heard about a father who allegedly threw his son over a bridge because of a custody battle. There is another father who killed his four daughters and himself because the wife cheated and allegedly abandoned her family. There are mothers who took the lives of children that they helped to give life to. I've heard of too many stories of children being drowned, shot, poisoned, or suffocated to death by their mother or father for whatever reasons they thought were valid. My heart and my prayers for peace one day sincerely go out to you if you have been a survivor of such horrible and tragic circumstances.

It just seems as if there's an unspoken war between most parents who are no longer together. The ideal way to end a relationship is with peace. I wish I could say that it would end in love and understanding. Sometimes we never understand something, and it's sad to say that millions of people really don't understand the meaning of love. Love is not something that we just say and proclaim. Love is what we do. You can't say you love the mother of your child and then beat the living daylights out of her. You can't say you love the father of your child and then cheat on him or make him feel he's less of a man when he's going through rough times. Most often, it doesn't happen that way because there is too much anger and hatred for what pain and hurt has done in the relationship. Sometimes the hurt caused in a current relationship is because of a past relationship that carried over into something that was supposed to be new.

It crosses all racial barriers, all economic and educational statuses. Pain has no color. It's that love that people carelessly proclaim that is supposed to protect our children, even from ourselves if need be. The children should never be so negatively affected because of it. Parents having a war within them is one of the major causes of dysfunction in the family. Those personal demons that we can or cannot deal with. There's that saying that says it's not what happens to you, but how you respond to what happens that matters. Evil things happen. You can overcome it with good and end the cycle with you, or you can knowingly continue to cause pain. I'm not preaching to anyone either. I'm encouraging myself. I made up my mind a long time ago when I was fourteen that if I was ever blessed to have

111

children, they would never grow up the way I did. With knowledge, patience, and determination, I can thank God's grace that I broke the cycle of drugs and abuse. I still sometimes struggle with the things that people have done to me. But I love my children enough to actively protect them from my fears by being acutely tuned in to our surroundings. I admit that I messed up and argued in front of my daughter a few times with my soon to be ex-husband. We both agreed that it wasn't a good choice. So we tried to go to a different part of the house, or even out of the house, to discuss what needed to be said. Over the last year or so, Whitney has said that she remembers just one time when Herbert and I *fought*. Her impression of arguing was like a fistfight. Although he never hit me, she assumed it to be a physical fight. After this divorce, I will never bring another man around my girls unless I'm absolutely sure in my heart that it's a good thing. Even then I might make another mistake, but I will try my best not to.

These problems start at home, then they spill over into the extended family, neighborhood, schools, and community. And so on and so on. It doesn't matter what color you are. There is some kind of trial and tribulation for every race, color, religion, creed, gender, and whatever else category there is these days. I'm definitely not an expert on relationships, just on myself, so I'll stick to what I know. I heard someone say that parents should love their children more than they hate each other. I can say that my soon-to-be ex and I have not been obviously hostile and argumentative in front of the children. They are so young right now, but they can pick up on things. A distrust of each other causes dysfunction for the child. I do agree that parents who are going through traumatic relationships cause their children to have a more difficult time in school. When a relationship ends, it isn't just the custodial parent's job to support the child. It takes two parents to tango, so it takes two parents to be there for their child, regardless of where each lives.

Tonight, after I left for work, I was just blown away by an unexpected situation for the evening. As soon as I left for work, I had planned on running to Walmart, the market, and Party City to return some items, and then take Melissa to the bank since she still doesn't have her car. Anyway, while I was sitting in front of our school building waiting for Melissa to come out, Whitney called me to tell me that her daddy was on his way to come get her. I found that very unusual because he and I had an agreement about who is picking her up. My school can be seen from her school. It takes me no more than a minute to drive down the hill. I immediately called him to find out why he was picking her up. He told me that the school's social worker called him and said that she needed to speak with him. He said that he was getting ready to call me, but I made the call first. I told Melissa that she could drop me off down the hill, and she could use my truck to go run her errands. Melissa took Faith with her, and I called Trianne, and she said it was all right for Trinity to stay late. When we finally got in the meeting to talk to the social worker, she began to tell us what my daughter had expressed to her. I know my daughter doesn't want me to put all of her business out there. So I'll just say that she was feeling so terrible that she felt as if she couldn't deal with it in a good way. To make a long night short, I was just devastated that peer pressure continues to be so prevalent in her life. She has a host of family and friends that support her and that she is able to go to and express herself. To hear what was wrong with her made a little tear fall down my right cheek. I know she can't grow up in a safe and secure bubble where no hurt and disappointments will come her way. I just think that there are some things they shouldn't even have to go through. I don't want her to feel so devastatingly torn between the world and how I'm trying to raise her. And now I feel like a failure as a mother because she couldn't come to talk to me. I feel like a failure because I feel as if her pressure to have and want things her friends have and desire puts me under pressure to give in to what society says.

I am not going to compromise my beliefs as far as training my daughter to be a woman of God, of character, of dignity, and of a strong mind. Some problems I wasn't going to address right now, but since I am going through some things, why don't I just put it here now. Why should this matter to all the parents who say that I'm there for my child, I go to the school, I ask questions, I don't let my child wear skirts up to their crack, shirts down the other crack, and pants down to the ankle? I govern what they watch, see, and hear on the television, radio, and video games. You have to care because our children go to school with children whose parents don't care. It is the just against the unjust. It's the spoiled versus the unspoiled; it's the rough, rugged, and raw against the sheltered. There needs to be some uniformity in the standards in the way the children are being raised. My daughter should not be called *weird* because I don't allow her to dress hoochie, hookerish, or like a slut. She should not be ostracized because she has manners, dresses like a young lady, and likes school. She should not feel like an outcast because she doesn't have a television in her room. She should not feel so overwhelmed that she has to have a boyfriend because everybody else's parents let them have a boyfriend or girlfriend at eleven, twelve, and thirteen years old. A child is a child. And my child is going to do what her family thinks is best for her development.

According to the legal system, if you are under the age of seventeen, you are a child. That same law says that seventeen-year-olds can have consensual sex and drive vehicles. In most places, children can drop out of school at the age of sixteen. Why do we even have such laws? The laws should be for their good and not for their failure. How about if there exists no such option to drop out of school? I'm not talking about extreme circumstances either. They wouldn't want to drop out of school if they didn't have to take care of their family and the school gave them the level of preparation that they need to succeed in the workforce. Another problem is that too many of our children aren't allowed to be children. Younger siblings and too damn tired grandparents are unnecessarily taking care of children.

Day 50
Friday, November 10

Today was a disastrous day for me because of my own personal issues from last night and the same foolish behaviors I have to deal with in this class.

Jaron was putting his middle finger up every day, all day. There is no regular educator in their right mind that wants to work like this on a daily basis. The children are so distracted by him. I can't teach with him in class. He needs to be in a setting that is conducive for him because this is not it. Every single time he does something, the remaining students respond with "oohs" and "aaahs" or complaints. There isn't even a point in complaining to headquarters. They would laugh at me in the face and say, "Do the best you can do with what you have." I don't have the resources, training, or expertise to deal with a child who is totally not ready for school. His behavior resembles that of a child who is documented as emotionally disturbed. He would qualify for any kind of services because he doesn't have any formal school training.

For example, if a child is one to two grade levels below his or her peers, the deciding factor for this child receiving services sometimes boils down to attendance, among other factors. A team that consists of a regular-education teacher, special-education teacher, one administrator, school psychologist, speech pathologist, a caseworker, and the school social worker come together in a meeting. One of the first things that's looked at is attendance. We need to determine if a child is slow because they didn't

115

come to school or because they actually have a learning disability. We look at when a child entered formal education. We see if the student had nursery school or preschool. Then we see how many days, if any, that the student missed school. If the child missed sixty days in kindergarten and fifty-five days in the first grade, then the child has had no consistent form of instruction. Young children learn from repetition, and if they repeatedly missed days from school, then they missed what was needed to be successful. That doesn't even include a child being in and out of five different schools in one year. There is so much red tape and bureaucratic crap that we have to deal with on a daily basis. I remember last year, a six-year-old that has never been to school came to my class. My principal came to me because he knew that I would "be sensitive to the child's situation." Well, this child's situation was unique. He was the son of two deaf parents. He was six and had never been in school. He was able to speak, but his oral language wasn't as developed as it should have been for a normal six-year-old. His language was limited because he spoke sign language with his parents and had no other way to develop his verbal vocabulary. I didn't have any problem with that. What I did have a problem with, was that before she left, she wrote me a note asking that I check his Pull-Ups and change it for him. My principal had already gone back up to the office by the time she had asked me this. I wrote her a note back saying that I could send him to the bathroom but that I could not and would not be able to change his Pull-Ups. After school, I went up to the office to let the principal know that I nicely told her that I wasn't changing any Pull-Ups. Children adapt quickly, and he would have gone to the bathroom just like the rest of the boys. I'm not getting near any children in any bathroom. It is inappropriate for me to do so. If that is what he really needed, then he would have to go to a self-contained class, where the teachers have aides to carry out those special needs. The boy ended up doing well in my

116

class. He adapted to the schedule and learned quickly. He went to the bathroom with the boys and didn't have any accidents. He developed some of his oral language for the last quarter, and I learned some sign language. It was a learning experience for the whole class. But this child I have in my class needs other professional help to just be able to socialize with other children and adults. He is too hostile to try to learn in a regular school day, in a regular school setting. I don't even want to go through it. If this same child was placed in a better-neighborhood school, oh, you best believe this child's behaviors would not have been tolerated by the parents or the administration.

We had a Poor Friday luncheon today. It's just basically a potluck on the Fridays that we don't get paid. I ate a little bit. I was too disappointed in myself to eat. I called my sister and told her that I still felt terrible about how my daughter was feeling. I did start to call around for a counselor that specializes in working with teenagers, but that didn't make me feel any better about doing my job as a mom. Being a single parent is a tough job. Just being a parent is a difficult task. I called up to the office and told them I was having a personal issue and I needed to step out of my class to get myself together. That was around the time that my sister showed up. My sister came around one, and I continued to fill her in on what happened last night. And my question to her and to everyone in this war of raising children is, what do you do when you raise your child one way and the world says raise them in another? The answer is keep on my brother, keep on my sister. Keep on. I know I will see the rewards later in life.

Saturday. I couldn't really sleep. I woke up early, around five thirty, crying. I could hear my pop was up, so I went downstairs in the basement, where he watches television. I needed a hug. I love my pop, but he was telling me things I already knew, but sometimes you don't want to talk. Sometimes you just need a hug. Obviously I didn't get any school work done.

Sunday. I got up and dragged myself to church. I cried the whole time. I really believe that I think too much about some things sometimes. Sometimes I think having a companion physically, by my side, would get me through things a little bit better. I know I'm not the only mother or father struggling with issues related to their children. But when it seems as if I'm the only one and don't have anyone to encourage me in my time of need, it's just a lonely feeling. Now I have to get myself together before I go teach my students tomorrow.

Day 51
Monday, November 13

I didn't go to work today. I wasn't in my right frame of mind to function at work. I need to get myself together. I got up, took the girls to all of their designated places, and then I went back home. I slept late, watched videos, and rested in between watching television.

Day 52
Tuesday, November 14

I went to my appointment at the clinic and ran some major errands. I feel a little bit better. I feel bad for my students. I hate taking off from work. Now I feel a little guilty about missing work. I know it's for the best. I wouldn't be any good for my students right now.

Day 53
Wednesday, November 15

I took my sweet time getting up. I ran a few minor errands. I think I'm ready to go back. I'm usually in a funk for about three to five days. I need to be there for my girls. I'm their sole provider and caretaker, so I have to pick myself up and move on to the best of my abilities.

Day 54
Thursday, November 16

I'm back! I was kind of out of the loop this morning. I had to get back in the swing of things. It isn't normal for me to be off three days in a row during the school week. I woke up late. Outside of that, I had a good day today. As soon as I came to work today, I thought that someone from the administrative team would have asked me how I was doing since they were aware of why I was out, but of course not. I don't even know why I thought anyone would have cared that I was gone. Teachers are just a wasted, replaceable commodity to some people. They have their favorites as to whom they really care about. Writing about the problem within America's school systems would be another whole book in and of itself. I would probably get fired for that book if I wrote one.

The students were happy that I came back. They are the only ones that really matter to me anyway. It's those precious feelings that are too few and far between that make teaching worth it for the moment. They all said that they had missed me. I heard all about Jaron's rampage on Tuesday while I was out. He gave everybody the middle finger. I think that's his favorite finger. He ran out of the building twice. Mrs. Siris had caught up with him in the street, but she needed help with him because he was too much for her. He isn't small either. He is average in height for his age, but he

119

is solid muscle all the way through. I know because I've had to refrain him in a hold called the a bear hug and tried to pick him up off the floor and, let's not forget, bring him back into the school after he ran out. I heard all about his behavior from everyone who had an interaction with him on that day. He kicked Ms. Hallow and got smart with several adults including the substitute, the neighboring teachers, and the secretary. One teacher explained to him that if he didn't calm down, they would have to call the school police. He said he didn't care and that he would shoot them. He also made the same threat to Mrs. Siris. He didn't get picked up on time at eleven thirty as he was supposed to. I was told that there would be an alternative placement for him. It wouldn't happen right away, but it would happen once all of the paperwork was taken care of. Yeah right! I've been in the system long enough to know that's not going to happen.

Day 55
Friday, November 17

It was chaotic today. Today was a half day of school because of report card conferences that were supposed to take place beginning at twelve thirty. I was able to talk to three parents as soon as they picked up their child. I knew I had to talk to them while they were there because I knew that they weren't coming back. One was rushing me as if she really wasn't even trying to hear what I was saying. One parent was really focused on what I had to say about her son. No other parents showed up until I was getting ready to leave around two thirty. Even though it was past the scheduled conference time and past my workday, I still stayed and gave the parents my undivided attention. I went over the child's report card thoroughly. I explained all the skills that the kindergartens have to master. The parents were very surprised by all the specific skills in reading, math, science, and social studies. They were very taken aback of how much is taught in a school day and that this grade is taken seriously. I had four parents out of twelve show up. That is horrible. When I took my sign-in sheet for conferences, the principal said, "Four, that's really good." No, it's not. Another poor average that has become normal.

Day 56
Monday, November 20

Ms. Brown didn't come in today. I had her students in my class until a substitute came. During the time that I had her class, a student couldn't get his locker open. I quickly stepped outside of my room and was down the hallway, about twenty feet, by the lockers when a parent walked down and asked me where Ms. Brown was. I told her that she wasn't in today and that three of her students were in my room. She proceeded to say that she didn't want them in the room unattended. In a matter of less than one minute, I was back in my room. I said, "Well, I'm standing right here in the hall and can see my class from where I'm at." There was a total of four students sitting on the carpet. I explained to her that a student needed help, and she didn't care. She said that she was going to go up to the office to complain. I told her that she could take her son out of my class and stand in the hallway until we found out where the children were to go. Before I could tell her that she could also just stay in my room until I was able to help all the students with putting away their belongings, she walked off and went up the hall. I knew that she wouldn't have stayed in the room, and I wouldn't have wanted her nasty attitude in my room or for her to help me with the students. Sure enough, they called down to the office to see if I was in my room, and I was. Later on, when I went into the office, Mrs. Landing asked me if I was in my room on time. I told her that I was in my room on time, way before that parent came in there. All the parents of kindergartens at our school know that we don't

121

have an assistant. If the parent really cared that much about her child, she could have stayed in my room for a few minutes, just in case other students needed my help. But no, they can't help us, but some parents expect us to break our necks to cater to their child. Some of the very same parents who complain about us are the very same parents who haven't spent one hour in our room for the entire school year. The parents who are fortunate enough to volunteer are amazed at all that we have to do. So if you're a parent that complains a lot about nothing and doesn't volunteer in the classroom, not even an hour in an entire school year, then put up or shut up!

The rest of the day was another hollering one. The children's behavior was totally off. It's the same pattern every week. Every Monday, they have to get used to being off for two days. Even without Jaron, their behavior wasn't good at all. Kevmani, Nerimiah, Tonto, and my special friend Leandre were all over the carpet jumping, wrestling, and tugging at each other. My throat was dry from continually getting them refocused and redirecting their energy into learning. Leandre's mother wanted a report card for him being in my class for fifteen days. For me it's enough time to assess the strengths and weaknesses of a student. To cover ourselves legally, we usually write *Not able to asses* on a report card for students who haven't been in school for a significant amount of time. I did let her know how he was performing low in class. He appears to be on a two- to three-year-old age level. I will definitely be making a referral for him to see if he needs services. Throughout the day, three other parents picked up their child's report card. All I could do was hand it to them and tell them that if they have any questions, then we would have to arrange a meeting time since I couldn't talk with all of my students around. Ms. Grasier got into an argument with a parent over a report card. They should have come on Friday or waited for an appropriate time to talk. A teacher cannot give a conference with undivided attention if there is a whole bunch of children around. You can't expect to have a conference during instruction time and expect the teacher to just stop teaching. I know how they would have responded if I didn't give them a report card. They would have probably cussed me out or argued with me, then run up to the office to complain, and then I would have been told to just give it to them anyway. Being prepared for today, I strategically placed the remaining report cards by the table near the door. I was able to quickly pick it up, give it to them, and continue with my lessons.

Day 57
Tuesday, November 21

Today they were better. But guess who decided that they wanted to bring their child to school today? Maytoria! Jaron's mother! I told you that he would be back. He comes back to school on my observation day. He was calmed down as he usually is when he first returns. And as always, I don't hold anything from a previous day against the children. Every day is a new day to start over. It's a new day to do better than you did the day before. In my mind, I did want to know who decided that Jaron was going to come to school today. I did all the cleaning that needed to be done anyway, and all of that stressing, and Mr. Shiller didn't even come yesterday. I can't understand, for the life of me, why principals schedule observations right before a holiday. The children are always off in their behavior because they know they are going to be free from school the next day. Not only that, but usually, teachers get to be a little more creative with the students because more holiday-related activities are done within one to two days of the holiday. Me, personally, no matter what the holiday is, I like to teach the children about all the holidays. I've learned a lot about different cultures since becoming a teacher. I've learned a wealth of information, period. I even learned how to make a small Jewish dish of latkes and applesauce to share with my students. Actually, my third graders used to help make the latkes in the classroom. I brought in all the ingredients and a grill too.

Anyway, Mr. Shiller didn't come in today and said that he would be in tomorrow morning, the day before Thanksgiving. Go figure. Now back to Jaron. He started showing off even with his mother there. He showed off, as usual, by not listening or following directions. She kept threatening that she was going to spank him. That's not the exact terminology she was using either, so that was another situation I had to watch closely. She tried to deal with him as long as she could. She took him out of the class and went home after about an hour.

After school today, we had a teacher-parent basketball game. Only two parents showed up. That's the kind of stuff I'm talking about. A gym full of excited students, teachers, and parents; and only two parents show up to play. It was crazy. How can we have a teacher-parent basketball game with no parents? Some of the teachers had to go on the parents' side. I'm not even going to try to figure that one out. Everyone enjoyed watching the game. The score didn't even matter because the teams weren't even what they were supposed to be.

Day 58
Wednesday, November 22

Mr. Shiller didn't come in again today either. He is either behind in observations, situations within the school came up, or he got a notice from headquarters to do something else. The big people in charge have a habit of notifying schools of last-minute information or paperwork that they want. I wasn't surprised he didn't come.

124

Ms. Nixon came today. She probably was getting ready for Thanksgiving dinner for tomorrow. The talk of the school staff was a student playing a practical joke by putting a specimen of fecal matter in the middle of the hallway by the front office. I think we might need cameras because there are too many students doing too many things, and their behavior is out of control. If another student doesn't feel the need to tell, then no one will ever find out who did that. Only a child who has no home training, no dignity, and no pride in himself would do such a disgusting and degrading thing. I've heard of practical jokes, but to actually pick up fecal matter and strategically place it in the hallway is not funny at all.

Thanksgiving Day- No school
Thursday, November 23

I'm so happy to be getting a break from work. This is proving to be one of my most challenging years ever. Even though I'm off from work, I'm not off from going to church and helping to cook dinner. There was a minute out of the day where it was kind of weird. Not only is it a happy Thanksgiving but, ironically, it's supposed to be a happy fifth anniversary for Hebert and me. If it could have been a marriage happily ever after then I would have taken that too. Oh well, I'm happy that this divorce process is almost over. I've only been married legally to him for five years. The last three years have been a mess and horror show. I accept ownership that I never should have married him in the first place. In my mind, heart, and soul, I am divorced. I just have to wait for the paperwork to say so. Anyway, dinner was later than usual for us. We didn't eat until five o'clock. My macaroni was overdone, so it wasn't as moist as I wanted it to be. I hate cooking when I feel as if I'm being rushed. I also did the ham, but my pineapples burnt on top of the ham. My pop's sweet potatoes were awesome, though. Overall, just like every day of my life, I was thankful for another day to spend with my family.

Day 59
Monday, November 27

Other than my sinuses acting up, today was a good day. While the children were in their computer resource, I entered some reading and math data into the system that needed to be done. I only had five children show up for school today, and two came late during resource time. We were able to complete our whole reading lesson because it was so short. Leaving the computer room, the boys kept playing in line, but they calmed down once we got in the classroom. I told them that I wasn't feeling well and I could always go home if they didn't want to make good choices. After that, they got themselves together because they didn't want me to go, and they didn't want to get a substitute. I got my first wonderful report from Mrs. Scott in the cafeteria today. Usually, my students give everybody a fit, but they all earned two turtle bucks for making good choices in the cafeteria. I was really ecstatic. I made a huge deal and went over the top about them having a good report from the cafeteria. Jaron also had a good day. He started getting restless around the time that he usually does. He left at eleven forty with a good report, probably because his mother stayed in the lobby down the hall all morning. Nerimiah and Kevmani got into a little fight because they wanted to be in control of a little rubber strip that came off my math mat. I sent them to Ms. Fields's class to get a time-out and to calm down. I wasn't really able to fuss at them since I could barely breathe. That left me with four children! That was only for a while though and then those two eventually came back.

Day 60
Tuesday, November 28

Oh my goodness! Let me tell you about today. First, I should have called in as I wanted. But no! I just have to feel bad if I didn't come in. I didn't get to sleep until after four this morning because of my sinuses. My face and head were in so much pain. Last night, I had to get up and take 1600 milligrams of ibuprofen that I had left over from my foot injury. Even though I still wasn't sleepy yet, the thought of getting up and moving was just as painful as actually moving. When I was finally able to close my eyes, it was time for me to get up two hours later. I already knew I was going to be late for work because I woke up late at about six thirty, when I need to be out the door by six forty-five. On my way to work, my radio broke as I went over a bump. Some streets are so screwed up you can't avoid those potholes. I just cut the thing off and continued on my way.

Today was the day, just as all the other days, that Mr. Shiller was going to come in to observe my class. I didn't believe that he was going to make it until he actually showed up in my room with his laptop. When visitors come in our classroom from time to time, I always tell the student who's coming in and what for. I explain to them that the visitors want to see how we work together. They want to see how I teach and how they learn. But of course, they weren't on their best behavior. The boys were off the hook. Jaron was calm at first, and then he did his normal routine. I'm still flabbergasted about how his mom ended up in my room, chasing after Jaron, during the middle of the observation. I'm thinking that when she saw that he was getting restless in the class, instead of letting me handle it, she fussed at him, and it agitated him further. Mr. Shiller and I stared at each other for a minute and we both were clueless and speechless for a moment. Even Mr. Shiller had a dumbfounded looked on his face. He would go one way around the room, she

127

would try to follow him, and then he would go around the other way. My desks are U-shaped, so I couldn't get to him because the remaining students were sitting at their seats. I wouldn't have been able to reach over them. Mr. Shiller is a grandfather, and I knew he wasn't chasing after him. I got him to calm down, but his mother said that was it for him for the day, and she walked him out of the room. I continued with my lesson as if nothing had happened. Later, my principal told me that he had never seen anything like it in all his years. He said he was ready to take him into the bathroom and tear his tail up. No home training! NHT! NHT! NHT! I tell you that's what it is. I locked myself out of my room for the tenth time this year. I move around so much, and I pick up and put things down that I easily lose track of everything. To top the whole day off, when I reached for my jacket from the side of my closet, a leaf was caught between my jacket and my coat, which pulled the plant and dirt down. I caught it in midair, but dirt was all over the place. It was the end of the day, but I still picked up what I could. I didn't want the custodians to think I was leaving a big mess for them to clean.

Day 61
Wednesday, November 29

Today was a good day. Of course, half of my children didn't show up again as usual. It's as if they play tag team for who is going to come to school today. I found out what was wrong with Ms. Grazier today. Apparently, some of her parents are upset over one of the report cards and didn't like what Ms. Grazier had to say. She came into my room to ask me for the teachers' union number. I just asked her if she was okay, and she told me the whole story. I feel sorry for her because she is a new teacher, and that is just one of the many kinds of situations that drives new teachers away. They never expected to teach children and have to deal with a whole bunch of unnecessary crap. Some teachers feel comfortable calling the union's numbers, and some don't. Teachers feel as if they may have some sort of retaliation if they call because they are having a problem or concern that may go past the principal, or even if the principal is the one that is the problem. I hope everything goes well for her.

Day 62
Thursday, November 30

Jaron desperately needs some professional counseling, help, and intervention. He hit Ms. Ann in the cafeteria today. She was livid when I went down there to pick up my class. She said so much I could barely remember what she said. She said that she was going to press charges, speak to the mother, and go directly to the principal and speak to him about Jaron eating in the office. I understood her frustration, and she is a volunteer. She doesn't get any stipend for her service in the cafeteria. She gets a formal thank-you on the parent-appreciation day luncheon. I really don't know what to say. I think his behavior from whatever goes on in his home life says it all.

Day 63
Friday, December 1

Today was an okay day. The students worked on their snowmen for their art time. Last year, when I had the parent volunteers, the projects didn't take that long to complete. Today we received a letter from the union talking about our rights if we are assaulted. Apparently, there's a surging problem of assaults against teachers and school staff. If the powers that be insist on limiting the discipline options that schools have, then there are going to be more problems with violence in the school. Instead of the repeat violent, offending students having appropriate consequences, they get a lecture and are immediately sent right back to the teacher they assaulted. We can press charges, but I know from firsthand experience that it is hard as heck trying to get any closure from that end. There are all these protocol steps to follow, and then there is no follow-up with the teacher. It's all becoming too much to bother with. Then people wonder why there is such a high turnover rate for new teachers. They don't have the patience and support to deal with it. There are many students that are dealt with accordingly, but then there are more who aren't.

My two little ones went with their dad this weekend. I talked to my lawyer today. I wanted to know if it would be okay if I went on dates and had a male companion in my life. I'm not trying to go all out and get my groove back or anything. I just want to feel comfortable hanging out and don't want anything negatively affecting my divorce. She said it was okay. As long as I didn't bring anyone around to hang out with the girls, then it would be okay. Well, I don't do that anyway, so that definitely would not be a problem. She said that he was the one that left and didn't want to be with me anyway. In all honesty, I've been alone for the last four years anyway, so I think I deserve to go out with a nice tall gentleman. I just want to go out to the movies or dancing. I don't like going to clubs anymore; that area of my life is way over. I did clubs in my twenties. I no longer want to be in smoke-filled rooms with sweaty people all over. All I do is work and hang around my family and friends. I have a crate of paperwork right next to me that I haven't even gotten to. I just want to start living life again.

Saturday. I had to go to the gym today because my knees are starting to hurt again. I don't think standing on my feet all day long is helping any either. It's probably making my knees worse. Since I can feel the grinding again, I need

130

to go back and build up my muscle mass around my knees. I put in a really good workout. Hopefully, I can keep this gym routine at least three times a week. After the gym, I went over to my pop's house to get Whitney. Some kind of way messing around with my sister, I ordered some stuff from a catalog and then took a nap for about an hour. I was exhausted from running Whitney to dance rehearsal every night this week at church. Last night, the dance ministry ministered along with Jonathan Nelson and his live DVD recording. It was an awesome night. I don't think he realizes how his music ministers to comfort my spirit. After I took my nap, Whitney and I went to Sam's Club. When I finally arrived back at home, I went to dry my hair after I washed it, and the dryer kept blowing a fuse. It never did that before. Not only was the hair dryer broken around the edge, I couldn't put a comb attachment on the end. I asked Whitney, did she break it? Of course not. She never does anything, if you let her tell it. After a half hour of running up and down in the basement to reset the fuse box, I decided it wasn't worth it anymore. I went way back across town to let my sister do my hair. She used to be a hairstylist. She still does great hair when she feels like it. She stopped doing my hair some time ago because she said it was too damn long like Pocahontas's, and I didn't keep it up. I just used to prefer my hair in a ponytail all the time. It is the easiest and quickest way for me to style my hair for work. Anyway, I went home to get dressed to go out. I wished Magic Man would have told me that the party we were going to was right around the corner from where I was. I just wasted gas going back and forth across town today. I went out with the Magic Man. He's my best male friend right now. I say right now because I told him only he can keep himself from being in my life. I had fun. I danced a little bit. I was just happy to get out of the house. He's good company to go out with too. I really don't feel ready and comfortable to *date*. Besides, my little secret is that I'm madly in love with him. It's up to the heavens above to decide if we will be an item. I do hope he will realize one day just how much I love him. After this horrific marriage, I just don't see myself going through all of the nonsense again. My patience is too short for foolishness right now. I didn't get to that crate of work done yet either.

Sunday. I went to church, JC Penney, Sears, came home to nap, cleaned up, and went to Bi-Rite for this week's lunch. I went to the gas station to pick up the girls, but they weren't there yet. He didn't even have the decency to call me and tell me that everything was okay or that he was running late. Herbert showed up a half hour late with the girls as if he was on time. I didn't acknowledge that he was late. I'm quite sure he knew and I'm not going to say a word to him about it.

Day 64
Monday, December 4

Today I'm feeling totally disgusted, and I don't want to be here. The passion that I had dwindles down even more every day. My fire and my spunk just aren't here in my heart. I have a little spark left that is going to be extinguished if something doesn't change. I try every day to change my outlook and perspective on the failures of our communities, but it is what it is. It's like when I was little, I used to like making mud pies. No matter what I said the pie was or imagined it to be, it was still mud that I couldn't eat and enjoy. This is December, and my students are usually further along than were they are now. All the boys want to do is play and wrestle. Their enthusiasm for learning isn't there. You can tell when I'm not happy. I'm at the point again where I'm questioning, even if teachers are making a difference anymore. I know that we are deep, deep, down inside, but the students and parents have no respect for teachers at all. Obviously, these exact problems are not prevalent at every school, but at our particular school, we are raising most of the children. I don't know what the statistics are, but I'm definitely positive it's a national epidemic. There are too many systems around the country that have only a handful of blue-ribbon schools. Every school should be a blue-ribbon school.

My sister just asked me over this past weekend, why is it I still teach at this school? I couldn't even really answer her question. I'm torn between leaving and staying, like a bad marriage. I used to insist that I can help change the world, one child at a time. But not anymore! My faith in what I'm doing is a little shaky. I would say a lot shaky. I'm addicted to working with children. (With the exception of my own preteen right now, who is trying to drive me crazy.) I feel comfortable doing what I've known for a long time and terrified of doing something new in an unknown territory. Yeah, I can do without the unnecessary paperwork that the system has us do, and I can definitely do without the favoritism and politics within the system. I just love teaching children and watching them evolve over the years. I hope and pray that something that I have said has captured their hearts. That's what I miss about the third graders. Older students like to have open dialogues with you. So they talk to you about their problems and how you may be able to help. I have no real clue as to what's going on with my kindergarten students. The most I get from the little ones is that someone hit them, or they're hungry and tired. The times have totally changed, for one thing. It has become socially acceptable for teenagers to have babies, and then their children have babies at or around the same time they had their child. Condoms are being passed out like candy. Parents are giving their children drugs and alcohol at home so the children don't get it out in the street. Now I'm looking at grandparents that are my age. How in the world are you going to be a grandparent in the early thirties? The younger children don't know what blues, classical, and jazz music are. They don't know why we shouldn't be calling each other names such as "nigger, white trash, motherf—ers," and any other derogatory words. I know of a second grader that told a fellow student to have his mother suck his d———. The little boy said it with no hesitation at all. How could a child come up to tell someone to tell their mother to do that? It's appalling. They have no concept of work ethic. The family members just drop them off and pick them up and their late at that. I am going to send letters home to all the parents, and if I ever find a number for the ones who sporadically show up, I'm going to call. Dimani was late again, as usual. Reshae has on clothes that are too small. The boys are still making bad choices. Jaron, Ponto, and Twan didn't come to school today. This is the poorest attendance I've ever had for a class. When I checked homework, eleven children didn't do homework. Two students were picked up late. I wish I had a tracking device sometimes to find out where the parents are.

I know all of this confusion is just confirmation for me to move to another school or make other things happen. I have dreams. I dream of reuniting with my father, whom I haven't seen since I was eleven, twelve or thirteen. I want to own and operate all childcare centers in the city I live in. Well not all, I want the poor-quality ones who claim that they offer good educational programs for the children but don't. There are a lot of people and places who say that they teach your child but don't. I want to travel to Italy and locate any Italian relatives on my mother's side; they may still exist. There's still a lot I want to do.

Day 65
Tuesday, December 5

Today I was frustrated because on my lunch break, I had to make phone calls to get some help for what happened last night. I will almost swear that ever since I started writing this book, so many things have been happening to me. It's as if the evil forces of the world don't want me to let parents know that there are little things they can do to make a big difference. Last night while I was on my way home, a Mass Transit bus was in the right lane trying to get over into my left lane, and it side swiped my truck. The bus driver didn't even stop. I followed the bus for a little over a mile before she stopped. When finally able to talk to her and let her know that she hit my truck, she said, "Oh well." Immediately the old young Philly girl in me wanted to come out and slap some respect into her. I called on Jesus so I wouldn't call some other stuff out. But I kept my cool. Eventually, the transportation and city police came. Names and information were exchanged. Tomorrow, I know I will definitely be calling to file a complaint about her attitude and disposition about the whole situation. Fortunately, no one was hurt. That bus driver's attitude is one of the attitudes that we don't want our children to have when they grow up. I don't know if she was having a bad day or not, but it is totally inappropriate and dangerous to have an unconcerned attitude while driving a large transportation vehicle.

If we don't get to put children together now, we are going to have a terrible group of grown-ups leading the future!

Day 66
Wednesday, December 6

This morning, I asked God to give me a new attitude, a new spirit and outlook for my class. I bought treats, changed the seating arrangement and the front primary teaching area of my classroom around. I tell them every day is a new day to start over. It applies to me as well. Jaron came to school today. His mother said that he was out because they went to her father's funeral. He acted his usual self anyway. Before lunch, I saw Jaron with his mother in the lobby. He walked off to see her. He was drinking orange soda out of a two-liter bottle that she had. There used to be a concept such as class. I don't think too many people care about that these days. It is really the boys that are driving me crazy.

Reshae had to walk around all day with her pants unzipped and unbuttoned because they were too small. I tried as best as I could a few times to try to get them closed, but I couldn't. I also sent her around to the other kindergarten teachers with a note to see if they had a safety pin. They didn't, so the zipper was all the way down all day long. It is times like this that you would want to ask the parents if you could donate some clothes, but her mother appears to be the kind that would be offended being offered help. I wrote a note to her mother. It was a nice note. It didn't say what I really wanted to say. Mrs. Landing called to tell me that Ms. Nixon wasn't coming in. I don't blame her either. However, today was a pretty okay day. The boys, as usual, ran their mouths and played too much. They are not ready to be in school. This is like an indoor playground or daycare center to them. Kindergarten is mandatory, but they don't understand that. Little children don't have the capacity to understand how significant their education is. That's why it is so important for the ultimate teacher, the parent, to instill that life skill in them. Ms. Meiskol had brought Shean into my class around noon because she had to go. But she wasn't able to leave right away because he was having an emotional disturbance. After she left, he still wanted to leave my classroom. With this child, I had to use my very calm, soothing side to coax him into staying with me in my class.

He's almost in the same category with Jaron. This little boy just hasn't run out of the building.

Tonight, in the mediation orientation class, I had to see Herbert. I still have some unresolved issue about that person. Anyway, there was a man there that said that he had a five-month-old and hadn't seen her since August. That's a shame! It's a trifling, no-good, low-down, dirty shame. There are some ignorant mothers out there too. It's not just the dads that do wrong by their kids. And that's all I'll say about that! Well at least for right now.

Day 67
Thursday, December 7

Outside of getting a run in my stocking, I thought that the morning was going very well. I went to bed early and got up earlier than I did yesterday. However, it still wasn't early enough to get Whitney to band practice at 7:15 a.m. I actually got to work on time at seven thirty, though. I was feeling good, looking good, and smelling good. Every day is a new day to start over, right? So I'm here in my room, ready to greet my students, listening to Heaven 600, and cutting out pictures of toys for one of the activities that I'm going to do with the students next week. Ms. Laquetta came in this morning and said that she was staying until eleven. I said wonderful. Dimani came in to school on time too. That really was like the icing on the cake. I was just in a very good-spirited mood after seeing her. What a beautiful day it was going to be.

Around eight forty, after breakfast, I moved to the carpet area for reading and asked the students to come sit on the carpet with me. All the students came over except Tonto. I asked Tonto three times to come have a seat. On the very last time I asked him, he threw his head back and made a loud grunting sound and then immediately went into his stubborn mode. All week, I have been explaining to the students that I wasn't playing games with them, and I had to keep reiterating that school is a place for learning and not for playing. I told them that I would call their parents and they would lose some of their privileges if they didn't get it together. What happened next was totally unexpected.

Tonto had a tantrum. He had a full-fledged, like a two-year-old's, tantrum. He was kicking and screaming and lying all over the floor. He was grunting, screaming, and yelling all in the same breath. I didn't get it at all. College classes don't cover this much child psychology. And even if it did, we have a new breed of children that don't even fit into a textbook diagnosis. While he was carrying on, I immediately called the contact numbers I had for his parent. I called all three numbers, and I got nothing but a long music recording. Then some parents wonder why we don't want to call. First, some parents just disappear during school hours. And when we call, we have to listen to a five-minute song just to leave a message. We don't have time to wait for a song to leave a message. Hello! I'm supposed to be caring on with my instructional day in the first place. If I wanted to listen to a whole song, I would turn the radio on. Why do people do that? I can understand a favorite verse of a song. But a whole song. People have things to do! Nor do we have the minutes on our cell phones to accommodate this foolishness. We don't have telephones in our classroom. It would be lovely if we did, but we don't. I'm tired of calling phones and then forget that I even called because now it's like listening to the radio.

So I carried him safely up the hall, which seems as if it is about almost two city blocks from my class. He kicked, and he screamed and yelled all the way to the office. Some of my coworkers came to their door, shook their head, and went back into their room. There is no need to even explain. We all understand, without even saying anything. I sat him down in the chair. I asked Ms. Landing to call for Mr. Shiller because I was going to leave if he did not remove this little boy from my room. I was filled with so much anger and disgust. I was overwhelmed with everything that transpired from my classroom to the office. Before I knew it, I walked out of the office and went into the bathroom in the teacher's lounge that is across the hall from the office. I slid down the wall onto the floor, curled up, and just cried until I couldn't cry anymore. This is not what I went to school for. This is not what I want to do. If I wanted to be a special educator of emotionally disturbed children, then I would have made that my area of expertise. I teach children, that's what I do. I don't babysit and continue the babyish mothering role once the children are dropped off at school. This is not the crap that inspires me to want to do this anymore. That is what I was thinking when I was squatted and leaning against that wall, on that floor. I'm just tired of it all. I went to the office to say I wasn't going back into my class until something was done. After about five minutes, I got myself together to go to the office to talk to Mr. Shiller. I did not leave that office until he came from wherever he was to talk to me. I explained what happened, and I told him that I will not go back in my class to work until Tonto was removed for the remainder of the day. I respectfully told him that he could write me if he wanted to, but I was not going to continue with the burden of having another problematic student in my room. Jaron was enough by himself. My principal was very supportive and understood. I rarely go to the principal for anything. I don't run and complain to him every year about my class that he assigns to me. I know he assigns me the more challenging classes because I can handle them. I am truly honored and humbled by his thinking, but this year is a little bit past my level of patience, which is already very high. I didn't know whom Mr. Shiller sent Tonto to, and I really didn't care. He also shared with me that he couldn't reach anyone at Tonto's home either. After about an hour, I was back at Ms. Brown's class picking up my class. I felt bad that she had to keep my kids. I know she volunteered and didn't mind, but the classrooms that we have are too small for one class. I know she was crowded in her room with both our classes. I went across to my class and picked up where I left off teaching, up until lunch.

While at lunch, I stopped at Ms. Hone's class. Somehow I was just checking on her, and the next thing I know, she gave me back the gift that I had given to her yesterday. Some of us here at the school signed up for a secret pal. Ms. Hone is my secret pal. I bought her a green tea lotion and body gel set. Since she and I are close, I thought I knew that she didn't like strong scents because she was very sensitive to them. I obviously thought I made a good selection. She said her secret pal gave it to her, but she knew she wasn't going to use it. I tried to explain that maybe it's rude to give a gift away and that she doesn't even know who her pal is. I also told her that maybe her pal really invested some time in looking all over for her gift. She kept insisting that I take it and enjoy. I told her I didn't want it, but she put it in another gift bag that she had and very discreetly gave it to me. She told me not to tell anybody. I thought that it was very funny.

When I picked up my students from lunch, Nerimiah got a bad report from a parent and grandparent about being disrespectful. He thought that he could just roll his eyes, suck his teeth, and walk away from an adult while they were trying to speak to him. These little five-year-olds are too grown. I knew his behavior folder or a note wouldn't make it home. After I reprimanded him for his behavior, I called his grandfather, which helped to run up my bill. His grandfather said that he would take care of him when he got home.

Kevmani's mother stopped in on her lunch break to check on him. He actually did pretty well earlier today. She was happy with the report. As soon as Kevmani's mother left, he slapped Lemonte in the face. Leandre did something to Lemonte, and Lemonte said he was going to tell, so all I saw was Kevmani slapping Lemonte in the face. Lemonte said something he didn't like, so he figured he would just slap the beeswax out of him. I then had to call Ms. Laquetta. More minutes on my bill. She couldn't believe he did it right after she left. I guess he figured he could get away with it because he knew she probably wasn't coming back. I don't know. I wonder from where he got the habit of slapping someone just because he doesn't like what they have to say.

After school, I got locked out the classroom again. I walked all the way up to the office to turn in some paperwork and to check my mailbox. I walked all the way back down the hall, only to have to walk all the way back up, to have a custodian called for the key to get into my room. I know Ms. Sharen gets tired of me and having to walk down here to let me into my classroom.

After all the foolishness of the day, I forgot about the meeting for math night tonight. I went around the hall to the meeting so I could see what my part is for that event. The meeting wasn't that long, so I went back to my room to clean up and water my plants. I delegated watering the plants to my goddaughter, Angel, and she overwatered the plants. Water was all over the top of the floors. She and I spent the remainder of my time at work mopping up the water.

Day 68
Friday, December 8

Today was a good day until Ponto had another tantrum. He just falls out all over the floor and screams and hollers at the top of his lungs. It interrupted the classroom instruction, and once again, I had to basically go through the same thing I did yesterday. The simplest request appears to set him off now. I didn't break down and cry, but I was very pissed off. I'm tired of this. I feel as if we're providing a babysitting service instead of providing a professional learning environment conducive for academic and social

141

growth. Some of our schools are beginning to be warehouses for defective and irreparable products. We simply just do not have the support we need from the home.

Everybody was here except Twan, who hasn't been here in three weeks. I heard he lives in Washington DC now. I guess since his mom allegedly didn't complete rehab, they had to move somewhere else. His pictures are still here and I'll have to go to the office to see if there is a forwarding address. Now I definitely won't have perfect attendance until his name is off my roll book.

Saturday. I did absolutely nothing related to school today because I'm so disgusted and exhausted. I've just had it with the whole tantrum episodes this week. I'm beginning to think that since Jaron comes back day after day with his behavior, then the other students are beginning to pick up on it too. They will eventually figure out that they will most likely get away with their behavior also. Outside of trying to figure out what more I can do to help my students, I spent the majority of my day relaxing and getting a Christmas tree with my sister.

Sunday. When I went to church this morning, the girls were having a difficult time. They were very restless and uncooperative because they were still sleepy. After church, I went over to Pop's and tried to make the little ones take a nap. That wasn't working because my nephews were making too much noise, and the girls didn't want to go to sleep. I had to send Faith to the boys' room and Trinity to my sister's room. If I didn't separate the two, I wouldn't have been able to take a nap. Getting a nap on Sunday is the highlight of the week for me sometimes. After we had Sunday dinner, we headed home, back on the other side of town. On the way home, Trinity started singing on her very own to the tune of "Frère Jacques": "Where is Herbert? Where is Herbert? / I don't know, I don't know." She sang it

142

over a few times. But by the time I tried to get my cell phone to record it, she stopped singing it. I swear parents have no idea what they put their children to do. She is only two years old and knows that her daddy is missing in action. To make a long story short, he really doesn't have a good bond with her yet. I pray that their dad gets himself together, at least for their sake. He thinks he does because when he does show up and takes them somewhere, Trinity is happy to see him. I just never told him that she responds that way to everyone. I know that in time they will have a great relationship with the girls. Divorce can just sometimes bring out the worse in people sometimes. I try to understand that but it can be very difficult at times to see the children suffer because of it. I know he'll be a great daddy when he's finish being pissed off at me.

I'm not directing this next comment to anyone in particular. All I'm saying is that court-ordered time is not enough if a child's time with the noncustodial parent is limited to a weekend visit every other week and two weeks in the summer. I commend all the parents who were able to amicably work out the divorce or breakup. It's a difficult thing to do, but it is possible. I have sat in a parenting class with the presenters telling you that younger children need more time because the first six years of building lasting relationships and connections are their most impressionable time.

Day 69
Monday, December 11

Today sucks already! At eight fifty in the morning! I really do try to believe in my own personal motto that every day is a new day to start over. But it is so discouraging to try to teach, and you really can't because of what goes on in the classroom. I don't feel as though I should just holler and not give a damn if my students don't show up on time to learn.

This isn't just a job, this is my heart. This is an investment in our future. Only three children were here for breakfast this morning. Three. One! Two! Three! It's free breakfast. The services are provided, and they aren't used. I know that the breakfast isn't a hot one, or the greatest, but it's way better than nothing.

Almost half of the entire staff is not having a very good day either. In the main building, there is no heat again, as usual. You would think a call would be made to close school, get the heater fixed for real, or bring in new heaters. Our school isn't good enough for those options. Maybe five of our parents will complain. The majority won't because we're their babysitters for the day. They can't do them if they have to watch their own kids. For my readers who don't know what the phrase "do me" or "do you", it means when someone wants to take care of their own personal needs. It means basically that a person is going to do what they want to do when they want to do without really considering others. It varies from different levels. Some people are discreet taking care of whatever it is that they want taken care of. Some people do what they want regardless of how it affects others. 'Doing you" can be whatever your heart desires. It can range anywhere from smoking, drinking, sexing gambling, drugs or whatever else. "Doing you" can also be positive like going to school, work, college, interviews, drug rehab, GED programs. So that's why taking care of personal needs can be positive or negative. With the population of parents at our school, the majority parents are on the negative side right now. We have fewer parents who are being good and supportive parents to their children and to the overall welfare of their child's academic career.

Back to the heat problem, let the truth be told, if our school was a better school in a better area, there wouldn't be a repeated heat problem. Our staff and students wouldn't be trying to go on as normal while they are freezing their tails off. About two years ago, when I was teaching third grade in the main building, the heater blew up in my room. I thank God that it happened over a three-day weekend and not while any of us were in the room. That room was one of the many classrooms that didn't have a working heater. It was a classroom that had a maintenance worker come in for five minutes and say it's working because it's blowing air. I wanted to say, "Cold air, you idiot." On a Tuesday morning, I came into my classroom and noticed that my room was in total disarray. Everything on the wall, as far as process, letters, posters, etc., was wet. You could see where the steam faded everything. I was pissed off. I had at least twenty charts full of information and notes that I had written for the students to refer back to. I don't know how much money alone was invested into everything on those walls. All of my time, money, and energy—all gone away with steam. And my charts weren't written with a plain old black marker. All my charts were unique and colorful. All the charts were strategically written to include visual learners. Most importantly, I was angry because I imagined for a moment us being in that room when that steam exploded from that heater. A tear welled up in my eye as I went up to the office because I know that my principal didn't expect me to teach in the room like that. Oh yes, he did. I didn't want to stay in that room anymore. I wanted me and my students to be in another classroom. I didn't care if he said the heater was fixed or not. I now had a new phobia of a heater. Besides, there was no other classroom to go to. The students asked why everything on the walls looked the way that it did, and I told them. I also warned them that if I said let's go, then they were to walk as quickly and safely as they could out that door. I was paranoid, and the damn thing making its normal noises didn't help either. I moved the desks as close as I could to the door. I gave the children busy work for that day while I cleaned up and put the room back together. The custodian told me that when they came into the building, water from my heater was all the way in the hallway. I think the heater finally got fixed this year, which is two years later.

I went to take my students up to resource but got stopped on the way by Mrs. Scott, who wanted me to fill out a paper that right then I really didn't have time to fill out. But she chose me so I had to do it. Ms. Brown was somewhere cruising in beautiful, warm weather while we were all there. I wish I was on that cruise with her. There is no resource class for my students today. One student came in late at nine, and another student came in at five minutes before lunch. It is already screwed up enough that lunch is at ten o'clock in the morning anyway. Nerimiah put his middle finger up at one of Ms. Fields's students, and he didn't even have anything to do with what was going on with the two other girls. Yuan's father came up to the school again to pick him up, and he wasn't here. He said that they moved and that they didn't know if he was coming back to the school. Parents don't let us know anything. If they are absent, they are just absent. If they are late, they are just late. I don't even ask for a note anymore. I can't even read the notes that they send in anyway.

Ms. Meiskol visited me as soon as I got my kids dismissed for the day. She was saying how a girlfriend of hers asked her if she wanted some balloons for her students. Ms. Meiskol said that she told her friend no because other students didn't deserve it. She basically said the same thing I said about the children not deserving it and being appreciative.

In reference to the repeated tardiness and absences, I teach the main and most important part of reading between 9:00 and 9:55 a.m. Lessons for smaller children are quick, simple, and to the point. Our program requires that the children gain repetitiveness of the letters and sounds that they are learning. Every day, they review a little and then learn a little more. But if our children aren't here to receive and absorb the information, then those children get left farther and farther behind. I try every day to get the drive, the heart, the passion for teaching that I once had, and it is a struggle for me. I question whether I care too much and whether my expectations are too high. We can't even get the basic respect from students to be able to work with them.

Now don't get me wrong, I have the drive, the heart, and the passion, but now it's for the parents of my students. I feel as if our school is just one big babysitting service. Why don't I just transfer to another school? There are a whole bunch of other schools that are worse than ours. I had a girlfriend transfer to another school in a better neighborhood. She loved the new staff, the free access to copies without having to get approval, and the neighborhood. When her new class walked in for the new school year, it was the same stressful behavior. She has some of the same kind of ignorant parents, tardiness, and lack of self-control and expectations within themselves. To be honest, our school is in one of the poorest, most aggressive, most transient, and most drug-infested parts of the city. It doesn't matter what the city is because it's in America. And in America, poorness is all around us as well as the other problems mentioned. But guess what, being poor is no excuse for lowering the expectations that we have for our children. I don't need money to talk to my child's teacher. I don't need money and an education to poke my head in the classroom or to sit for a minute. I don't need money to teach my child respect for adults and teachers. If so, then that's maybe why we need to start legislating for teaching parents how to be parents. People keep saying that there is no one perfect book on how to raise your child. That may be true. There isn't a book telling animals how to raise their offspring either, even if they were capable to read. Most animals' instincts tell them to care for and fend for their babies. So how is it that those blessed with the resources within the village have to be told to check on their child in school? I just can't believe that people having children are so ignorant or oblivious to the fact that they have to do more than to bring the baby home from the hospital. It is the parents' right and responsibility to go up to the school and check on their child. Why should teachers have to go knocking on doors to reach out to parents? The school's need to reach out is a huge complaint. We've been waiting for our parents to come in every day at the same times, at the same places. I believe most parents don't want to come in. Those parents who give a damn about their children will go through hell and back again. They are going to be intimidated by their own wall of insecurity that they put up. We love talking to parents about the students' academic-growth project. I do believe that one parent can make a difference. However, I believe our village needs every parent accountable to make a movement to regain our future again. Why can't we have a legislated baseline of expectations for all parents? Why can't we say that all parents will be responsible for ensuring that children aren't having babies at the age of thirteen? Why can't we get our village together?

Day 70
Tuesday, December 12

Dimani was here on time this morning. That was a nice surprise. I was happy to see her. That means that she gets the whole day of school and no interruptions from lateness for me while I'm teaching reading. Yuan showed up at school with his mother around eight forty-five, after the children were already in music. I fussed at the boys all day long. They are too babied. All they want is their mother or grandmother. We need our men back in the homes! These groups of children are not ready to be in school right now. And then when you talk to the parents about it, there are always some excuses, or the behavior is downplayed. "I'm going to talk to them when they get home." I think that is one of the top ten lies parents tell us. I finally got in touch with Tonto's mother. I told her that I was ready to have Tonto put out of my class. I explained to her in great detail his tantrums and how his behavior is now interfering with the learning of others. I'm not teaching but managing tantrums. She really didn't have much to say besides, "I'm shocked." I'm not shocked because the mother is young, and every time she comes up here, her mother, Tonto's grandmother is the one that fusses over him while the mother just stands by and looks. Good parents know their children well. And you know that if a child has a tantrum with the parent, then they will have a tantrum with everybody else.

Jaron told Mrs. Siris to kiss his a———. All she did was ask him to pick up the trash that he threw on the floor. His grandmother came to pick him up at eleven thirty, the time he is supposed to leave anyway. That's why he is supposed to have someone sit with him all the time. His mother hasn't been up here for two days. I was trying to get some more background information as to where his mother has been for the last two days. When I asked the grandmother if she or her daughter would be here to sit with him, she basically said no. She said she doesn't have time to be chasing after somebody. She wasn't chasing after her daughter, who wants to party all the time. She's got bills to pay. She feeds Jaron, gets him dressed, and sends him to school. I told her that I understand, even though I really don't. Magic Man always tells me that I'm naïve, but I guess I just have to believe in what could be. It has become normal for grandparents to take care of their grandchildren. Grandparents have to make their grown children accountable for their actions. I know a grandmother who complains about her thirty-three-year-old son living in her two-bedroom apartment. She enables him to do the things that she complains about. She goes to work to stand on her feet all day long and goes home to spend her money on him, and cooks for him too. The bottom line is, your family will treat you the way you allow them to. When parents spoil their

149

children when they are very young, then they will probably be the same spoiled way when they are grown. Grandparents should not have to feel obligated to pick up the burden of raising their grandchildren. It's not normal, and it's not okay, and it should never be all right. It just shouldn't be. And when parents come home from being incarcerated, they should make them do some kind of mandatory community service in their child's school. Now of course, if they are a sex offender or some other kind of violent offender, then they can do community service somewhere else. Everybody else can take a few classes on how to help around the school, give them explicit instructions, and assign them a teacher to work with. Trust me, we have so much that we need help with.

Faith got sick at school today. I think she just had an upset stomach. I was able to cornrow Faith's hair after school since her hair was washed on Sunday night. I still have to cornrow Whitney's hair when I get home. Fortunately, Trinity can just get some kiddy spray and go. Whitney has a holiday play on Friday, where she would be singing and playing her saxophone. I have to do what I can do when I can do it. I knew I wouldn't have much time for anything else this week because I have a lot of choir rehearsals, Christmas parties, holiday shopping, etc. I'm tired of being sick. I'm tired of the medicine that makes me nauseous. I can't even enjoy food and really enjoy my days. This dirty school makes me sick all year long. I've conducted my own one-person study. When I am away from the school in the summertime, I never get sick. A month after being in school, I have sinus infections every six to eight weeks. I'm tired of repeat sinus infections, pinkeye, and strep throat. If I don't get sick from the school, I get sick from the student who digs in their noses and mouths all day long. A lot of them even dig all the way down in their underwear and any other body part where they feel an itch. I guess I would be rude and get into trouble if I wore rubber gloves and a face mask in my class. I hope I don't become immune to sanitizer and soap.

On my way home, I saw Ponto walking home with what looked like five- and six-year-olds, walking home by themselves! I'm not even going to go there right now. I think that if I wrote "SOME PARENTS SUCK!" all over my truck and rode around like that for 180 school days, then maybe our parents would get back in the village and claim their lost and abandoned children. Nothing would happen outside of me getting beat up or my truck getting vandalized.

Day 71
Wednesday, December 13

It was raining outside this morning, and I already knew Ms. Nixon wasn't coming in today. She already forewarned me that she wouldn't be in on any kind of day that has even just a little precipitation or anything. I was so over animated with the children. I overdid the turtle buck rewards for behavior, treats, and using Mr. Lion. He's the puppet that we use for our reading program. It isn't as fun as last year because they keep going on about how the lion isn't real. That's another negative thing about letting children watch too much television and video games; the children aren't using their own imagination to think of what could happen. They don't dream, wonder, and create. My students this year don't even know how to draw. They have no imagination to pull from. Anyway, we had a good morning learning with a lot of fun. I told the boys and girls earlier in the year that I love to have fun teaching. Learning is supposed to be fun sometimes. I'm not going to lie and tell them it's fun all the time. When I was in grade school, I had a hard time with social studies and trying to remember all those names, wars, and dates. It just seems as if there were, and currently are, too many wars! While I was teaching, Kevmani hit Reshae when she said something to correct him.

He doesn't like to be corrected by other children, so he hits. I witnessed that again today, when she asked him nicely to sit down, he just punched her in the arm. He didn't care until he had to move his behavior card to yellow for making a bad choice. Green is for good choices, and red is for bad choices on the behavior chart. Jaron could care less about anything, so that's why the behavior chart doesn't even work with him. Nerimiah was talkative, as usual. When he came in this morning, he sat somewhere else. I told him to have a seat at his desk. He told me that his mother told him to sit by himself. I had to politely remind him that this is my classroom and that I'm quite sure his mother would have asked me to move him. He kept telling me over the next thirty minutes what his mother said. Finally, I took his desk out of the group and sat him literally by himself. That's when he finally closed his mouth. I asked him later, was he ready to go back into the group? After that, he didn't tell me anything else about what his mother said. The children know that if you are not sitting with the whole class, then they are not making good choices.

Jaron was even an angel this morning on the carpet. He was calm and nice. Even though he called out a little, he was trying to raise his hand. He was attentive to what I was saying, and he was asking and answering questions. I made sure I gave him praise for everything he did that was good. And he actually began to smile. I was so proud of him. When I let him know that he's doing well, then he becomes happy and eager to do more. It's a great thing when he has had a breakthrough. He really showed genuineness.

That man, my ex, called me at nine seventeen this morning. I didn't know if it was him at first. You know how every city has their own designated first three digits, so I knew it was someone working for the city calling. I thought the number was from Whitney's school. I picked up the phone because I thought it could have been Whitney's school. As he was talking, I really didn't know who it was because the students were making a lot of noise while lining up to take a break. I try to use my phone only in emergencies or urgent concerns. I always try to show my students respect, which means I don't have general, everyday conversations on the phone. So as the children were lined up to go to the bathroom, once I caught who it was, my heart started beating faster, and my hands started shaking a little bit. I was so nervous because I didn't know what in the world he was calling for. He basically said that there is no need for us to be angry toward one another and that he wanted to talk to me because he had some things that he wanted to say and get off his chest. I told him that I wasn't angry at him and that I would have to call him back and let him know if I would be able to meet him. Initially, I was elated because I was thinking that he might begin to cooperate and make this divorce process more digestible. I just wanted to scream with joy. I was so happy that he showed just a little sign of progress. I had to quickly get myself together, though, because the last time I agreed to talk to him, we ended up arguing again. We came to an agreement on something, and he reneged on his promise when I didn't act the way he wanted me to or when something didn't go his way. Anyway, I am hesitant because his not sticking to his word is another reason why staying with him is impossible. I'm just hopeful that this divorce can go on peacefully with no further heartache for me. Divorce is not something that I advocate unless the marriage is abusive or with infidelity, but it doesn't have to be so doggone traumatic. At this moment, I'm happy and hopeful. I called my lawyer at lunch to share the potential good news. I told her about my reservations because I didn't want to get hurt again. She said to follow my heart, make sure I stick to my guns, make sure he is still willing to sit down at our mediation appointment, and get everything worked out. I called him back and let him know that when I get out of school in two weeks, it would be better because I have a lot of running around to do.

Whitney has rehearsal for her performance, I have choir rehearsals, Faith has a Christmas party, and I have a Christmas party. The system doesn't call them that, but I do. I don't mind at all saying Christmas!

Anyway, back to my class. Jaron did get a little restless right before lunch, but I was so elated that he made it that far. His good choices were ruling for the most part of the morning. It is predictable of me to say that his good behavior didn't last the whole day. However, when the children were taking a bathroom break after lunch, he filled his mouth with that dirty, contaminated water in the bathroom and was spitting it out all over the mirror. Mr. Shiller was in the hallway at the right time, so I asked him to talk to him before he went off again. Mr. Shiller just kept him until it was time for him to be picked up and go home. He told the one-eyed man that picks him up not to bring him back to school anymore. (I keep forgetting to ask that man his name so I don't have to keep calling him the one eyed man.) We'll see. Twan is finally off my roll. The attendance monitor saw that he missed three weeks in a row. She was finally able to get in contact with someone who said that he moved to the Washington DC area. I told her that I needed the number for whoever she talked to because his first school pictures with his homework book are still sitting in his mailbox in my classroom. Maybe I can also get an address to send them. I'm going to miss him. Not just because he was an overall good student, but because he was sincere about learning. He was eager to please me, and he asked questions about everything he was doing. Now I can really have perfect attendance when all of my students actually show up on the same day. I'm still trying to figure out why I'm so worried about getting perfect attendance. We don't have awards and prizes for perfect attendance at our school for the individual classes. The classes that have perfect attendance just get their names announced at the end of the day. Well, I just want all of my students in here learning. The individual students who have perfect attendance get awards or special activities. I can't wait until I have a day where I have all my students here on the same day. Tonto and Leandre didn't come to school today.

One of Ms. Meiskol's students who were giving her problems was moved to Ms. Kaylor's room and she isn't happy about it at all. This particular boy appears emotionally disturbed or off in some kind of way. Now if we've been teaching long enough, teachers can usually make an generally accurate diagnosis about what is possibly wrong with the child. We never ever tell the parents of certain types of findings. We will make a formal referral to have the child evaluated to see if they qualify for testing and services. Sometimes we are like mothers and fathers who can just look at their child and know that something isn't normal. Getting a new student from another team member is just like having one of the many students that transfer into your school and get assigned to your class. If they don't know anything, it's just absolutely terrible. Our students are already set a given routine of how things are done in the classroom. We have the students working the way we want for the most part, knowing the procedures, routines, and rules. Having a new student put in your class in the middle of the year is another nightmare, especially if they come as a clean slate. This little boy obviously has some emotional issues. But the children are just sent to school in any kind of way. We're like a potter trying to take and form something beautiful from whatever condition it was given to you. The rest of the afternoon in my classroom, the boys got restless as usual and started getting out of their seats and talking too much. The three girls that I have are starting to play too. I have to stay with them as far as their behavior, though. The children I usually don't have to talk to are beginning to display some of the characteristics and behaviors that they see daily in class in the other students.

Day 72
Thursday, December 14

Only some of the children brought their homework books. I was curious about their homework habits, so I asked the students if their parents helped them with their homework. I got all kinds of answers. Some students told me that their parents tell the children to leave them alone so they can watch television or take a nap. Some of the children told me that their parents did their homework for them. And some told me that no one helps them with their homework, but they try to do their best. Only two raised their hand and said that someone helps them with their homework every night. I like having open conversations with the children. They are so honest and unashamed of the things that go on in their lives. It's sad to see that they think that their lives are supposed to be that way. The only time little children tell stories is when they are in trouble. Outside of that, they are open books to the truth.

There were no major events today. It was like sixty degrees outside in the middle of December. I called Herbert to see if he wanted to pick up the girls early since I had to get to Whitney's performance. We actually had a nice conversation about the girls. I'm still thinking about what it is that he has to say. He might want to be nice because tax time is coming again, or because he doesn't want to have to pay a lot of money as a result of the divorce. I don't know, but I'm still thinking. I really don't trust some men right now, so I don't want him or any other man in my personal space like that. I'm going through enough and have been through enough with men period that I don't have the patience for ignorance, stupidity, and childish games. If I ever get involved with anyone ever again, I'll pray that they have already gone through their midlife crisis and all of the foolishness that some men bring.

Day 73
Friday, December 15

I am so angry right now that my hands are shaking as I try to get this latest event down. It is ten forty in the morning. I took my children to lunch at nine fifty-five, and I'm just now getting back to my room. "I have to work," is what the mother told me. Trust me, taking a half hour off work to speak to your child's teacher or just to pop up on them and check on them is better than spending a lifetime in the court systems, okay. I am so sick and tired of the crap that teachers have to go through with other people's children. This is insane. I just came back from telling my assistant principal that if they don't remove Tonto from my room, I will not be back until they do so. I will call the union and North Avenue headquarters if I have to. I don't want to do this anymore! I can't! I refuse to go through this tantrum process with Tonto every single darn day for the rest of the year. I don't like using the word *can't*, but enough is enough. They don't pay me enough to do this day in, day out. I worked and paid my own way through eight years of higher secondary education to teach, not to babysit spoiled little brats with no home training! I am not trained to be a counselor, psychologist, psychiatrist, or any kind of therapist . I have natural teaching talents that I have been blessed with, along with the several years of teaching under my belt, but this is my limit.

Let me start at the beginning of the morning so you can understand why I'm ready to tear up a little child's behind. I mean, a put-him-over–my-knee kind of spanking. He needed the kind of spanking where you pull down the pants and the underwear and tear their little tail up with a switch. I'm talking about getting a switch as they did back in the day when I was growing up. All a child really needs is one good whoopin' to remember. Anyway, the students didn't have resource class this morning. I was going to wait

157

until next week for them to start working on their Christmas presents for their parents and guardians. However, I decided that I would get started today since I don't have anyone to help with the projects anyway. The students and I went to the back of the classroom where the reading center is. The main focus area in the reading center is a three-dimensional fake fireplace that I decorate according to the seasons and holidays. My fireplace currently has cutout pictures of candy canes all around it. I have white lights that hang year round on the fireplace. Currently it has shiny blue and silver garland draped all around. On the top of the fireplace is a small Christmas tree with a girl and boy angel on each side of the tree. Then I have a girl and boy snowman on each side of the angel. It's just really decorated nicely, I think. How many teachers have a fireplace in their reading center? All of the students were happy that they were taking pictures to make projects for their families to take home. Everyone was waiting patiently and enjoying themselves along with me. Getting back to my frustration, I placed each child in front of the fireplace by themselves to take a Polaroid picture of each of them for one of the projects we were working on. As I was about to take Kevmani's picture, Tonto jumped in front and stuck his hand in front of the camera. Well, of course, I was curious and asked him, why would he do that? I wasn't screaming or yelling at him either. I just sternly reprimanded him for about a minute or two and was ready to move on when he went into one of his tantrums magnified by ten. He laughed and obviously thought it was a funny thing to do, but I didn't. It was probably something that he and his family do. I was mad that I wasted film, and all of the other children followed directions and stayed where I told them to. I explained to him that I had to spend my money to buy the Polaroid film and so on. I know he didn't understand where I was coming from about the time, energy, effort and money put into these projects. He went off as he usually did, but this time, it was a higher-pitched screaming. This time, he was kicking and rolling all over the floor. He would not calm down, he would not respond to anything I said or tried. I tried walking him out the door to calm down, but he didn't. I walked my remaining students across the hall to ask Ms. Brown to watch my students while I took him to the office. She could hear him all the way from across the hall. Other teachers came out of their rooms because he was that loud. For some reason, I was so embarrassed, as if he was my own child acting like a fool. He obviously wasn't going to cooperate, so I picked him up and carried him like a football underneath my arm. He never stopped kicking and screaming. He was screaming and yelling all the way up the hall to the office. It was so intense. My colleagues were coming to their doors as I passed by with this child under my arm. I don't know if he was easy to carry because he was little and light or if my adrenaline level was that high. I was calm the whole time I walked with him up the office. I was in shock or disbelief or something almost like an out-of-body experience. When I finally reached the office, I calmly sat him down and went to go see the assistant principal, Mrs. Scott, while she was sitting in her office. That's when I expressed my frustrations and feelings about going through this every day with him and having to deal with the other behavior problems in my room. I meant what I said too! I would walk out of my room and go straight to the union if Tonto is in my room on Monday. And I left it at that, calmed down, and went back to my room and taught the rest of my students for the remainder of the day.

An old colleague of mine called me today, Mr. Dopp. He tried teaching here for two years and then left. He took all that he could take. It was nice catching up with teachers who have left or moved on to find out if they are happy or regretted their decisions. Most of them are happy. A lot of people love children. But it's different when you're working with them every day. You don't understand what it's like in anyone's shoes until you walk their walk. I knew I couldn't be in the medical field, which would have to use needles. When my Nana Bea was first diagnosed as a diabetic when I was fifteen, that's when I knew I definitely wouldn't be a doctor or nurse. I went to the doctors with her and learned how to give her shots. But when we got home, I couldn't stick her with the needle. I always filled the needles for her because she couldn't see those small numbers. But that was it. I just couldn't inject her medicine. A lot of things are easier than they look.

After all of that crap I had to deal with at work, I still had to go to the store for my daughter's village potluck at school. I purchased four big bags of loaves of bread. I then went home and cut over four hundred slices of bread for the potluck. The potluck was nice and a much better way of starting my weekend.

Saturday. I woke up early and went to the bank. I had to fuss at Whitney for not doing the chores that she was supposed to do. I've been asking other seasoned, more experienced moms about their trials and tribulations when their children were teenagers, and I'm coming to the overall conclusion that she's normal. I just have to stay on her to make sure my soon-to-be official teenager doesn't go too far off the deep end. I had to go to the toy store to go get a birthday present for my girlfriend's daughter. I really hate going out shopping around Christmastime because too many people get out of control and go crazy shopping, spending money they don't have. I used to be one of those people, but no more! I have a budget now that I try very hard to stick to. Whatever I buy after October 1st, I hide it away and add it to the presents for Christmas. Anyway, that was the only reason I went to the toy store and bought a gift card. Then I had to go to the military exchange and commissary. That took up my time from noon to four in the afternoon, and that didn't include putting all of that food away. I was just happy and blessed that I was able to have food to put away. After all

160

that running around, I took a late-evening nap, which made me stay up until four in the morning because I couldn't go back to sleep. And I still didn't get any schoolwork done!

Sunday. I went to church, and then to the movies to see *The Pursuit of Happiness*. I'm a huge Will Smith fan. After that, I proceeded to Kinko's, and I ended up spending $30 for copies. I copied all kinds of alphabet, Christmas, Kwanzaa, and Hanukah activities! Even though it costs a lot of money, I get a natural high of just knowing that my students are going to have added skills and activities that incorporate fun and excitement. I went to Walmart, AC Moore, and Michaels to get some more needed materials for the student's upcoming activities. My family might say I bought a whole bunch of unnecessary junk. But you have to work with children to understand that when children have tangible items to work with, they learn so much more and retain more information. I can't just teach about something, I have to show it to them or bring the experience to them. Finally, I went home and swept and mopped the floor before I had to pick up the girls.

I accomplished a lot this weekend but never heard from one of my buddies. I'm still upset with Magic Man because he wasn't there for me when I needed him. I'm beginning to see that he really can't be there for me like he said he would. Either he can't or don't want to. I know that we are just friends, but it's not that often I let a close friend know that I needed a hug. It's days like this that I miss my Nana Bea the most. She was the only person in the world that never hurt my feelings when I was younger. I could pick up the phone and hear her voice and her laugh. She would say, "It's going to be all right, baby." Anyway, after the week that I had with Tonto and then him hitting me and all, I set myself up to think that my friend would always be there for me. For some reason, I placed him on a pedestal, and I'm going to have to take him off. Oh well, I guess I have to build a bridge and get over it.

Day 74
Monday, December 18

Today was a pretty okay day. Tonto didn't come to school today, and if he did, I was not allowing him back into my classroom. The children were probably tired from the weekend, and that's why they weren't all fired up today. We were able to successfully complete all of our lessons and activities that I planned for today. The boys were still displaying their moving, jumping, touching behavior, but it wasn't interfering with instructions as they usually do.

I know I desperately need a laptop so I can produce an even better book. I am limited to typing here at work when the school day is over. I have to hurry up and put notes down and then go back and recall the day's events. So far, the Lord has blessed my mind indeed to remember most of what I want to share from day to day and points I need to expand on. There are so many other things that go on; I can't possibly document it all in a book. Maybe, I'll do a video documentary on my next school year. That's if I don't get fired for writing this. Who knows? If I could get it all done here, then it wouldn't be a problem. The number one reason right now I want another computer is because of these darn mice. I lock up all my snacks into containers, and then they are locked into my cabinets. I don't know what in the world they are coming up here on the desk for. I don't eat over the computer, so I don't have crumbs in or around this work area. I think that it's just a large ratio of mice, which have enrolled themselves into the building this year. It is so disgusting and unhealthy for me, coming in close proximity of the mice feces that I have to keep wiping off the keypad and around my desk. I really hate working here in this corner now. The mice droppings are all over the room. I didn't have this problem when I was in the main building. But moving over here to the portable has really just made me even sicker than I usually am in the school year. No matter how many glue traps and how many times I sanitize, they never go away. There are too many openings, holes, spaces, and nooks and crannies. Everything is really adding up to say, leave. I wonder if there is a certain phrase for when teachers hit this kind of particular roadblock in their careers.

When I first started, I thought I was going to teach for the next thirty years and retire. I don't see that at all right now. It seems practically impossible. I see retired teachers, or those who are eligible for retirement, that are disrespected every single day. Why are they still teaching? I think they still want to eat! I know myself, and I know I will not be able to tolerate much more of this. Our parents have to step up, or we're just going to continue to go down the drain.

I wasn't joking about what I said to Mrs. Scott on Friday. I went up to the office and asked her if she already took him off my roll. She asked me who had the least number of students with severe behavior problems. I told her that all my team members, or any class for that matter, everyone had at least one or two challenging students in their class. I think that it would be Ms. Kin and Ms. Kaylor who had the least amount of severe behavior problems. I felt bad because I didn't want anyone else to have a problem with him in their room. But all the severe behavior problems in my room are a little too difficult to maintain control with now, what with having to juggle in another temper-tantrum child too. No one wants to have their own student going into another classroom and causing more problems. Ms. Brown has a borderline special-ed student in her class. Mrs. Brown also has some children who are a little unruly. Ms. Fields, Ms. Meiskol, and I have just about the same ratio with about eight to nine boys and three to four girls. I don't have any idea as to what changes she is going to make, if any. I just answered all her questions and once again reiterated my concerns with the behavior in the classroom. I've been told that I'm good with challenging behaviors, but I know my limits. I'm not that good for emotional and social problems. I think that the regular-education college course for becoming a teacher should have more special-education classes. I think that would allow us to have more needed training in specials situations. We should just be trained in special education and have certificates that goes along with our degrees. That would also help increase our pay. Ha, yeah right!

Before the students were dismissed, I sent a letter for their parents, attached to their shirts, asking their parents to make sure that they send their child to school every day this week. I also reminded them about the trip on Wednesday to the college theater and the Christmas party on Friday. I'm thinking I should have reminded them to be on time too.

Day 75
Tuesday, December 19

I am so tired. I just don't understand. I fell asleep last night at seven thirty. I've been training Trinity to sleep in her own bed for the last week or so. Last week, I lay down on the floor, next to her toddler bed. This week, I'm still in the room, but I was halfway between the door and her bed. By the time next week comes, hopefully, I'll be able to sit by the door and then all the way out in my own room. Anyway, I've been taking vitamins, drinking water, exercising a little because of limited time in my schedule. However, the thought of even coming to work just drains me. At the beginning of the school year, I was here every day early, and now I don't want to come at all. I was so excited and full of life, and then reality stepped in. It is very hard for me to separate my personal emotions from what I do because I care so much. I know I can't change the world, but I try with the students I have in my class and with all the other youth that

I come in contact with. How can I believe in the dreams of my children if they don't have any? First, I have to teach them to dream and to dream big. And how can I encourage them to dream big if their parents don't even care? A lot of parents don't even make sure their child does their homework. It reminds me of how my many goals and dreams seem to be nowhere close, but at least I do have dreams and goals.

Sometimes I feel as if I just can leave the classroom for good right now to follow my own dreams because I would feel guilty about not directly teaching and working with children on a daily basis. I want to go to Italy. I want to find a long-lost so called loved one. I want to meet a whole list of people who have inspired me outside of my family and friends. I definitely want to meet Diana Ross and Maya Angelou. My all-time favorite film is *Mahogany*. At the time I was growing up, I didn't know where I was going, and I didn't like the things that life was showing me. As a child, I said to myself, *If she can go from being poor to being rich, then I could too.* I didn't know at the time it was a movie for entertainment. It was one of my lifesavers. And Maya Angelou, all I can say, is spectacular. I want to publish this book and have someone actually buy it because they want to know what they can do to help. I want to give big to the community that I have taught in for so many years. I do have dreams. A lot of times, it seems as if my dreams get smothered and suffocated by everyday life.

Anyway, I think I should have reminded the parents to send their child to school on time. Thirty minutes into the school day, and I only have two students. Ms. Fields came to tell me that Tonto was in her room. First of all, he was not supposed to come back to school unless Mrs. Scott and I spoke with his mother. That's the kind of stuff I'm talking about. How is it that parents don't make a sacrifice to go to their child's school for ten minutes but will spend many days in and out of the courtroom or jail? Prevention is the best medicine! Breakfast didn't come on time this morning, so I took the children to music. I went to the office to let them know about not receiving breakfast and to let them know that Tonto came to school. While I was in the office, I found out that there were two staff workers in the cafeteria for breakfast. The problem was that the gate was locked at the top of the steps from the cafeteria. They couldn't get the breakfast up the steps even if they had help from the fifth-grade students as they usually do. Breakfast didn't come until eight forty-five, after the students' resource class had already started. At this point, I had to decide if I wanted my students to eat breakfast. If the children ate breakfast after returning from music, then they won't eat lunch, which would be only an hour after they eat breakfast. I still can't understand, for the life of me, why the schedule can't be changed. I know we can't please everybody, but that time is a little too much for them. They are so hungry by one o'clock, they want food not a snack. You just don't eat lunch at ten in the morning.

Anyway, parent number seven turned in her child's money for the trip. She didn't give for the party on Friday because she said she didn't know about it and that Shamira doesn't even like pizza. I'll make her some finger sandwiches. I called Leandre's mother about the trip because I would need to find a teacher compatible enough to understand and help with his needs. His mother said that she would just keep him home. I reminded her of his attendance and that it was her decision but that he would still receive quality instruction and activities in whatever class he was placed while we went on the trip. She also said that she didn't have the money for the party on Friday. I wanted to say fine and do whatever you want to do. I had five students today. You would think that I would be elated and excited about having five students, but my brain really isn't used to it. All these years, I've had anywhere from twenty-one to thirty students in my class. My five students that came today were

Dimani, Yuan, Lemonte, Nerimiah and Shamira. Jaron didn't come to school. Jaron threw up in the cafeteria yesterday, so he might still be sick. Before he left yesterday, I sent a note for his mother attached to his shirt, saying that he was sick. Nerimiah left for a little while because he had a doctor's appointment. I wonder if he is going to get his medicine. I told you, it's the NHT. Nerimiah came back at twelve forty, and Lemonte left at one thirty. When you have five children, it can only be three things. One, the children are yours; two, it's a special education or pal class; or three, I'm babysitting. Earlier today, Ms. Hone said that a new student came in at nine and left early. So she said the exact same thing I was thinking earlier today. She was a babysitter just like me for a couple of hours.

It is challenging to teach and work with a class when half of your class is missing. The students who aren't here miss the work. Today we couldn't make the gifts for the parents because I have to instruct them on every step. I can't have two different groups going on at the same time if it is a hands-on activity, and I don't have an aide. It is possible if you have the cooperation of the students. But the combination of the children in the classroom is not conducive for just a regular lesson. So I had to wait when everyone is here.

Day 76
Wednesday, December 20

Today was the field trip from hell. We went to a college theater to see a traveling program called "Dance Asia." The children had no clue as to how to behave or act. Before the trip, I talked to my students, and most of my students behaved themselves. But the kindergarten class as a whole was horrible. They were up and down and in and out of their seats. They were arguing and fussing over who knows what. They were so loud. We weren't even in there long, and the children were complaining, and they all seemed to want to go to the bathroom at the same time. Only our children embarrassed us all. All the other students from the other schools were quiet and attentive. Two parents showed up to chaperone. I'm just disgusted. My stomach hurts too much to type.

Day 77
Thursday, December 21

The holiday program went beautifully. All of the classes that performed did a great job. I was really impressed with the assembly this morning. Our kindergarten class did a Rudolph performance. All of the teachers went out and brought antlers to put on top of the children's heads. They looked so adorable. I think I have stomach virus. I have just one more day until break.

Day 78
Friday, December 22

YES! YES! YES! YES! YES! All I have to do is to just make it through the day. I must have had something that didn't agree with me. I'm feeling much better today. I've just been eating lightly so I don't agitate my stomach again .

Saturday. I was well enough to finish shopping with Pop and my sister, along with Faith and Trinity. Whitney was hanging out with her dad and didn't want anything from the toy store. So Pop will take her Christmas shopping later.

Sunday. I went to church and sang in the choir for our Christmas play. They had live animals this year. I cooked and cleaned all day in preparation for Christmas dinner on Monday. Katlyn and her mom came over and wrapped all the girls' stuff. They wrapped every last thing. They wrapped stuff I wasn't even thinking about wrapping. They were such a blessing. I went to sleep at six thirty. I didn't even get to eat Sunday dinner. When I woke up at around nine, everybody, except my girls and my nephew Gregory, was gone. While I was asleep, I remember my sister saying that the kitchen was clean. I got to go see what was left. I just had to put the containers of food into the refrigerator. All the kids came into my room to watch *The Ant Bully*. We went to sleep after that.

I didn't do anything that exciting over the winter break. I just enjoyed being off and not having any real time constraints on every part of every single day.

WINTER BREAK!

Monday. I stayed up until three in the morning, and I am tired as I don't know what. Next year, I'm going to do an easier and different menu. I enjoyed the day beginning with church and ending it with dinner with my family.

Tuesday. All of us went to the movies to go see *Charlotte's Web*. When my sister and I go out with our children together, it automatically becomes a small team. Today it was me, my girls, my nephews (the boys), Pop, and my sister, Lez. Later, around five, we went over to my friend's home, way out on the boondocks. We played all the new games that their family got for Christmas. Then we ate and watched a movie. It was fun, and I wanted to stay longer, but it was already late.

Wednesday. I took all the kids to Jeepers for a couple of hours.

Thursday. I took my nephews back to my sister. I intended on keeping them the whole break, but I needed a break from children. Anyway, the girls went with Herbert, and Whitney went with her dad. But before the girls went off with Herbert, he and I did meet at a diner to talk. It wasn't anything that I hadn't already heard. He thought that we should socialize as a family for the girls' sake. I'll be honest with you and say that right now, I don't want to. I told him that too. I don't think it will be in the near Eternity either. I don't want my girls to think that their father and I are going to be together. I think that it just confuses them. The situation is confusing for me sometimes. They are used to doing their thing with him and then their thing with me. At the end of our conversation, he did mention that for the sake of the family, he would go to counseling, which he doesn't even believe in. When I wanted to go, he didn't want to. I basically said that it has just been too much pain and heartache along with the bad memories. His words were like something about two big mountains. I did think about it. I don't understand how people say that they didn't think about something to come up with what their decision is. You have to think, even if it's only for ten seconds. Anyway, I came to the conclusion that our marital relationship has truly come to its end. Yes, there are some mountains so beautiful that they are worth every climb to the top. And some mountains you just drive by and take them for what they're worth. I don't even have the energy and effort to try anymore. A lot of things you just have to let go and let God. God gave me the confirmation for me to know that it's okay to appreciate the last five years for the lesson and testimony that it is. I have two beautiful, hilarious, inquisitive daughters that resulted from something just about tragic. That's a miracle for me. Now he and I must continue a journey of our individual restoration and healing. Leaving those mountains behind us and just continuing the unexpected scenic view of this journey we all call life. My daughters will experience the beauty from both mountains for as long as the mountains remain beautiful. Unfortunately, the other "mountain" will one day be of no good or value for the girls. One mountain, if he continues in his own self-made man, womanizer, arrogant and narcissistic beliefs, he will slowly but surely deteriorate and will no longer have no substance of "beauty" to offer the girls. He's not a good person and if he turned on his first two kids I don't see why he wouldn't turn on our girls.

Friday-Saturday. I relaxed and enjoyed myself. When I'm home alone, it's just nice to get a break from taking care of other or the girls. I can sleep late, watch what I want uninterrupted. Run errands without anyone asking for something extra. I can do chores or work on projects. I can take naps or extra special bubble baths. I enjoyed my quiet time to myself an no one asking me what for dinner.

This weekend I able to reflect and thinking about my "mountain". Most mountains I have seen from a distance are so majestic and breathtaking. It's not until you are on a mountain that not only see the beauty of the mountain, but you also see its massiveness, its grooves and possible dangers of the mountain. I know I will have a tough climb moving forward after this divorce, but I will move forward one step at a time. I will get the supports I need when I feel like I don't know what step or move to make nest. I will appreciate the mountain for what it is and continue to remember that I must climb this mountain to get through to the other side. I know I will slip or even fall, but I also know I didn't come this far to fail. My faith tells me that I didn't get this far for God to leave me now and He won't leave me stranded with my children on this mountain and the many more different mountains of trials and tribulations to come. I reflected on how I want to continue my journey with my children in a future divorce. Ten years from now it is my prayer that I will still be beautiful person on the inside. I pray that the things that happened that shouldn't have happened don't scare my heart for life. I want to be able to keep getting

171

up every day and see the beauty in my girls and their well-being to inspire to be the best I can be. On our mountain, I know I can't keep them from all hurt, including their father, but as for me and my house, we will be loving, positive, encouraging and we will successful in all areas of life. I will do whatever it is that I need to do to be healed, to get myself esteem back.

Sunday- Today I went to church. Service was good as usual, and I'm fired up for the week and the new year. I love positivity and encouraging words to keep in my spirit. I also made my to-do-list for the year. Every year I write down ten things I want to accomplish for the and at the end of the year I open the envelop and see how much I accomplished on the list. I've been doing this for probably the last 20 years or so. I can honestly say that for the most part I usually get seven to eight things accomplished on the lists every year. All the girls came home today. It was good to have a mini break but I'm always glad to see them and they were happy to see me. They missed the morning service but we all did go to the midnight church service to bring in the new year.

Monday- Happy New Year! Just like that, it's a new year...2007. Wow times flies. I already wrote my to do list for this year, so I look forward to checking off to see what I accomplished this year. Today is a day of rest for me. Tomorrow we go back to work and school so at some point today I will get some things done, ready and prepared for tomorrow.

Day 79
Tuesday, January 2

Happy New Year students!

I actually got to work a few minutes early. I'm trying. Every day is a new day to start over, right? Even Whitney said that I didn't want to go to work this morning. I didn't. I hate my job now. I had passion like Steve Irvin had for his love of his animals. He loved what he did without question. I want the passion that I had before. But now my passion is empowering parents to be parents. I just have to keep encouraging myself until something good kicks in. I just want to teach. It's challenging enough to be a single parent of three. I don't want to be a single parent of even more children. It would probably be easier to feed and clothe my students instead of trying to teach them.

Happy New Year! That's what I've been saying this morning since I signed in at the front office. I went into my room, and I was automatically sick to my stomach. It smelled like a dead rodent. The smell was so strong that it made me want to you-know-what. It was so nasty! After I got Faith and me situated by taking off our coats and hanging them, I started to walk around the classroom. After a long break, depending on the area of the school, the staff knows not to just come in your room and start touching things. We have to get out our rubber gloves and Clorox wipes and start disinfecting things. As I walked around the room to observe everything that needed to be cleaned, I came to the conclusion that it was basically everything. There were mice droppings on all of the desks, student's desks, bookcases, and chairs. The mice even ate several leaves on one of my plants. In another plant, the mice made a burrow, and there was dirt all on top of the bookcase and the floor. I got my cleaning wipes and tried to clean the desks before the children came in to have breakfast. I opened the windows, but I still had to keep going outside in the hallway to get

173

fresh air. I know that there has to be some kind of study on how mice droppings make you sick. While I was cleaning and moving stuff, I found the dead rodent. It smelled awful. I guess it ate too much construction paper. I don't know. After work, I Googled *mice droppings*. The search found over 480,000 results. I think that there should definitely be a more aggressive approach to help us with mice in the school. I understand not being able to put down chemicals because of the safety of the children and staff, but the mice droppings are a danger themselves. It took me all day to clean the droppings. I still haven't made it to my desk.

Daytoria brought Jaron in to school late again. I overheard her tell another parent that since she got here with him an hour late, then he can stay a little later today. Hello! He is supposed to be staying all day in the first place. I must say that all the kids had a pretty good day.

Day 80
Wednesday, January 3

Jaron didn't make it to a whole day. After lunch, he started acting up. The last thing he said to me was "Get out of my face!" It was the same old drama with him. It was the normal tantrums, yelling, fussing, giving everybody the middle finger, and turning his behind to our face. I'm tired of it! His mother was asleep in the teachers' lounge. She was probably high or something. Either her eyes were red and glassy, or she smelled of liquor. She was dressed for the occasion too. She had on pajamas. But she had on men's bottoms. So that meant that she had an opening in front. I think that it is tacky to go anywhere away from home in pajamas. I don't ever recall seeing anyone out in the street in pajamas when I was growing up. I can see it in the case of an emergency. But to actually know that you have somewhere to go even if it may be across the street or around the corner, it's just tacky.

174

Words can't even capture what goes on with this boy and all the other dynamics in this school and others like it around America. If I had the resources and permission, I would have done a video documentary of all this stuff. People outside this profession just don't believe the behavior we have coming to us every day. We're told often that the parents send us their best. I don't believe that. I don't believe that some parents are giving their best to their children at all. Well, sometimes their best are little mean-spirited children with no home training. It seems as if the school system doesn't want the truth about what goes on in the school because their system doesn't want to lose funding from the city, state, and federal governments, or wherever they get money from. Only tragedies such as someone getting shot, stabbed, attacked, or raped at schools are reported in the media. Then the community is upset for a little while, and then it goes back to the same old thing. But the problem starts way before it even gets to that level.

Day 81
Thursday, January 4

Dimani hasn't been here all week. Already she has missed the formal lessons for letters D and P. I guess she is still on vacation while the rest of the city is back to the business of education. Jaron and Leandre didn't come today either. That left me with only six children. I feel as if I'm babysitting. Most teachers and people would say it would be a dream class to have only six children. It would be an ideal class if the students and the curriculum were compatible. As I mentioned earlier, the population of students I have this year are not even equipped to be in school, in the first place. Earlier today, I was explaining to Ms. Brown how frustrated I was that my students were not listening for the sounds that I was giving them. I would ask them if the word ended with m or p. They would call out letters and sounds that I didn't even say. These children have not been trained to think. It doesn't even seem like they are trying. It appears as if they just blurt out answers of what few letters they have retained in their head. When I ask them questions, they still just look at me as if I'm speaking another language. Television and video games just suck the imagination and thought process right out from them. I explained that there were two children whom I retained last year, but they ended up in the first grade anyway this year, when the school year started in August. When the administration goes ahead and passes the children, it sets them up for failure. Sometimes they have to be passed on because of their age, or they have an IEP and can't be retained. I agree with that; however, a lot of children are already set up for failure by their parents before they even come to school. Somewhere there is a huge misunderstanding that teachers are supposed to be a child's first teacher. That is an indisputable lie! How can we continue to allow generations of children to wait for five years of their life to begin living? The whole point of the book, in case you missed it, is that parents are the child's first teacher. I'll say it over and over again if I have to! A parent is the child's first teacher!

There was a little funny moment today. Nerimiah was supposed to be returning to his desk to take out his workbook. We had just finished working on words that end with *p*. Anyway, after all the children were at their desks, I turned back to look at why Nehemiah wasn't at his desk. He was still sitting on the carpet, but it looked as if he was meditating in a yoga position. He was sitting in Indian style, or as some teachers say, crisscross applesauce. Why? I don't know. Anyway, he had both of his arms up and extended out in opposite directions. To top it all off, he had his eyes closed. He finally opened his eyes and started laughing. I couldn't do anything but laugh with him.

Not so funny! Reshae was a little off today. While we were working with our workbooks, Reshae blurted out that her daddy killed her mommy last night. I immediately and naturally frowned, thinking about how horrible it sounded. But before I could ask her if it was for real or a bad dream, Yuan asked her, was she "for real" ? I had some doubts in my mind since she told me when she first came in that her mommy did her hair. Not only that, I believe she wouldn't even have been in school if that really happened. So she says that yeah, it really happened. But this time, when she said it, she said that her mother was running away from him and that she hid under the kitchen table. Her daddy found her and killed her. She was telling the story as if it really happened. This was my first time having a child share such violent information out of the "normal" someone-getting-shot scenario. I went over to get Ms. Brown to see if she would tell the same story, and she did. Ms. Brown asked her, was it a dream? Reshae hesitated for a minute and looked at me. Then she says it was a mistake and that she was dreaming. She said what really happened was that her mommy killed her sister. Once things settled down this afternoon, after school was dismissed, I did call her mom to let her know that maybe she might want to talk to her daughter about how when someone dies, they can't come back alive. I also let her know that she might want to explain what dreams are and how most things on the televisions are not real. I was honest with her mother and explained that I thought that it was unusual for her to do that and that the statement itself was so graphic and violent.

On the afternoon radio show, the question of the day was, "What should Oprah do with her money?" The topic came up because she apparently donates more money to school in Africa than she does in America. I haven't heard the whole story about how this all came about. The radio host stated that the children in Africa were more appreciative of getting an education. First of all, Oprah, and whoever else is blessed to help others, can do what she wants with her money. Someone used to tell me that no one wants to help someone who doesn't want to help themselves. Sometimes, I don't see the people that need help trying to help themselves. I believe that there is too much that is taken for granted in America. Even foreign students come over and do better because they get their education by any means necessary. They take it as a golden opportunity and not just something that will be there whenever they feel like taking their education seriously. How many girls or guys have you seen gone wild that were foreigners? Don't get me wrong, I haven't forgotten about that tragic day in history caused by terrorists. I'm talking about the everyday people who come over here from around the world to have a better life for them and their family. It just isn't the norm for immigrants to come over and cause problems. They come over here with a mission and get the job done. They don't have time for that foolishness, and why should we make it acceptable for our youth and young adults to think so? *It starts at home!* If you didn't do anything else back in the day, you went to school to get your education and took it seriously.

Day 82
Friday, January 5

When I looked in the mirror this morning, I felt disgusted by the many little scars that have been left on my face from my stressing out so bad in the first part of the school year. My face breaks out in pimples, and then my nerves are so bad I try to pick them just because I know they are there, which annoys me. I feel disgusted from the little pouches and cellulites here and there. When I walk the halls, or even in my house, going up and down the stairs, I feel so heavy and slow. My knees hurt with every step. Not just because I tend to eat when I get stressed, but I haven't been able to take my vitamins the way that I want to because of the medication that I take for my sinuses. Sinus infections that started with this rat-infested and moldy school. I had to

178

walk to the storage room to get the vacuum cleaner to vacuum the floor before the children sat down on the carpet. As far as my day in school goes, I am very frustrated at the little to no progress that my students have made this year. These children are so much into playing that it is taking them too long to calm and have some kind of discipline to learn. Discipline that should have started at home. I want so desperately to teach parents some strategies to be more effective, encouraging, and disciplined parents to their children.

I talked to some lady from Phoenix, Arizona. She asked me what I wanted to get my doctorates in. I now know what I want to get my doctorates in. I want to earn a doctorate degree in parental education. That's it. I want to empower parents with a wealth of knowledge to be empowered to empower their own children. Anyway, Dimani still didn't show up to school this week. Jaron didn't come either. Ms. Hallow has been looking for him and his mother for the last two days. When I saw Ms. Hallow in the hallway, she said that she was working on some information to get Jaron some mental health services. Thank you, Jesus. I don't know if it will all go through, but it's a start.

I was very frustrated today with how much energy it took for the students to still try to do the bare minimum. I don't ever want to lower my expectations for my students, but now I am questioning whether or not some of my students this year are even capable of successfully completing the kindergarten level. Out of the nine students that I have on roll, only three would really be somewhat ready for first grade. These children need a lower-level curriculum like a pre-K–level reading program. They are still unable to identify their letters, sounds, numbers, high-frequency words, or anything else that they should know by now. I have only two students who can write their first name and last name legibly. It might not even be legible to others because no one but me is used to their handwriting. Usually, only the teacher can tell what in the world a student in their class is writing. On my lunch break, I pulled a whole bunch of letter activities off the Internet for the students to complete. This year, we are having an even harder time getting copies made. Remember I told you how I spent all that money on copies before winter break? Well, I don't have money to keep getting copies made. Younger children always need hands on manipulative and realistic pictures to work with. The principal said that if we use all of the ink in the cartridge, then we have to replace it. So that means I have to be selective about what activities I copy. But it is so time consuming waiting for the information to download and then waiting for copies of each sheet to come out for each child. I just go to Kinkos, do it and get it done.

As usual lately, I am at the point where I'm questioning how I can help my students' dreams come true, and even mine, when I can't even get them to dream in the first place. I want my students to know and believe that they can be anything that they want to be when they grow up. I want them all to be someone great for themselves, their family, and their community. I remember asking the children on one of the first few day of schools what they wanted to be when they grow up. Some children didn't know. One little girl said that she wanted to be a mommy. Some of the boys said they just wanted to be a football player. I remember four years ago when I was teaching third grade, one of my memorable students, Nicolas, said that he wanted to be a pimp, and he never wanted to go to college. Bless his heart. I was so proud of him near the end of the year when he told me he wanted to go to college and become a physical therapist for athletes.

Today the question of the day was a continuance of yesterday. Apparently, a lot of people are upset that she built a $40 million school in an African country because those children have more passion. A lot of times, I think people blow things out of proportion, concentrate on the negative and not enough on the positive. I know I'm guilty of it sometimes, but I'm working on it. As I said before, I don't know all the details about the school, and I really don't. Even if I never get through to getting tickets for her show or meeting her in person, I still appreciate her and all the others who are about the business of making a difference in the lives of children instead of just talking about it.

Saturday. I went to the mall to exchange a gift. I went over Pop's house and played games with the kids until nine thirty at night. Earlier today, I finally saw what everyone has been talking about on the news, as far as Oprah donating her money. She said what she felt. It's not as if my opinion matters, but I agree with what she said. I support anyone who uses their wealth, influence, time, talents, and gifts to help make something and the world a better place. However, I don't think that there is anyone who donates money, time, energy, or efforts to children, people, or causes that can't benefit them. I don't think those who do have it would help people if they didn't want to help themselves. It's their money, and they can do what they want. If you ask me, the majority of urban-school children could care less about getting an education. Their family problems are so bad that they are just trying to survive. Their coping skills are terrible because most of their family members don't even know how to cope. I see a hunger for surviving. In the children's eyes, I see a hunger for an understanding of what goes on in their home life. I see a hunger for wanting to feel as if someone truly loves them and won't hurt them. The children are so down and depressed when they come to school. And if they aren't down and out, then they are angry and aggressive, causing havoc and chaos in the classroom and around the school. The future looks very scary. Instead of just moving to the suburbs, people are going to be moving out of the country if America doesn't get herself together. I just don't see passion in my children's eyes. All they want to do is to stay home all day with their mommas, watch television, and play video games.

Sunday. In church, the sermon had me really refocused and thinking about how hard life really is for a lot of people less fortunate, aside from having added pressure and stress. To be a parent and have your child do better than you is no guarantee. I look at my oldest daughter and think about how I wish she could understand that everything that I do is, and always has been, inspired just by the day I knew I was going to have her. I know my expectations are high, but I hope my girls realize when they get older that I just want them to do better than I did, and with less obstacles.

Day 83
Monday, January 8

I called Leandre's mother about sending homework home. She said don't bother because she has six other kids at home, and that she couldn't deal with his problems. I reluctantly let her comment go. I would usually try to convince the parent of all the benefits of helping at home with their homework, but I knew that it wouldn't get done because his homework wasn't really done all year anyway. I believe that every little bit helps. I told her that I would see her at his meeting on Wednesday.

I started going back over to Ms. Brown's class for math again. I just can't take looking at a mini copy of a textbook and not having a real guide or materials. I really needed the teachers guided, not just because it is color-coded into the various sections that I need to teach, but because I was getting tired of looking at the much smaller version of a black-and-white copy that they didn't even staple in the office for me. You should see me trying to use copied manual while the pages keep slipping and falling apart. When I try to use them to plan my lessons, they fall all over the floor or get mixed up with all my other stuff. It's bad enough that I have to wear glasses, but with these copies, I'm making my eyesight even worse. Anyway, while in Ms. Brown's class for math, I asked the students, "What year is this?" And Leandre called out, "Two thousand dollars." Every question that I asked, he kept yelling, "Two thousand dollars." Although I didn't show it, it was hilarious. So the third time, Ms. Brown (I guess she was listening) yelled out, "Now who yelled out that answer?" I told her and the class that Leandre did a very nice job trying to answer. Once she found out who it was, she just looked at me and shook her head. He was very close by saying two thousand, being this is 2007.

Jamon visited me today, giving me an update. He left his school at third period. Once he showed up at my school, I tried to encourage him to go back to school so he didn't get into trouble. Before I could finally get him out of the classroom, he just shared the trials and tribulations that were on his mind. I feel so bad for him I wish I could do more to help him.

Nothing else much interesting happened today other than Eternity giving Rayshire a lip gloss, and she put it on her eyes. Dimani and Jaron didn't come to school. Twan is in Ohio. They called for his records. I took his school picture up there to see if she could mail it with his report card. I didn't want to throw them in the trash. Hopefully, he'll get to see his first school picture. I really miss Twan. He was so eager to learn.

Today, I found out about some more bureaucratic bull crap. Some new teachers who aren't even tenured got student teachers. You have teachers who have been teachers for eight, ten, and even thirty years in the system and one in this school for an entire thirty years, and they don't get a student teacher. A student teacher in your room sometimes means that you get extra pay, have help in your classroom, and you get to help impart helpful techniques. It's just crazy.

People just don't understand the crap that we go through. Society treats us as if we are expendable. You can't replace teachers with computers and electronics as you can everything else. Teaching as a career has fallen off the radar. We had to sit in a faculty meeting today to talk about more paperwork that we have to do. Why don't some of these parents have an audit? It seems as if every day, I get more agitated by the way parents can just send their child to school and walk away. I feel like an overpaid babysitter. I want to teach! I want to teach! I just want to teach! Raising other people's children seven hours a day isn't exactly what I went to college for, for eight years. Raising other people's children is more difficult than teaching because the children know that what I say doesn't apply to them after the bell rings at two twenty-five. Most of the time, it seems as if we don't matter while they are in school. I really need a laptop. There is so much that I see in my travels to and from, that I just want to share that the lack of parental responsibilities just doesn't happen in the schools. It happens in the malls, supermarkets, and even churches. Everywhere there are parents or guardians and children, there is some confusion and huge scenes because of undisciplined and spoiled children. I see adults arguing, debating, bargaining, and fussing with children. The parents are supposed to have the power and control, not the child. For example, a four-year-old wants a toy, and you tell them no, and then all hell breaks loose. Children are impulsive and naturally want everything they see. As parents, we have to teach our children from a very early age that they can't get everything that they want when they want it. You explain to them that you don't have the money, or that they have enough toys already. Then everyone surrounding the adult and the child has to hear screaming and crying because the child was told no. And I hate to see an adult walking somewhere and the person has a little one-year-old or two-year-old dragging behind them. Then some have the audacity to yell and cuss at the child

184

because they are walking too slowly. Hello! Why in the world would they think that their little legs could keep up with them?

Day 84
Tuesday, January 9

The first thing this morning, I had to deal with a phony, lazy-behind, ghetto fide, in-denial parent. First of all, I didn't even have a chance to get situated before Mr. Shiller came into my room right after morning announcements. After he asked me what resource I had because we had a meeting this morning, he asked me if I sent a particular note home. I looked at the letter he was holding that I sent home yesterday and said that yes, I sent it home as I always do in January. He proceeds to tell me that numbers 1 through 4 were fine. But then he says that number 5 is a problem because any issues with behavior requiring a parent to sit in class with their child has to be a case-by-case basis. Well, I already knew that, so I asked him whose parent came up to the office to complain, but he wasn't going to tell me. I kind of already had an idea of whose parent it was because there were only three of my students in school so far. Kevmani's mother is the only parent this year that is involved with her child as far as keeping in contact with me on a daily basis. I knew it wasn't her because she already knows that her son has challenging behavior in class most times. I knew it wasn't Yuan because his brother or some other girl usually brings him to school. So that only left Nerimiah's mother. Not only that, Nerimiah's mother walked into my room while she was on the phone talking, looked me up and down, turned around, and walked right back out. Apparently, she had a problem with number 5 because it basically says that if your child continues to display the behaviors that disrupt instruction and prevent others from learning, then someone is going to have to sit with them in the classroom. Now instead of coming to me and finding out exactly what it is that her child is doing, she runs straight to the principal. I think she believes that she has some kind of clout because her step-mother works here.

I wouldn't care if a famous person's child was in my class. I would treat them the same way. I dare not show favoritism to anyone. I don't want any one of my children getting off scot-free when their behavior gets off track. I'm not lowering my standards or expectations for anybody. For God I live, and for God I die. He is the only one that can judge me. I spend more waking hours with these children Monday through Friday for one hundred and eighty days out of the year. I know these children as if they were my own. I know what it is that I'm talking about. You see, parents like her only want to come up here when their kid's problems at school mess up whatever they have going on. They don't want to be inconvenienced. I keep trying to tell parents, "You better invest your time wisely with children while they are young. Once they get older and set in their own ways, it gets a little more challenging to try to help them and for them to turn their life around." So many parents don't even understand or know that they are the ones that have sentenced their children from twenty years to life. Her coming up here is proof that parents don't want to take responsibility for their children's actions in school. It can't be just one parent out of every class accepting responsibility for their child's behavior. It has to be every parent and every family. She came up here because there is a possibility that someone may have to sit with him, but she can't come up here any other time. For the first couple of months of school, the excuse I was given for her not being active in school is because she was pregnant. After she was pregnant, it was because she just had a baby. So I guess her excuse now is that she has three other children other than Nehemiah and can't come up to school. People really need to think about how many children they have, who they have children with, how old they are when they have them. And can they be an active parent in all areas of their children's life. Having a child is just not about feeding and clothing and sending them off to school. They need to think about more than *Dang, I didn't use protection for the sixth consecutive time.* I have three girls, and being a parent is difficult. I love my girls. But we all know that life is not perfect. Sometimes I don't like the behaviors, attitudes, and sickly times, but I don't see my life without them either. Right now, at this exact moment, I don't want any more children. I think that's because of the marriage that I'm coming out of, and I'm happy with the three blessings that I do have. I don't think I would want to bring any more children into this world. If, and that is a big if, I do have another child, I have until the age of thirty-nine to have one more. And if it doesn't happen, then it isn't a problem for me.

After Nerimiah's mother was up here for half of the morning, telling him to have a good day and to behave, he still got into trouble in music. I'm not the only staff member he gets into trouble with. He is too smart and sassy with his mouth, and his attitude is really smug.

Leandre didn't come to school. I wonder and worry if he's getting appropriate attention and supervision when he is home.

Dimani showed up. Her mother said hi and walked right past me as if today isn't her first time coming to school in the new year. No explanation, no note, nothing. The first couple of years I was teaching, I used to inquire why the child was absent. But then I came to the conclusion of why. You get the craziest excuses or the same excuses every other day or every other week. No doctor's note or anything. Only children with chronic problems are the ones who usually have legitimate documentation. I had had students who have had legitimate excuses for emergencies, illnesses, asthma, or other breathing problems. Last year, I had a little girl who had sickle-cell disease, so sometimes her legs or back would

187

start hurting. She also had a doctor's note when she returned to school.

All the kindergarten and pre-K teachers who had a resource this morning had to meet with Ms. Rooks from the Office of Early Childhood. I was thinking, here we are in another meeting that we have to sit in, and I say, for what! The purpose of the meeting was to give us more options for documentation of children's work. As if we didn't have enough. Everybody from the top to the bottom and everyone in between is up to their necks with paperwork. Employees on all levels in all areas have had enough of pulling the parents' weights. It seems as if every day we are required to do more and more. Are the parents required to do anything more? We are all busy, from the custodians and cafeteria workers all the way up to the chief executive officer. From the school police, cafeteria workers, teachers, principals, school board members, all the way up to the government. I'm not pretty good with paperwork, but it is so stressful trying to keep up with all of the different kinds of paperwork—report cards, progress reports, in-school testing data, city and state testing data and documentation, attendance, progress monitoring, materials and textbook inventory, fund-raiser money, field trip money, permission slips. I've always wanted to be the principal of my own school but refuse to because of all the paperwork. I know I would get into trouble for paperwork alone. When I have to go into Mr. Shiller's office, it seems as if he has at least one hundred big, thick binders of documents. He has what seems like eight different pockets for information on his bulletin board in the office. Then he has more piles of paperwork on his desk and other tables in there. More and more paperwork because of the No Child Left Behind Act. Which once again supports the whole title of this book. Where is the parental responsibility in all of this? It has come to a time in our society where we have to make parents accountable for their actions. Especially with the younger children. There does come a time in a person's life where you have to accept that you can't keep blaming bad choices one makes on what their mommy and daddy did to them. But our children's parents should be held accountable for the damage, hurt, harm, danger, disrespect, neglect, abuse. Hold parents accountable. Parents are only held accountable by the law when it is a life-or-death situation. That is usually after the fact. All the technology we have access to, and you mean to tell me that we can't keep better track of what parents are doing with their children. I'm held accountable along with all my other colleagues around the country. Let them go through training, classes, workshop, and paperwork. I bet things will start to change. Nothing will be better until there is a paradigm shift of increase in parental responsibilities. Nothing. I take that back. It is going to change for the worse.

While walking in the hallway, I overheard the fourth-grade girls talking about how they stayed up last night and was watching the new show *I Love New York*. Now it just so happened that I watched some of the show. I try to stay in contact with some of the worldly things so that when my almost-thirteen-year-old comes home and starts talking about the things that they talk about in school, I can have some reference point. There is no way that any child in elementary school should be up past nine. Yeah, I said nine! And they definitely don't have any business watching a show of that magnitude. These young girls actually look up to some of these women who totally degrade themselves on national television. Do we really need our children to have any more distorted views of relationships in their lives? It is already bad enough that even in our own day-to-day lives, we as a society have a 50 percent divorce rate. Our communities are now turning into blended families. I'm in no way saying that there is something wrong with it, it just takes a lot more work than the traditional two-parent household. I included! I think we all know all the different households that now exist. It doesn't mean that we have to change our standards and lower our expectations, it just means to work it in a different way. I will try with everything in me to teach my girls of how men and women should courtship one another. I don't even think anyone really knows what that is anymore.

At the end of the day, Nerimiah's mother picked him up and didn't say a word about the letter. I told her that he had to sit by himself for the same reasons I've been calling their home since September. She said that she talked to his doctor and decided that she wasn't going to put him on any medication. I never suggested he needed it in the first place. Then she proceeded to say that he didn't even sit down at home. And in the nicest, most serious, and professional way I could, I explained to her that his behavior had nothing to do with sitting down. I told her that I don't expect five-year-olds to sit down all day. I told her that his problem is with basic listening skills, following directions, and his mannerisms. He thinks that he knows everything, but he doesn't. He is very sassy, and he is making slow progress because he wants to play all day. She said, "Well, I'll talk to him again." Thanks a lot. The world is going to change now. Sorry for the sarcasm. It needed to be imbedded in the children from birth. Talk to the baby about going to college as soon as you feel that first movement in the womb. Wow, what a day. It was just another typical day here at our lovely institution of learning.

Day 85
Wednesday, January 10

I must say that today was a very interesting and full day. As soon as school started, I only had three children. Yuan's brother came in and said that Yuan had an asthma attack and had to stay home to get his treatment. He gave me his note, and I just told him thanks for the information and to tell him that I said hi. Leandre and Jaron still weren't in

190

class. Dimani was here on time at seven forty-five. I didn't have a resource class today, so the children stayed with me. By the time I was ready to work on the carpet, I had six students to work with. Mrs. Siris, the intervention teacher, came in today to chart their progress of sound and letters for me. That is always a huge help to have someone help you with anything, really. While she worked with one student at a time, I tried something different and new for my students with the remaining five. I decided that I was going to revamp the teacher's guide directions for the day that I have to use. I'm going to do as many concrete activities as I possibly can. So today, instead of orally blending three-letter words, I gave each of them three different colored cubes, one for each sound. They did pretty well with it. They were really getting the hang of it when Ms. Utler came in the door. So I knew that it was time for me to go to the IEP meeting (Individualized Evaluation Process).

Today I had to have our very first meeting for my special friend Leandre. His meeting was just about the basics of what he can and cannot do for his age. He is basically like a two-year-old. Every day my youngest daughter and Leandre remind me of each other. Anyway, what it boiled down too for Leandre, is that he hasn't had enough formal education for us to be too concerned for his lack of academic and social growth. I disagreed of course, but who am I to say anything different. I'm just a seasoned teacher that spends every day with him. I wanted to say just forget it an walk out of the room I know in my gut that there is something more wrong with him other than the lack of formal education.

When I came back to my room, Mrs. Nixon was there. Yippy! I was so happy. I thought that my class had run her way.

Jaron's cousin came in and told me all the background info on their family. She also said that I had to feed her if I wanted her to stay and help him. She was a character too, just like everyone else I've met. I wanted to laugh so bad. First, it was the grandmother, then the one-eyed neighbor, grandfather, mother, and now crazy cousin. I guess every family has their own assortment of chocolates in their box. As in the movie *Forrest Gump*, where the mom used to tell Forrest, "You never know what you're going to get." Coconut comes to my mind when I think of my family. But you know what? I love coconut!

Day 86
Thursday, January 11

Dimani beat me to my classroom today. Can you believe it? Whitney didn't get up this morning, and it threw my schedule off. I was proud of myself because I was ready to go. Whitney just had to get herself up and either help with the girls or make the lunches. I think from now on, she will just have to make the lunches at night. She and the younger two really don't get along at six in the morning. Today was a much calmer day. I talked to Mr. Shiller again today and showed him some activities that I was talking about in reference to my students. Yuan made it to school today. Jaron and his chaperone never did make it today. I forgot to call Ms. Haith (Jaron's grandmother) yesterday, what with all the commotion that was going on. I almost had perfect attendance today. I think my class has only had perfect attendance only one time this year. The students did much better today, working on the more simplified activities. They were really engaged in what they were doing. I made sure that I had enough work so that as soon as they finish, I have another assignment for them to do. Most of them will probably go to first grade even though they are not ready. So I'm going to try to get them to some kind of level where they can work independently and not have to have me to sit right beside them.

Day 87
Friday, January 12

I was late and I apologized to the parents for my tardiness. I explained to them that Trinity soiled her Pampers as I was going out of the door, and it went all onto her T-shirt and pajamas. So I left out later than I needed to. I told myself last night that I was going to focus on smiling as much as I can. Today I was still a little frustrated and overwhelmed anyway because Leandre was very off for the last three days. I went to Ms. Abrams and asked her if she could copy some of her communication icons that I could use with Leandre because his behaviors this week have worsened and magnified. He was out of his seat more; he was even calling out to and mimicking the students and me more. Even some of the students were a little annoyed with his behavior because he was going into their personal space.

Jaron and Lemonte didn't come today. All the children were displaying bad choices today. Kevmani got into trouble in the cafeteria again, so I called his mom. Yuan got into trouble following him. Shamira was being mean to Dimani and Reshae all week. So I guess she's coming out of her shell now. I wanted her to talk, but not in a negative and mean disposition. She even threw a crayon at Dimani today. I called her mother on the cell phone, and the man told me to call the house phone. I called the house phone, and someone picked it up, but when I said hello, they hung up the phone on me. I said okay. I didn't call back because I didn't even feel like being bothered. I had to call Kevmani's mom earlier. I don't have the time or money to be playing around with people. Reshae's mother just insisted on letting her do what she wants to do. So today, I called her and told her about her behavior and that Reshae continues to be unprepared for school. I couldn't tell you how many boxes of pencils, crayons, and tubes of glue I have bought.

For the remainder of my Friday, I spent the evening with Whitney, going to see *Déjà Vu*.

Saturday. I went to support our mentoring program's production of *The Nutcracker*. It was nice to see all the families supporting the children. That's what it is all about. Once you become a parent, most of the time, you have to sacrifice the things that you want to ensure that they get the things they need such as positive activities to keep their wandering minds occupied.

I went hanging out with the Magic Man. He just lets me talk and talk and talk. The only time when he really has to cut me off is when he is at work or on his many side jobs.

Sunday. I went to church. Pastor J seems to be eavesdropping on my life or something. He has been talking about everything that I've been thinking on the inside but only sharing with God. When a child has been told over and over again in so many different ways that they aren't anything worth loving, that's what they believe. Everyone wants to feel loved. I believe every person needs to know at least one person in the world loves them. Because of all the heartaches of my journey in life, my heart has become somewhat of a refrigerator. Most days, I feel as if I can't let anyone in my circle because they will just try to destroy the wall that I have built around myself. When people hurt you, it sometimes takes a long process just to be okay enough to accept it for what it was. Adults truly need to be educated beforehand what and how negative situations can cause long lasting damage in a child's life.

I didn't go to the performance for today because I had a terrible headache. I stayed in bed all day. I finally made it out of bed around five in the afternoon. I really needed to wash the truck before the girls came back. Ever since Whitney spilled her cappuccino in the truck, it has that stinky coffee smell. It was drizzling outside, then it had stopped by the time I got to the car wash about a mile away. Herbert dropped the girls off early again. I was right in the middle of shampooing the rugs. So he went and did something else and came back. I could tell by his sly comment that he didn't think that I was washing the truck, since it was raining, as he commented. Anyway, any negative comment that he says is just a soft, gentle reminder as to why we could never be together again.

Monday, January 15

Happy birthday, Dr. Martin Luther King Jr. I was finally able to make it to the parade. I asked God to make the weather warm enough for me to be able to take the girls. Today I really thought about, would Dr. King be happy about what's going on in the world, especially here in America? To see so many youths smoking weed and men dressed up as women in front of the little children is just sad. People have no respect for themselves anymore. There used to be a time when people didn't know what was going on behind closed doors. Now it just seems as if people bring their personal business outside.

Day 88
Tuesday, January 16

I woke up this morning and said that I would be at peace with my job from now on. And today, I was at peace. I can't change these children's parents and their circumstances at home. But I will give a damn while they are in my presence. I'm going to stay with them on their level and try to take them to the next, every time I see them. They had their typical talkative behavior. Not listening and following directions. Kevmani is the ringleader, and Nerimiah is second in command. They both just always have to run their mouth about something. What I can say about

Kevmani is that his mother has obviously worked with him because he is where he should be for his age. Nehemiah, however, doesn't know a thing. He still doesn't even know the letters in his name.

Day 89
Wednesday, January 17

The kids were, as usual, Kevmani, Yuan, and Nerimiah, bad. Yuan brought his uncle's cell phone to school and was passing it around in the cafeteria. I called his father, and both parents were up here in an hour. I wasn't expecting that. I truly appreciated that response, though. I'll take what I can get. I wasn't expecting them to come up here for that. I just wanted them to know so they can expect him to bring it back home.

Jaron and his mother and cousin came today. They got here at about nine fifty, which was ten minutes before lunch. So he was able to get five minutes of work. his mom and cousin carried on like fools as usual. I just tried to ignore them. I talked to the counselor about Jaron and she eventually spoke with his mother. No one discussed the outcome of the conversation and I didn't ask. More than likely it was nonproductive. Ms. Nixon called me and said that she woke up late and wouldn't be in. she'll probably stop coming soon. Well, at least I'm almost finished with the Open Court testing for the reading program.

Leandre wrote the uppercase *T* today. It brought tears to my eyes. I had to walk out into the hallway to regain my composure. The students asked me why I was so happy. No one can ever take back that knowledge of the *T* from him. That's why.

In a general conversation with an acquaintance of mine, I found out that he doesn't want to talk to his nine-year-old son. What kind of man doesn't want to talk to his only son out of four children? It's not as if a nine-year-old, who doesn't even live with you in the same state, can do something so terrible that you don't want to talk to him. The child lives six whole states away. Ignorant! He is just trifling and ignorant. It is the parents' responsibility to keep up with a child. It is the parents' responsibility to call and visit the child on a regular basis. You can't hold a nine-year-old accountable for calling you every week. Parents!

Jazmyn, my previous student from the third grade, had on four-inch wedge sandals today. First of all, it's January, and secondly, four-inch heels. You got to be kidding' me. I swear, people may be angry at the thought of federal laws dictating options on how to raise your child, but I think some parents really need it.

I saw a young mother in the ob-gyn's office who firmly corrected her two year old son. I wanted to commend her on how she handled her son's behavior but I didn't want her to think that I was crazy. I don't remember exactly what he did off hand. I just remember that she didn't go crazy by cussing him out or smacking the mess out of him. You can tell from the way that they responded to each other that she wasn't consistent with her parenting with him. You've seen it before where a child does something and the parent looks around to see who's watching. Then the parent pretend like they enforce rules, so the child doesn't respond the way the parent wants, and then the parent gets mad at the child for embarrassing them.

Day 90
Thursday, January 18

I had perfect attendance again today. All were eventually here, present and accounted for. Jaron came in at nine fifty again. Only his mom was with him today. Kevmani came in at 1:20 p.m. He came in one hour before school was to be dismissed. And you know what, I didn't even have anything thing to say when he came walking in. I was

197

speechless. I had no idea why he was late other than him saying that he was at the doctor's. Hey, the saying goes that it's better late than never. He came in with one hour left and still managed to get into trouble anyway. I just chose to continue to go with the remainder of the day and not even worry about it. I had to call Nerimiah's mother first thing this morning and I see where he gets his smart mouth from. He didn't have pencils this morning. When I asked him why he didn't bring his pencils, he said that his mother said I shouldn't have sent his pencils home if I knew that he would need them the next day, and then said oh well. Did she ever come up today? Of course not. She can run up here to the principal's office when I send a note home about her sitting in the classroom with him. But she can't come up here when he is just absolutely horrible. He's the worst kind of student to have, other than violent. He is very sassy and always gives you that smirk. You know that face that somebody gives you that just makes you have to think twice about your actions. His mother has exactly the kind of mentality that gets our children on the wrong road that they are on.

I saw a child today in Ms. Kaylor's class with three pounds of hair on her head. I guess it's just me. Because I don't understand why girls with perfect heads of hair have to have a whole bunch of fake hair on their heads. I don't understand the philosophy behind a lot of these decisions. I guess I have to keep saying that they don't know any better.

The counselor was looking for Maytoria again. I found Maytoria in her normal resting place, the teachers' lounge. She was asleep of course. When the counselor was leaving for the day, she walked to my room to ask if I had found the mother. I told her that I let Maytoria know that she was requested by the counselor and what room number to go to. Maytoria never got up from the table. That's where the counselor caught up with her. Once again, I don't know what resulted from the conversation.

The children were their normal selves. And I just smiled. I've done all that I could do as far as letting administration know about their behavior. If they haven't made any class changes other than Tonto, then nothing else will happen. I do the very best that I can do, and I do it with as much love and patience that I have.

I'm tired of cleaning up mice droppings. I came in this morning, and one of the children's paper decodable books was all chewed up on one side. It seems as if it never ends. The only good thing is that the mice aren't visibly running around while we're in the room. I only saw a mouse one time when I went over to my desk to cut some paper, and I saw the mouse crawl from behind the paper cutter. I wore rubber gloves all day today. And I'm going to try to do it every day from now on. Calling the health department won't change anything because there aren't enough people complaining in the first place. When you work for any government agency long enough, you just know how things are. When I took my gloves off at the end of the day, the gloves were so disgusting. Ms. Brown wore gloves today too, I think. She said she did. She threw her whole lunch bag away because mice are just everywhere. I am now paranoid that the mice are going to start jumping on me or come out while I sit here at this computer. I really need a laptop. I plan on buying myself the least expensive one I can find for a birthday present for myself next month. I talked to Lemonte and Yuan's fathers today about their behaviors. I got the usual response that they will talk to them. How about putting them on punishment or taking a privilege away. All that the boys want to do is play. They were truly not trained or prepared to be in any kind of school setting at all.

I turned in my Open Court test scores. Now all I have to get done are my report cards, which are due by the end of the day on Tuesday, the twenty-fourth. I'm tired today. I've been doing good, taking my vitamins and exercising, but I know I just have to keep hanging in there until I build my endurance back up.

Day 91
Friday, January 19

TGIF. Kevmani punched a carton of strawberry milk all onto Nyaa at lunch. I just don't understand him. He has to be acting for some reason. His mother reprimands him and he just keeps on getting into trouble. One whole side of her shirt was soaking wet with the pink milk. She had to go up to the nurses office to get a dry one. Luckily, they had something up there that she could put on. Jaron and Leandre didn't come in today.

I started DIBELS (Dynamic Indicators of Basic Early Literacy Skills) testing, which I was supposed to do yesterday. Since we can't test our own students, we rotate, and I had to test Ms. Fields class. I tested Ponto today, and he acted as if he was so happy to see me. He said that he didn't want to go back to Ms. Fields's class. I just told him that his behavior showed me that he didn't want to be in my class. He even asked me where his desk was. I showed him that it was still in the same place.

Ms. Nixon came in today and I was happy to see her. She helped out as usual so I had a very productive day getting things done.

Saturday. I dropped the girls off, went to mediation, went to pick up the girls, and got to sit with my girl Trianne for an hour to talk, then I picked up Whitney from school. Went over to my mom's house. Ate oodles of noodles, tried to get the girls to lie down. Finally, Faith went to sleep. Trinity wouldn't go to sleep. Around five, I helped a girlfriend move.

Sunday. It was the choir's turn to sing today, so I stayed for two services. It was just awesome, as usual. My sister was supposed to come to church today so I could stay for both. She didn't show up because she couldn't get off the couch. However, she did come to get Faith and Trinity in between the services. So Whitney ministered with her dance ministry, and I was able to minister in the choir.

Went to Mom's house. The girls were asleep, so Whitney and I went home to clean up. I got most of what I needed to get done before my sister got there with the kids. Whitney got a butt whoopin' for not having any of her chores done, her room being atrocious again, and then went to top it all off with an attitude problem. Then I got my first verbal "I HATE YOU!" It was an interesting situation. So I told the child that if she hated me so much, she didn't have to be here, and she could get out if she wanted. So she stomped past me down the two levels to the front door. She acted as if she was waiting for me to open the door, so I opened it, and she went out. So of course, I don't want to go to jail for hurting this little girl who thinks she's grown now or for having her sit outside on the porch with no coat or shoes. She is sitting on the porch in her pajamas. It was eleven o'clock at night, with fresh snow all outside, forming the first snowfall of the season. It was only about an inch, so I know we are definitely going to school tomorrow. Maybe we'll get a one-hour delay or something. Anyway, I immediately called her dad. He's the calmer one between the two of us. My sister was in the other room braiding my goddaughter's hair. I really try not to get my sister involved with anything that I might be a little emotional over. My sister will lay her out with no hesitation. My sister hates to see or hear me cry. So this night, I did good with this new situation because I kept cool. Her dad appeared to be shocked by what I had just told him. So I told him the story again, and he said he was on his way over. He asked me if she had coat and shoes on, and I said that she went outside with nothing but her pajamas. He seemed to be under the impression that I put her out, which I didn't. I know from now on to give her a different option. We hung up, and then he called back. He told me to tell her that she better have that room clean and those chores done, or she was going to get it from him. I told her and I went to my room and lay down. I tried settling my nerves by watching television. I was processing her words, "I HATE YOU!" I've come to the conclusion that it is best that she hates me now and love me later.

She messed up on the wrong day too. Her thirteenth birthday is in two days. And as she told me before she got into trouble, she doesn't care about anything. So she saved me some money for Tuesday because I'm not taking any flowers, balloons, or a platter of sandwiches up there for her and her friends to share on Tuesday.

Quarter 3

Parents Who Drugged Their Children
Author Unknown

God bless Parents who drugged us!

The other day, someone at a store in a town read in the paper where a Methamphetamine lab had been found in an old farmhouse in the adjoining county and he asked me a rhetorical question: "Why didn't we have drug problem when you and I were growing up?" I replied, " I had a drug problem when I was young". Looking at me dismayed I said:

"I was drug to church on Sunday morning. I was drugged to church for weddings and funeral. I was drug to family reunions and community socials no matter the weather.

I was drug by my ears when I was disrespectful to adults.

I was also drug to the woodshed when I disobeyed my parent, told a lie, brought home a bad report card, did not speak with respect, spoke ill of a teacher or the preacher, or if I didn't forth my best effort in everything that was asked of me. I was drug to the kitchen sink to have my mouth washed out with soap if I uttered a profane four-letter word.

I drug out to pull weeds in mom's garden and flower beds and cockleburs out of dad's fields.

I was drug to the homes of family, friends, and neighbors to help some poor soul who had no one to mow the lawn, repair the clothesline, or chop some firewood; and if my parents had ever known that I took a single dime as a tip for this kindness, they would have drug me back to the woodshed.

Those drugs are still in veins: and they affect my behavior in everything I do, say, and think. They are stronger than cocaine, crack or heroin; and if today's children had this kind of drug problem, America would be a better place.

Teacher objective: Teacher will continue preparation of students for city/state testing by reinforcing test-preparation skills and strategies.

First and foremost, we do not teach for tests. I don't. I'm quite sure there are probably a few teachers here and there who may teach for a specific test, but for the most part, we don't. From the first day of school, we are educating the children for their life, for themselves, for the next grade level, and for their overall academic Eternity. Every day of formal classroom instruction is a deposit made into their brain that no one will ever be able to withdraw. In between the end of the second quarter and the beginning of the third quarter, we have more academic materials for the students to practice the skills tested in the format of which they are given on the standardized tests. Some are teacher-generated, and most are already generated from different programs. In addition to the daily instructions *we provide* according to our curriculum guidelines, we provide even more practice based on where the student's individual needs are. Through daily instruction and monitoring of students' progress, we know what skills a child needs. Some children need intervention if they are struggling, extra practice if they are right on target, or more challenging work if what they have is too easy. For example, a kindergartener should know all uppercase and lowercase letters and sounds and some high frequency words. A first grader should be able to read a certain number of high-frequency words and read sentences fluently. A second grader should be able to identify all parts of a sentence's structure and be able to expand those sentences. Obviously, the skills are more specific and precise, and a

204

child moves to the next grade. Now here is where the problems begin to come. If I have a second grader who doesn't even know his or her letters, numbers, and sounds, then they are already two grade levels below. And every year, they will be farther and farther behind. That's why we really can't teach for a test even if we wanted to. Either they know it or they don't. Helping them with testing strategies won't help if they don't know the information in the first place. We can keep the hope alive all we want to, but if parents don't support and encourage their children to be successful, in partnership with the school, then it will just continue to get worse. So quarter 3 involves standardized tests and more in-depth detail focus on taught skills.

Parent objective: The parent or guardian will ensure that that their children will come to school every day for testing. Parents will make sure their children will go to bed at a decent time to ensure children have been well rested. Parents will study and review with their child the practice-test materials and homework that are sent home.

I won't get into all of the controversy about standardized tests. We have to give them, and we need the support from home. That's the bottom line. I know I have sent letters home to parents, letting them know when testing would be and a list of things they can do to help their child during those weeks of testing. And what will happen? Some students will still come to school absent or late. I have called, or even gone by their homes to talk to the parents of children who showed up absent for testing.

To make a long story short, the data from the students' test give a lot of information about the student, teacher, school, and the system as a whole. Absent children add zeroes to the scores that are calculated. All of the students' scores are calculated, and it affects the overall school grade. We need every child in attendance to take their tests. There are way too many parents who do not support their children doing their homework as well. Some parents feel as though that homework is not their responsibility, but the teachers responsibility. Now the last time I check, homework was done at home. I guess we're supposed to help with the homework too.

Day 92
Monday, January 22

Before Whitney got out of the truck this morning, I prayed that God will bless her today and told her that I loved her and to have a good day. I think she said something, but I wasn't sure. We almost had a snowy day. But as Brandy said in one of her songs "almost doesn't count." The surrounding counties had a two-hour delay. The inner city only got an inch. But it was enough to have a one-hour or two-hour delay because of the slipperiness. Everybody came today except Jaron. Lemonte came to school. Kevmani has school suspension with Ms. Fenwick. When I talked to his mother this morning, she said that he was also suspended from recreation.

I saw Nerimiah's mother in the hallway on my way to pick up the children from lunch. Before I could even open my mouth to speak to her, she intentionally turned her head the other way. That's okay. She didn't hurt my feelings any. That's on her if she wants to be ignorant.

I threw two plants away because mice were using them for nests. I cleaned a whole section of the room with mice feces. It took up the rest of my time at the school.

I also started to hang February decorations and black history papers.

Day 93
Tuesday, January 23

I thought I had a productive day. I cleaned another section of the room, hung some more of the students' works, rearranged the students' desks and my front teaching area. I wanted all the children directly facing the front. I finished report cards and turned them in on time. Since I spoke with Mr. Shiller about modifying the instructional day to include more hands-on work, I wanted to use Reading Rods because the little cubes have pictures on them that correspond to the letters. Today when I started to tell the students about working with Reading Rods, I said as soon as Mr. Shiller brings us some Rods, we'll work with the Rods, and Mr. Shiller walked right into the room with the rods in his hands; it was the most absolute, perfect timing I've seen in a long time. Attendance has been low this week for everybody.

Day 94
Wednesday, January 24

Jaron came to school today and at least he's consistent with giving unfamiliar staff a hard time. Ms. Hone and Ms. Nixon were here also. Ms. Hone came in to see me on her resource time. I had to go to the bathroom this afternoon because I didn't get a chance to go. I asked Ms. Hone and Ms. Nixon if they felt okay for me to use the restroom; they both said yes. Five minutes later, when I came back, Ms. Hone told me that Jaron had kicked her several times and gave her the finger. She said that she was really scared, but she wasn't going to let him know. She's never worked with little students so she wasn't exactly sure how to handle my precious little one. The two of them had already handled him, so I just reaffirmed what was said to him. By now I don't think there really is a point for me to feel embarrassed about his poor choices. I didn't raise him. I just went on with my day.

I cleaned another section of the room. I was actually proud of myself for throwing three slightly bulky items in the trash since I don't use them anymore. I collected the field trip money for next month. I also started scheduling conferences for Friday. I wanted parents to know that school ends at eleven fifteen and that conferences are scheduled starting at twelve fifteen. So far, I have three parents signed up. I'm curious to see who else shows up. I'm tired today. My feet are really bothering me. You would think that they would automatically make a different flooring for people who work on their feet all day long. I take that statement back. There probably is a more shock absorbent flooring system, but the city needs to be willing to pay for it. I've been giving myself foot massages every evening, but it isn't helping. I didn't finish cleaning my room because I had to go pick up Trinity early. Whitney has an appointment tonight.

Day 95
Thursday, January 25

11:00 p.m. Ms. Nixon called to tell me that she was sick. Ms. Nixon said that she didn't even go to her line dancing class last night. She also told me that her throat was sore and that she didn't even have any cold as symptoms. She was highly under the impression that it was the mouse droppings that is making her feel that way. I believe her too. I was not as sick as I am now when I was in the main building. I've been off my antibiotics for almost two weeks. Yesterday my throat started itching really bad. I haven't had a chance to go to Rite Aid to pick up my allergy medicine. My doctor said that maybe allergy medicine might help. I have an Advair inhaler, but that makes my hand shake and makes me all jittery. I don't like that, along with my heart racing. And the allergy medicine makes me drowsy. The Lord knows I don't need anything else adding to my being tired. Anyway, yesterday, while Ms. Nixon was here, she tried helping me to clean up and probably inhaled fumes from the droppings.

12:30 p.m. Jaron started another tantrum during gym. He wouldn't move off the wall. Apparently, he was upset when he came out of the gym because he owed Mr. Handler some time for misbehaving. He was still able to participate after he gave Mr. Handler his time, but I guess Jaron wasn't happy with that. He was crying when I first picked him up. After I started walking the class down the fourth/fifth grade hall, he just stopped and leaned against the wall. Ms. Sott saw him and tried to get him to catch up with the class, but that didn't work. I was going to get Mr. Shiller, but he suddenly ran all the way down in the breezeway of the portable building. I did see Mr. Parnette and asked him to go get him. Although he is assigned as the music teacher, he does other stuff too. I asked Mr. Parnette to get Mr. Shiller because I didn't have the energy to physically get Jaron to where he needed to go. Anyway, Mr. Parnette was able to get him situated in his class. when I finally got down to where they were at, I went to get Jaron so he could finish his work. It just so happens that Mr. Shiller was now by the music room also. Mr. Shiller reaffirmed my request for Jaron to get himself together and to join the class again. Well, he obviously wanted to stay in music and watch the movie, so he came storming out of the room and started screaming and yelling. Then he walked over to the lockers and started to kick the lockers. He walked up some more and was hitting the wall. I knew that Mr. Shiller saw his behavior and would be going to get him, so I just continued to walk my class to the water fountain. Jaron walked passed all of us and all the way back to my classroom but couldn't get in because the door was locked. Mr. Shiller kept calling him, and he kept on walking as if he didn't even hear his name. Mr. Shiller kindly walked up to him, held his hand, went to the teachers' lounge to wake his mother up, and told her that Jaron was ready to go home for the day. He didn't come back when Mr. Shiller told him to and I knew it pissed him off.

1:30 p.m. Nyaa Carr's shirt was torn from the wrist all the way up the arm. Her mother told her to put something on and that's exactly what she did. I told Ms. Brown that she should take her to see the social worker. Ms. Brown said that there always seems to be something wrong with her clothes. They are either too big or too small. I can't believe that she was allowed to come to school like that. I know that someone could have sewn the sleeves together if the shirt was really needed.

3:00 p.m. On my way to run an errand, I saw a kid hanging out the car window up to his chest, playing a game that involved what looked like blowing something out of a straw. He had no coat on a cold January day, without a seat belt, and hanging out the car while the adult is driving like nothing in the world is wrong. That would definitely be driver irresponsibility. But it would be someone else's fault if something was to happen to him.

Day 96
Friday, January 26

Today was a half day. Only four of my students came in today. Only Lemonte, Reshae, Leandre, and Kevmani. Another low-attendance day. All the teachers knew that it was going to be a low-attendance day. I was told that Nerimiah had a fever, and that's why he didn't come. The schedule for the whole year is given to parents in advance. I think that it is important that they try to make the first three report conferences a year. There are only four quarters, you know. Anyway, I finished up Ms. Fields's class. I'm so glad testing is over. Looking at scores sometimes is depressing. I think that parents are under the impression that all their children are supposed to know when they leave pre-K and kindergarten are their letters, numbers up to 10, shapes, and colors. They are so wrong. Those are the basic things that they should know even before they set foot into a school. In the school system, when it's all said and done, the teachers are the ones held accountable for the students' achievements. They don't care that parents don't bring the students to school or bring them late, they don't care if they do homework or not. We cannot make children do what they are not ready to do. And with the school system not having appropriate level curriculum for children who have never had any kind of learning experience, then the children are going to continue to be behind. I've said it so many times that it is impossible to catch a child up from five years of nothing in a matter of months. Impossible. All I can do is try. My students are making some progress, but it is nowhere where it should be. My heart is just really solemn today. I just pray, wish, and dream so much for them.

On a personal note, today is one of those days that I feel very overwhelmed. After the early dismissal, I had to drive back across town to get Whitney's birth certificate and social security card so she can get a state identification card. she has to take her SATs (Scholastic Aptitude Test) tomorrow. At noon, I drove all the way home to find out that her birth certificate and social security card weren't in the safe where I thought they were all along. So I found a copy, praying that it would suffice. While I was at home, I checked my mail. I got a letter from the transit insurance company saying that they weren't going to pay for the damages to my truck because basically, the driver said it was my fault, and they have to believe the driver. That driver told a bold-faced lie and got away with it. But that's okay. She told the wrong lie on the wrong person. What goes around comes around! There's apparently nothing more I can do. While driving on the way back to my job, I spoke with the chief of claims, the supervisor, and the claims adjuster on the speakerphone. It's situations like this that confirm that all some people care about are themselves, and they couldn't care less how they affect others. I can't afford a $500 deductible for my insurance company to fix my car and, in turn, sue the MTA(Mass Transit Administration). I guess I have to chalk this up as a loss. But as for that so-called woman who hit my truck with my daughters and nephews in it, she said, "Oh well!" and then lied about it. I'm quite sure God's vengeance for one of his anointed ones will be just. I went back to work to do a little more work. I left at two forty-five to take Whitney out of school a little early because her school day is until five o'clock, and the Motor Vehicle Administration is closed when she gets out of school. I got her out of school, took her to the MVA, and stood in this long line, only to be told that a copy would not work since this would be her first time to be included in the system. I just prayed that her other ID card will work tomorrow. After that, I had to go pick up my truck and then take Whitney back to school. I returned to my job, where I started cleaning my classroom again. And that still wasn't the end of my day.

I did have Magic Man help me out with a lot of stuff that I can't do or don't have time to do. For example, he took my truck to get four new tires that I desperately needed. So that was a blessing for me today. I will focus on the good and the expectations of great times ahead for me.

At least I'll have time to refocus myself since the girls go with Herbert this weekend. He called me earlier today, but I was in the middle of getting Whitney and trying to get her situated. I must give him credit for trying to hang on to this relationship to the end. But I just can't go any farther with him. I definitely can't be with anyone who would knowingly not want to see his girls for a whole year at a time on every single holiday. I couldn't be with a man who doesn't want to talk to his only son of nine for no legitimate reason. Sometimes, I think you can tell how a person would treat you from how they treat their own flesh and blood. Adults can have so many relationships, but a relationship with a child is one that is different. Children are irreplaceable.

And so on that note, I think I'm going to treat myself to some coconut shrimp at the Bahama Breeze. I've never been to the Bahamas, but I it is on my list to go. I like going to Bahama Breeze because I can completely relax in its environment and forget about my worries for a few minutes.

Not a very good night. I got into it with Herbert again as usual. Same stuff different time of day that's all. He's an arrogant narcissist and he's not even worth talking about it right now.

Saturday. Today was another typical errand running day. I dropped Whitney off at school, went to the Home Depot for new doors, filed taxes, picked up Whitney, went to go finish complete filing taxes, and stopped at church. And after all of that I still had to go to the skating ring for Whitney to be surprised at her birthday party. She's really blessed because her birthday party was too late to cancel. I forgave her for her dlittle angry outburst. I wasn't hurt like I thought I would be when I heard the first "I hate you!". Finally, I took the boys to the mall to get their birthday presents. They wanted those sneaker skates, so our time at the mall went fast

Sunday- I cried at church today. I'm sick and tired of being sick and tired and going through it all by myself.

Day 97
Monday, January 29

Today I got a new student who appears to be at least on grade level if not above. She's is very well mannered, sweet and I know she has home training. I'm really glad about that because I don't think I would've been too happy

213

if I was to have another low performing student. Outside of my new little girl coming, the day was uneventful. There isn't anything I feel like is worthy of going over again. It's just about the same crap every day. I guess I'm just tired of having to deal with the dame thing every day every year. As usual I cleaned up my room. Picked up my taxes after getting Angel from school.

A man from the tax office called while Herbert was there. Herbert called later, being ignorant. He just had to assume that I was claiming both of the girls instead of just one like I promise. I know what he's thinking without even having to talk to him. I didn't answer my house phone or cell phone. I just went to my dictionary to look up the word *scum*. I don't know why I wanted to know the word *scum* after I talked to him.

Day 98
Tuesday, January 30

The custodians took the water dispensers out of the school today. There was apparently some report that said the water in school water fountain system is clean. I hope they don't think my students and I are going to be drinking that water. There is no way they can say that after all those years of the water being contaminated that it is now clean.

We had a team meeting with Mrs. Green and Mr. Shiller. The point of the meeting was just more work and more paperwork to show the work that we are supposed to be doing in the first place. They also wanted to tell us that a whole bunch of people are going to start visiting our classes. I didn't ask what for because it doesn't matter to me. When you're doing what you're supposed to do in the first place, then it really doesn't matter when people come in. I admit that there are days when my room may be a little junky from not being able to put all of my instructional materials right away. But for the most part I'm doing my job, well at least trying to teach.

While the students were in music class, I got my girl Melissa to listen to the message because I couldn't take the sound of his voice. Herbert was being the ignorant person that he is. I'm trying to figure out why some demonic people don't know that their blessings are not from God but rewards from the devil. It was just a thought. I wish he would leave me alone.

Once we started reading, I had a problem only with Nerimiah. We were reviewing the short sound for *aa*, and he refused to open his mouth and say anything. I gave him three chances to do what I asked him to do, and he blatantly refused. So I told him to go down to his grandmother, and then he wanted to do what I asked him to do. It was too late, though, Nerimiah is the kind of child wherein you have to mean what you say because he plays too much. His mother doesn't think he that he does anything wrong. I'm not playing any games with him. Then he wanted to get an attitude when I told him to go down to her classroom, three doors down. Even Jaron was having a good day. He was just whining about being sleepy, but that's it. Anyway, once Ms. Gracey got to him, he came right back in, and I had no problems the rest of the day.

I had a wonderful afternoon with the children. They did their work so wonderfully that I had to bring out the doughnuts. All the students were doing everything that they were supposed to do. They were listening, following directions, paying attention, doing their work, helping each other. I was truly elated and happy, and the students knew it too because I told them that this is how it's supposed to be all the time.

I cleaned my room some more. It never seems to end. After work, I graded papers and hung up a lot of the children's work. I won't be so extremely stressed and overwhelmed until testing time and report cards come again.

After that, I spent the rest of my time at work typing lesson plans.

Later after work I picked up Trinity from Trianne's and stopped to get something to eat. Then I headed toward Whitney's school for report card conferences and a mandatory meeting about their end-of-year trip to Boston. I think that every school should follow the KIPP model. They are very strict about behavior management and parent involvement policies.

There was a news report on the radio that said something about parents letting their children drink while they are in the with them. Permissive parenting just may be at the top of the lists of how parents go wrong with their children. There are way too many parents letting their children do whatever they want to do. No parent should be allowing their teenagers to be in the house with them engaging in illegal activities and participate in things they really aren't ready for. I was under the impression that we are supposed to want our children to do better than us, not worse off.

Day 99
Wednesday, January 31

Today was a productive day with the students. It was an overall pretty good day. A little frustration during math time, but that's the norm for my group. Anyway, I only had three students absent early in the day. Mr. Parker stayed with Yuan this morning for about an hour. Since I usually let the children have art time, he was able to help his son with making a card for Valentine's Day. When Yuan was finished with his project, Mr. Parker had him complete the assignments in his *Sounds and Letters* workbook from the days that he was absent. That was a big help. When the children miss a day, they miss the entire day's work and aren't able to catch up or make up for it if the parents don't help them. We were able to complete our entire reading lesson this morning. They did better at rhyming words today. After lunch, we were able to work with the language arts book. I've been praying that my students begin a miraculous blooming process where all of the lightbulbs just go off in their heads. The students did an excellent job with the book. As I was explaining to Mr. Shiller, as long as my students have pictures, they are able to do the work.

I told my students to make sure they worked on knowing their birthdays. They have four days to learn it before I see who knows it on Monday.

The whole class was good at lunch.

Kevmani, of course, acted up throughout the day.

Lemonte is in everybody's business but his. He is so nosy and talkative.

The children didn't know their birthdays when it was time to discuss it at math. I sent a typed note home with each child, saying that they needed to know their birthdays. I have three children's birthdays that I have to know. I could go all the way up to the main office and pull their cumulative folders, but it would just be easier if they knew their own birthday. As usual, since I don't have a math kit, I was in Ms. Brown's room, so I didn't have anything to reference their birthday from. Only the new student, Aleesha, knew her birthday with no hesitation. Ms. Brown and I were both frustrated with the lack of knowledge the children had about the four seasons. It was insane. They couldn't describe anything but snow for the winter. No matter how much I drew pictures and gave them clues, they still couldn't give any answers. The only thing the children could think of for any season was watching television or playing a video game. What happened to outside games such as tag, hide-and-seek, jump rope, double Dutch, riding bikes, and flying kites? I make sure that my children are outside every day when it is nice outside. I wouldn't even think of having them sit in the house all day watching TV. If it isn't deadly hot outside in the summer, then the children are playing outside.

Professional Development Day
Thursday, February 1

Professional development on math. Today wasn't really anything major for me. A lot of these workshops that I go to now are just redundant information. I guess when you've been teaching for a while that's what happens. They just went of the math program as it is. They used the teacher's guide from the math kit, but I couldn't bring a guide because I don't have one. So I just sat quietly and completed some paperwork that I needed to do.

Professional Development Day
Friday, February 2

Professional development on MMSR. The MMSR is the Material Model for School Readiness. It's just a survey that we must do on each child that basically gets an assessment of where the child is as far as being ready for school. After teachers fill out the survey on each child, the information is sent to one central location for the data to be compiled and analyzed. Overall, they just want to know and compare the differences that home schooling, no schooling, daycare, nursery school and preschool make in a child's academic career.

Saturday. Got up early, went to women's Bible study, went back to Mom's to pick up the girls, but I stayed until about four. I was going to take the kids to see my pop, but he wasn't feeling well. Took Whitney to get her stuff so she could go to her girlfriend's birthday party, who mother happens to be one of my best friends. She got mad at me because I thought I was going to have to pick her up from

218

the slumber party early. I didn't care if she had an attitude with me. I have to do the best that I can do, being a single parent. I love my daughter and Chantel dearly, but I have to go to church. Church is a form of therapy and rejuvenation for me. It works for my ninety –nine percent of the time. Anyway, later on her sister said that she could bring Whitney back to her house, and I could pick her up from there. Faith and Trinity and I went home and ate dinner and played and watched a movie. The three of us were in bed around nine.

Sunday. I dropped the girls off at my mom's and went to church, picked up the girls, picked up Whitney, went home, changed my clothes, went over my old coworker's house to see him, his wife and his daughter, whom I haven't seen since she'd been born, went to Walmart, went home, started dinner, went over to Andrea to talk to her for about thirty minutes, went back home, and got the girls ready for bed.

Day 100
Monday, February 5

It's cold again today, around nine degrees this morning. The social worker came looking for me first thing this morning. She said that Jaron's mom was high. So now after I've been reporting his family's problems for five months, now someone wants to notice and take action.

Today was the one hundredth day at school. Pre- K and Kindergarten teachers make a big deal about one hundred because it's up to that number that we teach our children to count to. Today was the worst day, as far as family participation, ever. Ms. Brown really had a rough day. She has had it and is totally disgusted with the lack of participation from the parents and family support. Just as I said and most of the teachers complain about, we put all of this effort into the children, and we don't even get half of it back. Only half of the children from each class brought in their one hundred objects. We asked for these objects three weeks ago. Teachers spend their own personal time, money, and effort on fun learning activities for not only the one hundredth day of school but on all important days and milestones in school. All we ask is that the parents send in what we ask to be sent in. One of my students who was absent today walked in the door right at dismissal with her one hundred pennies. I told her right in front of her mother that we already celebrated the one hundredth day of school and that she could take her pennies back home. Her mom just looked at me and smiled, with no explanation as to why she wasn't in school today. What else was there to say? And neither one of them looked sick. There was no explanation as to why she wasn't in school today. And I didn't ask. I did want to put the parent in a guilty mood but why bother? The world isn't going to change until parents change. And I'm willing to help teach them. Our parents and their children and everyone around them are perishing because of that lack of knowledge. All government systems and community organizations are overwhelmed with problems related to permissive parenting or no parenting at all. We've been in this cold school all day long. I made sure Faith had on enough layers to be warm in school. If there are four hundred students in a school, if half of the parents called headquarters, something would have been done. But we can't tell parents to call and complain about heat and lead-poisoned water. We'll probably get into trouble or get fired. But parents, collectively—parents can rule the world.

The children still didn't know their birthdays. Today seemed like a long day. It always does when you haven't seen your students for more than two days.

Day 101
Tuesday, January 6

It is cold outside! I was so cold in my classroom that I had to make hot chocolate. I tried not to drink anything but water to keep my throat wet because teachers have to do a lot of talking. Then after I made the hot chocolate, I almost burned my insides because I was freezing and wanted to drink it. It was too hot to drink. Mr. J kept laughing at me because I had on my coat and hat every time he came in the room. I took it off when I had to write on the board, but I was still cold with the blue jean jacket I had on. I know they only keep the schools open because of numbers, money, and politics. Apparently, if the boiler system is working, we can come to school even if the system hasn't heated up the school yet. Oh well, that comes with the territory of my career choice.

This was the second day in a row that my students and I didn't have a resource class. So I put on a movie for them to watch while I finished my lesson plan for the day. We are supposed to have three resources a week for us to plan and to do the things that we need to do. Around nine thirty, I went over to Ms. Brown's room because the children were getting a little cold. I have a heater in my room, but it is so cold in this corner-end room of the portable; the cold overrides the heat. My heater unit is just taking off the chill. Today I was dressed as I was supposed to be dressed for winter. I had on jeans and a sweater. It is too cold to be dressed up. Half of the teachers, staff and students in the school were wearing coats or hats and gloves. While I was in Ms. Brown's room, some lady just busted in the door around 9:55 a.m. in the middle of math and didn't even say good morning. She just said that Rayshire woke up late. How does a five year old child wake up late for school? It is an adult's responsibility to get a child up for school. I was sitting at the table that is right by the door. She opened the door so hard that it slammed against the table. I'm glad that I wasn't sitting any closer to the door.

We had the state people and the area academic officer come in today to check out the classes and school. They didn't make it to my class. I don't really care one way or the other if they come in my room or not. I have everything that they want to see. The objectives written on the main board, lesson plans, and students actively engaged in learning or working. The children know when outsiders are in the building because they're people they never see on a regular basis. I had perfect attendance again today. I didn't think many would show up because it was ten degrees outside when we got up this morning. It is really freezing outside. Nehemiah got an attitude because I had to take his dry-erase marker from him because he was not using it appropriately. I sometimes hate letting the children use stuff that I have to touch because they have such disgusting habits. So many of the children just pick their nose all day and don't care where they put the body samples. And all day, the children had problems with flatulence. I kept the air freshener close by because I had to use it often today. The children did surprisingly well with the dry-erase boards today. I have to find more hands-on activities to captivate their attention like the video games do. We teachers, by ourselves, cannot compete with the television and video games. No matter how animated you are, the children just look at you as if you're dumb. The class I had last year was so excited about everything. Even though they knew that Mr. Lion wasn't real, we still had loads of fun. My class this year is distracted by the lion. They keep going on and on about how it isn't real and where I put my hand and so on.

I saw Kaluan Glinn today. The last I heard, he was living in a juvenile detention or group home. I think he's been in both. One year, I had him in my class, four years ago, and I had his sister the year after that. He was an unforgettable youngster and gave me a run for my money.

Snow Day
Wednesday, February 7

SNOW DAY! YEAH! WOOO HOOOO! I was able to go back to sleep and relax today!

Day 102
Thursday, February 8

Children aren't an excuse to stop your dreams...
They should be the fuel to go for it!

Today was a pretty good day. Everybody came to school today except Leandre. I went over to Ms. Brown's today for math, as usual. Jaron was starting to act up first thing in the morning. The children had trouble identifying things they eat or do in the mornings, afternoons, and evenings. I got the finger from Jaron today. He wanted me to get out of his face too. I just looked at him and told him to have a good day.

One of my former students, who come to see me almost every day, saw me on the computer, looking for publishing information. She asked what I was doing. I told her that I was looking for someone who can publish my book when I get to finish it. I also added that one day I was going to be a millionaire. She said that I couldn't be a millionaire. I was in shock. I asked her why I couldn't be a millionaire, and she said I had three reasons. I asked her was she serious and she said that yeah she was. Well, you know I had to asked. Not only did she say it again, but she also told me I had three reasons. I curiously and anxiously asked why. She looked right over to Faith, who was sitting at the computer, and said, "There goes one reason right there." Then she said, "And the other two children you got!" I asked her if she was saying that the reason I couldn't be a millionaire was because I have three children, and she said yes. I went on to explain

223

that my having my children won't keep me from doing the things I want to achieve in life. It's amazing how children get a perspective on things at a young age. Maybe for her it was good that she thought that about children so she wouldn't have any at a young age. I just didn't want her to think that about me.

Day 103
Friday, February 9

It's my lunchtime, and I don't feel like eating. I lost my appetite, so I had to force myself to eat. I didn't even enjoy my chicken salad as I did yesterday. The time when I usually don't take the time to type is when it seems as if more stuff happens. But I feel a cry in my heart. It's a cry of anger and frustration. I'm not going to cry. I just really feel like it. Jaron started acting up first thing this morning and I'm not going to bribe any student to do any work. I'm not going to offer promises that I can't keep. I can't tell Jaron I'm going to give him candy or take him to the store if he does his work and behave. Doing what he is supposed to do is an expectation that he should already have in his life. If I have to do it for one, then I'll have to do it for all. So from now on, anyone that comes in contact with him has to suffer the consequences from his being pacified for his five years of life. He ended up punching Ms. Kaylor in the face. I feel bad because he's a student in my class. I see these children more than I do my own in the daytime. I wished Ms. Kaylor would have called the police and pressed charges. This is one of those situations where it seems as if the extreme problems need extreme intervention.

I saw one of my previous third-grade students from five years ago. Damont Yirby. I asked him how he was doing and if he had gotten himself together; he was one of the students that had issues and gave me problems.

On a personal note, Herbert is back to being his true self. You fill in the blank with what you like. He wants to meet back at the gas station because he thinks that I claimed Faith on my taxes. That's what he gets for making assumptions and not wanting to talk to me. He arrived at the gas station at five, knowing that we have always met at six, and he left at five fifty, from what his text message said. Oh well. It was his loss from spending time with two of the most beautiful spirits in the world. So all four of us went big-grocery shopping. It was quite an adventure for us all since I usually don't take them with me for big shopping. They had fun.

Saturday. I took Whitney to school and dropped the girls off at my mom's, then I went to a workshop at my job led by Mrs. Green. It was fun, and we were able to make stuff. I dropped the girls off at my mom's because I had to go *mediate*. Went to mediation. It didn't work out the way I wanted it to because he had an attitude. I went home, lay down for three hours because I had a terrible headache. After that, I went to the mall to get out of the house. Then I went back home and watched television until one in the morning. Around that time, I was really bummed out, a little depressed late in the midnight hour. I called Magic Man, but he didn't answer his phone. I called Melissaattie, and she didn't answer her phone. Anybody else I would have called would have been awakened by the phone, so I didn't bother. I was especially disappointed with Magic Man because he, out of all my friends, always answered his phone no matter what, or called me right back. So I called on God to just comfort me in the middle of my distress.

Sunday. Went to church. Went to my mom's. I picked up the girls, went home, fixed lunched, and lay down. Whitney watched the girls until I woke up. Fixed dinner for the next two days.

Day 104
Monday, February 12

I got a new student and the child doesn't know a thing. Jaron didn't come to school. Mr. Shiller said that he'll have to go back to half a day, which is fine with me. We all had a pretty good day. We are working on digital and analog clocks in math. We are still working on letters, sounds, and words in reading, among other skills. Everybody is hoping for snow tonight so we don't have to go to school tomorrow. I told everybody that I would see them tomorrow.

Day 105
Tuesday, February 13

I told you we would be in school today. When I got out of the house this morning, there wasn't any snow to be seen. By the time I dropped off Trinity and Whitney, it was obviously snowing. I had six children come to school today. All the girls came, and so did Kevmani. I felt bad because when I saw Kevmani, I lost a little of my smile. I had the children work in partners today. They worked with the reading blocks. I don't like teaching new skills to only half of the class. I also needed to work on finding some already-preprinted activities for my new student because she is a total clean slate. She doesn't even know her name, which is apparently new to her or something. I was confused from the mothers explanation. So I just made it seem like I understood but didn't. Jaron was still his normal self. He likes to always do something he doesn't have any business doing. All the girls were lined up nicely, and he's dancing and playing in line, being a clown. An attention seeker. We got out two hours early.

Wednesday, February 14

Happy Valentine's Day. I got an awesome present today in the form of a snow day! The girls and I and hung out all day at home. We didn't go anywhere. We were being lazy bums all day.

Thursday, February 15

Another snow day. I thought that we were going to school today with a two-hour delay. I went to the gym for two hours. The girls got out of the house. Went to get some water from the Home Depot, but they didn't have any. Went to Sam's Club to get Trinity some Pampers because she is obviously not ready to be potty-trained. She is very stubborn when it comes to that. Went to choir rehearsal.

Day 106
Friday, February 16

We had a two-hour delay today, and I was still late. Kevmani's mother called at 7:20 a.m. and woke me up again. She wanted to know about the trip. I told her I wasn't sure since this never happened to me before. The side streets on the way to Trianne's house weren't cleared. Most of the way to work was one-lane traffic. The school parking lot wasn't even cleared. There was nothing but ice covering the lot and the sidewalks. We assumed that since school was called into session today, all the schools had been treated. The field trip to "Dance Asia" was cancelled. So we rescheduled the trip for May 7.

Monday, February 19

No school for Presidents' Day. Another short week. I guess that's why the month of March is always a long month because we have all the professional development days, holidays, and snow days in February.

Day 107
Tuesday, February 20

All my children came today except Jaron. I was told that since he is half a day again, I should mark him as present. It probably has something to do with meeting AYP (Annual Yearly Progress) for attendance. I think if you are absent for no legitimate reason, then you should be marked accordingly. I haven't even seen him in almost two weeks. So his mother doesn't even know that he's back to half a day anyway. Oh well. That's why I don't get into the political things because if you are at the bottom of the totem pole, you're never heard. It's just like the war in Iraq. We have the leader of our nation representing everyone, and the majority wants our troops back home helping here. Anyway, I do what I'm told for the most part, especially when it is something that is being checked every day.

Day 108
Wednesday, February 21

Leandre's pants fall down while walking. All day long the students and I were helping to keep them up. I finally found some ribbon that I looped through his pants. The pants looked to be the size for an eight year old. Ms. Frasier shared her dismay to see that a student who has been absent has come back to school with a head full of braids down her back and a tongue piercing that is a stick-on. The

228

girl swallowed the thing before the end of the day. I tell you on some days I don't even know what to say.

Day 109
Thursday, February 22

Happy birthday to me. I am really excited about being twenty-nine-plus some added numbers. It's not old, and it isn't too young. Today Tonto's suspension was in question, as far as attendance. Yuan's dad said that he would be in today to sit and work with his son, but neither one of them came in. I just decided that I would have a good day since it was my birthday. I didn't do anything special to celebrate it either. Every day I wake up is a birthday celebration to me! I usually have cake and ice cream with my students, but I didn't this year. I really haven't been in the mood for doing anything extra with my students this year.

Day 110
Friday, February 23

Leandre had on a T-shirt with an oversized shirt and a long sock and an ankle sock. I started making high-frequency word cards for both our classes while Ms. Brown was making high-frequency word games. My hand was hurting and cramping by the time I got the fourteenth word on the list, which was *four*. I had to stop after that. Since I was making a set for each student in my class, as well as Ms. Brown's class, that would be thirty set time fourteen words that I have written so far. In case you didn't feel like adding that up it amounts to four hundred twenty words that I have written so far. I'm only on the *f* words.

Nyaa said that she didn't eat dinner last night because her mother said that she needed to get some rest. I told Ms. Brown to add that comment to her records she was keeping on her. She had too many things going on with her that didn't always seem right.

Day 111
Monday, February 26

Ms. Meiskolf shared her concerns about her class. But I told her that there is only so much that she can do. I told her to just smile as if she is on candid camera. Even though we know no one is going to jump out and tell us that we have been on some hidden-camera show all year long. She didn't give birth to these children. She hasn't raised them from the moment of conception. Ms. Fields was a little bewildered today when one of her students told her that he was big enough to beat the white off her. Since when did five-year-olds become big enough to whip anything and conscience of using skin color in that tone anyway?

Day 112
Tuesday, February 27

Every day you think that you can't be surprised with something new. Ms. Brown came over first thing this morning, sharing with me that one of her students glued their homework pictures in the book by using hair grease. Yeah, grease. For any parent who is reading this, grease will not make pictures stick down. It will just make the pages oily. While checking homework, she also found that another parent used Band-Aids to "glue" pictures down. Now before I go any farther, we do commend the parents that make sure that their child gets their homework done. It's a shame. I really don't want to say too much because I don't know if the parents can't afford a bottle of glue or if they are just too damn lazy to go get it in the first place.

Ants are all over the place. Ms. Brown is making score sheets for the students' decodable books. We are going to use them to show parents what their children can and cannot read.

Mrs. Lacey has helped me tremendously by printing all the labels for the students. She walked in my room to borrow something form me and saw what I was doing. She immediately offered her services and I graciously accepted. That was such a huge relief to me that I did have to finish writing the rest of the sets by hand.

Day 113
Wednesday, February 28

Today was okay. Just another typical day in the neighborhood. Children are not performing where they should be for this time of year. It is a struggle to get the children to learn. We need more counselors here at our school. The schools in America are only as good as the lowest-performing school. There is no reason why our children should come to school hungry, tired, dirty, and unkempt. There is no reason why parents should not be made or held accountable for their children's success and failures in school.

This afternoon, after school, I went to get Angel, but I had to just come right back without her because she had basketball practice. When I was pulling into the lot, I saw two young men, who obviously didn't attend my school. They were walking around two of the teachers' vehicles, looking in the windows. So once they saw me pull into the lot, they walked toward the way I was coming in. I got out of my truck to go back into the building, and by this time, they were in speaking range. One of the boys said something to me, and I asked him, did he call me a girl? He said, "No, ma'am," and I told them to behave as they pretended to keep walking off the parking lot. They kept on yelling something.

And they had the nerve to have a piece on the news last night talking about tracking teachers. They can track the teachers all they want. There's a large population of the parents they need to track. Nothing in the school system, neighborhood, community, or world for that matter, is going to change until the basic family foundation is rock solid. Nothing!

Ms. Fields's student, who said he was going to beat the white off her, was in my class since lunch. She needed a break from him, so I made him come into my classroom so she could have a breather from his behavior.

Day 114
Thursday, March 1

Picture day, crazy day. The children are just all off today. All over the school. All my students came except Yuan and Jaron. Dimani came late as usual. Her mother said that she was sick this week. Some of my class didn't even look as if they were going to have their pictures taken today. Half of Ms. Brown's class showed up. One child almost knocked the camera down playing around. Another second grader was doing cartwheels in the hallway behind his teacher's back and then got an attitude when I said something to him. Then he had the audacity to talk about telling his mother. I don't care whom he tells. If he had manners and respect for himself in the first place, then he wouldn't be fussed at by anyone.

Friday, March 2

Professional development day. I was very productive today. I checked all the students' cumulative folders for the school audit next week. I hung decorations for March, checked the math test they took yesterday, and finished putting the labels of high-frequency words on the index cards. Altogether, I created one thousand cards. Just as my typical day would go. I didn't get to do as much as I wanted.

I was preoccupied about the Magic Man. I talk to him every morning and every night. It usually isn't anything special. I talk so I don't keep my day's events bottled up inside. I haven't heard from him since yesterday morning. When I don't hear from my family and friends that I usually hear from, I start to worry excessively. I don't know why I do that. I guess I'm used to things always happening or something. I'm going to break out of that one day. I know that he is going through some things in his life, but he still always listens to me vent. I was so worried that something had happened to the one who's been helping me get through this divorce. Anyway, I finally heard from him as I was on my way over to his house at about three fifteen in the afternoon. But by then, the damage had already been done.

Saturday. I took Whitney to have an eye exam and get glasses. I had my nephews and the girls with me too. We had an adventurous morning. I took all of them to breakfast at a fast-food restaurant. I waited in a long line. After the food was ordered and ready, I gave Whitney her food and watched her walk across the parking lot to the eyeglass place. The remaining five of us sat down to eat. I had to pack them up after they took their first bite. Whitney was back and said that I had to come in with her. I forgot that quick she had to have an eye exam, so you can't leave a child in a room without an adult. After I ate that greasy sandwich, I had a migraine headache. It was delicious and everything, but I know that my stomach can't handle certain foods and beverages. My head stopped hurting long enough for me to go to the gym and let the kids play outside at the huge community playground for an hour.

Sunday. I managed to make it to church. I still had a headache.

Day 115
Monday, March 5

What a weekend! On top of the war overseas and in other parts of the world, America seems to just be going straight crazy! I just felt so depressed coming in here today. The news is so depressing. Toddlers smoking weed; a man chopped up his wife while children were home (they found the torso); a fender bender happened, and when the elderly man got out to get the driver's information, the driver took off and crushed the man's pelvis; too many people fighting over Anna Nyaa's daughter; five children found alone in DC area, living in filth and feces. And I haven't even started my workday yet.

Ms. Kaylor had a substitute in her class today. They seemed to be having a pretty good day until around one this afternoon, when I heard a little bit of a commotion. I got out in the hallway to see what the problem was. And the substitute, Ms. Milliams, was very upset because one of Ms. Kaylor's girls just cussed her out. Now Ms. Milliams is an old retired educator. You know, back in the day, you *never* heard of a teacher being disrespected. The little girl told her to "get the f—— off me, you b——!" a few times. The substitute called the office, and Mr. Shiller told the student to get up there immediately. Yup! Five years old. Insane! Just absolutely insane!

Leandre didn't have any socks on again today. I'm going to have a talk with Ms. Yizeman to see how she wants to handle this one. It is still cold outside.

Day 116
Tuesday, March 6

Leandre had on no socks again today. Terrible shoes, no T-shirt, clothes too big and dirty, face dirty, and hair not combed. I'm going up to the main building to see if Ms.

Yizeman was able to call and get a feel for what was going on at home.

Ms. Kaylor's girl, the one that got into trouble with her foul mouth didn't, come today. Ms. Kaylor was infuriated when she found out about her student today. She said that she couldn't wait until the profanity-filled student came back to school to lay her out. These children have no respect for teachers. Why would they when they don't even have respect for their own parents?

Day 117
Wednesday, March 7

Today was almost a snowy day. After school, for two hours, I scrubbed, cleaned, mopped, and bleached the desks, chairs, and floor. I wanted to make sure I could deter those ants from coming in my room.

The girls were good, the boys were bad, jumping around on the ants in the classroom all day long. Leandre had on mismatched socks that didn't look any better than the ones he had yesterday. I was just happy that he had socks on. The little girl came back, and Ms. Kaylor told her about how she isn't supposed to disrespect adults.

Ms. Kaylor laid her out. She also made the little girl write an apology note for Ms. Milliams. The little girl said that she got a spanking at home.

Day 118
Thursday, March 8

Do you know that all those darn ants were all over my room this morning as soon as I walked in the door? I was so pissed off (excuse my French). I did all that work for nothing. Later on when Mr. J came in, he said that he would caulk the seam where the portable wall and floor meets. His job never ends around here.

I'm thinking today that the title of this book should be Nobody Left Behind because what's going on in the world affects us all. No amount of words could describe all the little things that children do to add up to a big day. Children falling asleep and drooling on the work that we take time to create and prepare for them; juice dripping all on the floor in the hallway from an unclosed bottle; the amount of tension that is released in the air daily from the bodies calling, yelling, screaming out; students disobeying authority; digging of the noses and other areas; tattling, bickering, name-calling, teasing, cussing out teachers, huffing and puffing and talking under their breath. Then there are the older students that take it to an even more challenging level, and the older children are much more aggressive and physically challenging to control.

Ms. Brown got a fresh, uncooked egg first thing in the morning from one of her students. Ms. Brown was so proud of her raw egg. Ha! We don't get apples and cards and beautifully drawn pictures anymore. We get headaches, no appreciation, and raw eggs. It's the thought that counts, I guess. It is better to have an egg than to have nothing at all.

Nerimiah got his butt torn up by his grandmother, I heard. He still came back into my room, playing on the carpet while we were trying to blend words. I was told that he can't go to the circus next Friday because of his behavior.

Day 119
Friday March 9

Mr. J is the man. He sure did seal up the seam. There were less ants today. But I just found them in another area of the room, All the ants that were left just moved on over to another location of the room. I have been fussing and yelling all day long. Ms. Fields has been out for the last three days and her class has been split up the entire time. The two girls that I had for the last two days, felt comfortable to be

236

themselves today. So in addition to my regular students who have abnormal behavior, the temporary students threw them off and it was like a field day for them, so they thought. If Ms. Fields isn't back on Monday, I'm going to ask Mr. Shiller if it is possible for him to get a substitute. The group of children I have do not need any extra stimulation, especially not from other misbehaving children.

I went to Mrs. Kin's baby shower tonight. It was really nice. She was truly surprised; that's how a shower is supposed to be. It's a success when people actually show up and the guest of honor is really surprised. It was nice being with my friends and coworkers out of the school building.

Saturday. Went to Ms. Yabourn's baby shower. Her shower was so beautiful, but it wasn't a surprise because she always have to be in the details of an event. The girls went over Pop's.

Sunday. The usual, went to church, then home. Was able to take a nap. Laundry and dinner.

Day 120
Monday, March 12

While I was typing my lesson plan this morning, Leandre's older sister came in and told me he couldn't go with the trip on Friday. I said, "Why? Because he got into trouble?" And she said yes and proceeded to tell me the whole story. She watches Leandre. But she and her older brother got into trouble because Leandre broke some kind of glass or mirror. So now neither she nor the older brother can go on their trips. I asked where her mother was, and she said downstairs with the baby. The young lady said that she was trying to get her book report done. The bottom line is that an eight-year-old should not be responsible for watching a developmentally delayed five-year-old who is really like a dysfunctional two-year-old. It is the adults' responsibility to watch the children, not that of a child trying to fulfill a grown-up's role.

I asked Leandre's sister at the end of the day if she was sure she didn't want to take homework today for him. She said no. I'm quite sure her plate is full with taking care of the other children. I'm waiting for the day when people need licenses and classes to have children.

Day 121
Tuesday, March 13

Dimani and Leandre didn't come today. I had to talk to Kevmani all day today. He has been really showing off since the new girl came. I think he is showing off to get attention from me because she has proven herself to be smarter than him. Mrs. Scott, the assistant principal, had to call his mother because of his behavior in the cafeteria. I told Mr. Shiller about the children's behavior downstairs in the cafeteria. The children have no respect for authority. Ms. Yonson looked as if she has been working out down there with all that sweat dripping from her face.

Late in the afternoon Mrs. Scott brought me a gift for the day. I had a volunteer for the first part of the day. Her name is Ms. Tia. That's all I know. Since I had an observation first thing this morning, I was running around trying to get my stuff together for my observation. So I asked her, could she cut out the sight-word cards for me? So she did that for the time that she was in my room. while I was cleaning up Ms. Brown said that she smelled something in her room by her door. I didn't smell anything, and everyone that she didn't ask didn't smell anything either. It's probably a dead mouse somewhere. I am so happy that I didn't have the mice right in my room his time.

238

Day 122
Wednesday, March 14

It's a nice day outside. Ms. Brown's room smells terrible. Not only her room, but some areas in the hallway. I guess the warm weather is really cooking those mice in the wall or where ever they died at. Her room smells absolutely disgusting. Mr. J, bless his heart, couldn't get it because they are in the walls. He said that he told whoever was fumigating not to put down the rat poison stuff because that's what would happen. Every time I went to her room, I held my breath. It wasn't funny, but throughout the day, I could hear her briefly fuss about the smell. How is one supposed to concentrate, teach, or learn with that smell that makes you want to vomit? It is supposed to be like seventy degrees today. Leandre came to school today looking a hot mess. Now I talked to the mother last week, and he still comes to school looking terrible. I am so angry and infuriated that he has on filthy, dingy socks that look as if they belong to a grown man. And the socks smell absolutely horrible. His clothes are too big, as usual. And his hair isn't combed either. Now if I went ahead and bought the stuff for him to have, she would have been offended because as she told me last week, "I am very capable of taking care of my children and providing for them." Whatever! I had to call Yuan's father because of his behavior yesterday, and already, he was playing this morning. So his father, Meatball, decided to show up with one of his friends. Dimani came in today sometime during lunch.

Nyaa's mom got locked up today at school. Apparently she has been abusing the oldest girl, her daughter Micole, whom I taught last year. Micole came to school with a busted lip and scratches and marks around her neck. Apparently Nyaa was being abused too the whole time and Ms. Brown had her documentation she was keeping but they didn't needed because someone else saw the bruises before she even made it to her class today. Nyaa's abused wasn't as severe as her older sister's though. What a shame. When will the abuse and violence against children end?

Kevmani continued to get into trouble all day.

Nerimiah and Leandre got water all over the bathroom floor in the boys' room. I tried to walk back and forth between the two bathrooms, but it only takes a few seconds for a child to do something. I kindly went into the utility room and brought out two dry mops. I made them go into the bathroom and mop up all that water. I just keep writing the same stuff over and over again. The sad part about it is that each year the children's behavior gets worse.

Day 123
Thursday, March 15

Ms. Moore was substituting for a class today. I can't remember whose, but one of the little boys was telling Ms. Yizeman that he didn't cuss at her. He just said, "Get the *F* out of my face." So because he didn't use the entire word, even though we all know what he is talking about, he doesn't think that he should get into trouble for the abbreviated profanity. It's not funny but all I could do was laugh.

We kept receiving these flyers for workshops around the country that are supposed to give teachers effective intervention strategies for so many different categories. Now they have a workshop for chronically disruptive students. I don't know how many times it has to be said, if you don't start with the parents, guardians, and caretakers, nothing is going to change.

Day 124
Friday, March 16

Today was the trip downtown to the circus. It was a cold and rainy day. Nerimiah went on the trip when I was

240

told that he wasn't. Nerimiah stayed with his grandmother the whole time. I told Ms. Laquetta that Kevmani couldn't go because he just would not listen to me. I wanted a parent for Yuan too. But he followed directions during the trip. The circus was okay. The children enjoyed it. That's all that matters. I love going to events and seeing mothers and fathers with their children. It makes my heart happy. I just love to see a child having a positive learning interaction with a parent. And every time I use the word *parent*, I already know that it does not necessarily mean the biological mother or father. So many people have stepped up to the plate where others have failed or are not capable of being a parent. Parents are now overworked and tired senior citizens, grandparents, aunts, uncles, cousins, siblings, the list goes on and on. I remember when I first started teaching seven years ago. I used to only address my letters home to just the parents. However, I soon learned that I needed to say *parents and guardians*. I'll never forget my third year teaching, but my first year teaching third grade. I had a special little support group for children who had lost their parents. In that one third-grade class, seven children out of twenty-three had lost one of their parents to death. Millions of children lose their parents to AIDS, violence, addiction, poverty, jail, and just whatever circumstance in their life. I can understand. I almost lost both of my parents. One I almost lost to drugs, and the other I almost to mental illness. If it wasn't by the grace of God, I would have been a totally lost one. I've seen it all as a child in my own life. My grandmother prayed for me. That's what happened for me to be where I am today along with His mercies.

Saturday. Just tired and don't feel like doing anything. It seems as if laundry never ends. I wish I could hire somebody just for laundry alone. I will one day. I don't need a nanny. I'll care for my own children, just a person to do laundry.

Sunday. I woke up early and couldn't go back to sleep, so I watched a pastor on television at six thirty in the morning. He said something that I've been saying all along, that just confirmed some of the things I've been trying to share on this journey. Parents used to make personal sacrifices so their children could have a better life. Now the parents sacrifice their children's lives so the parent can have a better life. It's as if he was reading my mind. Sometimes when I feel like giving up, I hear a word of encouragement or confirmation that keeps me motivated or gets me back on track. So many parents and family members have pimped out their children for sex, drugs, alcohol, rent, a hairdo, a car note. So many parents have already messed up their children's credit. It wasn't enough that they messed up their own credit. The mentality of the parent is supposed to be wanting the child to do better than we did. It just seems to get worse day by day. I was wondering if from now on, children can have some kind of small tracing device that triggers an immediate call to authorities if certain things happen or are about to happen. I just have so many ideas in my head about possible solutions. Tracking high-risk parents. I just believe with all my heart that some people should not be allowed to have children. And that people should be required now to take classes and get a license to have them.

I eventually went to church and followed that with going to a birthday brunch with my girl Melissa.

Day 125
Monday, March 19

Nyaa and Micole are moving with another relative since their mother was locked up. I taught Micole last year in my kindergarten class. I was touched that she wanted to say goodbye she just walked up to me and gave me a hug. I

242

was happy that they were going to be in better hands until their mom got herself together.

Back to the normal abnormal stuff, the first thing this morning, Reshae just blurted out that her daddy was locked up again. Then another student said to her, "Your daddy is always locked." So I nipped the rest of the comments in the bud. I told Reshae to come to where I was sitting at my round table. I asked her, was she sure, or was it a bad dream or something? She said that it was true. So I asked her, did she see him get locked up? She said no, that her brother told her. So I asked her if she knew why, and she said because he was just walking down the street. So I encouraged her that he would be back home again and that he would be okay.   I didn't know if her story was true or not but I wanted to comfort just in case. She didn't seem upset at all. It was as if it wasn't even a big deal to her. You never know with her if she's telling the truth or not.   Sometimes you just have to pretend right along with them just to go in with the day.

Leandre wasn't here. The children were terrible in the cafeteria.

Day 126
Tuesday, March 20

Today was an overall good day. Dimani didn't come to school today. The students were a little more cooperative with their behavior, so we were able to have fun today and get more work done. We especially had fun while talking about the different kinds of sentences. We've been talking about the types of sentences for the last week or so. After I finished teaching, I let the students say different types, and I had to pretend to be the student to pick the right answer. They really liked that. At math time, we worked on *fourths* and *halves*. The students had to draw something that is round or the shape of the plate. For the most part, they did pretty good. The problem is that the children have a hard time using

243

their own imagination. As teachers, we always have to model or make a model of something. And the children copy what they see or hear instead of creating their own. Anyway, it was a nice teaching day for me. I actually got to teach a lot.

Ms. Tia came in today, and a male parent came in today. I don't want to say which one because he opened my eyes to a lot today. While I was eating lunch, he saw a picture of my girls, and that started a whole conversation about children. Eventually, I found out, through his openness to talk, that both of his twelve-year-old sons are sexually active. He makes sure that they have the condoms they need. The father also talks to the boys about sex-related topics such as AIDS and pregnancy. I also was listening to how he doesn't talk to his fifteen-year-old daughter about boys or anything related because as a man, he doesn't want to even think about what boys might do. So I was truly puzzled as to why his sons had full permission and support to engage in sex and he doesn't even talk to his daughter about it. Inside I was pissed off. But I didn't want him to know that.

You'll never guess who walked into Ms. Brown's class at the beginning of math class today. Did you take a guess? Jaron. Yes, Jaron Smith. I haven't seen him in a month. The "aunt" that he was with said that he was moving to Pennsylvania with her dad because she couldn't take it anymore.

So I was wondering if today was his last day. I didn't want to ask because I knew I would have been happy while asking. At close to dismissal time, Ms. Brown was in my room sharing with me about her day's events when I scanned the room and saw Leandre's little butt in the air with his too-big boxers wedged in between his butt crack. That was a sight that I didn't expect nor wanted to see. I immediately told him to stand up so I could fix his clothes before leaving.

244

I feel sorry for Mr. J. He looked as if he was going to pass out today. In the past month, his schedule must have been changed at least ten times. When I saw him this morning, I asked what he was doing here. I automatically knew that something must have happened with one of the other custodians. They just work that poor man to the bone.

Day 127
Wednesday, March 21

You wouldn't believe that I got Whitney to school on time today. I got there, so proud of myself, to see all the teachers standing outside. I thought that they were going to tell me that I had to drop her off on a new location. But I found out that school was closed because of a water main break. However, I did find out, without asking, what happened to my daughter's glasses. She said that Trinity broke them on Sunday. I asked her why I was just finding out about it on Wednesday morning from her music teacher. He saw me in my truck, walked over, and just came out, said that he tried to fix her glasses, but he couldn't get it. I tell her all the time that when she tries to hide stuff from me, I find out anyway without looking. The Lord will shine the light on a situation whenever he wants to. She just got these brand-new pair of glasses ten days ago. Ten days. And she was talking about how she wants to go to a private high school. She would be a terrible roommate, as far as taking care of stuff. That's exactly why I made her pay for half of her bill for the glasses out of her allowance money. And she's going to be on punishment for lying and breaking her glasses. I made her stay with me all day at work and help out. That was just the beginning of her punishment.

I had another good morning with the students again. It seems as if they are beginning to blossom. I pray that they are blossoming. Whitney and Ridge helped out a lot. Ridge is Whitney's classmate and the son of a staff member here.

The kids were, overall, good today. No ants that I saw in the room. I take that back. I just looked down at the floor under my computer desk. There's a few here. The children decorated butterflies for spring. I got glitter all over the place. I didn't mean to because I tried to use my materials wisely. I used the glitter over a big sheet of construction paper so I could put it back into the little jar. I still made a mess. We were talking today for the new letter *R*, and they didn't know what a raccoon was. Technology would have been really nice. I wish I could have talked to a voice-activated computer screen and say, "Find me a picture of a raccoon," and everything else they've never seen or experienced. They might already have them. But of course, I wouldn't know if it's not in my room to use. Anyway, it just isn't any fun after the fact to go and look for the picture or information. That would just be nice. I'll find the picture and show it to them tomorrow.

A lady at the bus stop, around six forty-five this evening, was doing drugs right in front of the blue-light camera. Her two children were about thirty feet away, playing unattended while she hooked up her fixes. How do I know, you ask? Well, let's just say that when I was fifteen I got a crash course in watching some family members getting high. When you've seen it enough you know. I could see her very clearly. I just prayed for her and her children and went on.

Day 128
Thursday, March 22

I'm tired. I did three loads of laundry last night. I'm going away to treat myself to my once-a-year pampering trip.

My good buddy Magic Man made me upset with a comment. He insinuated that he might not be able to attend his daughter's function because his work comes first. That sent me into a whole funky attitude. It just reminded me of being with my soon-to-be ex. Family comes first. Yes, we have to go to work and make a living, but there comes a time when you have to be there for your child for some event or experience of their life. In this situation, when you have a job, where you can take days off and you can attend everyone else's affairs, then it's hard to accept the "I got to work" excuse. But people have to do what they gotta do. I knew I was real angry with him for not being there for his daughter when he seems to be there for everyone else. But then to not continue to be pissed off with him, I just told myself that if you're not your own boss, then you must do what you're told to do. It's because of him and not his job though.

Personally speaking, I don't think I could be in another relationship, where a job seriously interferes with spending time with the family. He would have to be a really good man for that. There is no point in being in a relationship with someone if it's not of good quality. There isn't a point if you can't get to spend time with the family.

Day 129
Friday, March 23

Originally, we were scheduled to go on this trip today on May 7, but some lady called me a few weeks back and said that we could come today. I was totally embarrassed by the students on the field trip. After the trip, we had our discussion about it, then they had to draw a picture and write a sentence about something new that they saw or learned on the trip to "Dance Asia." It was obvious that most of them had never been to a live theater performance. They were lost and barely remember anything. I don't even think they understood what was going on before their eyes to appreciate in the first place. I think that every elementary school should have an auditorium. And I don't mean a gym that is used as one either. And each school should be made to give students different kinds of performances for the children to experience. I called Ms. Laquetta like three times while I was on the trip. I was so angry with Kevmani. I know his mother has taken him to different places. I was so glad it was over when it was.

Mrs. Lacey was upset because Ridge didn't come straight to her after school. She called me on my cell phone to see if Whitney was with him. He left Whitney, so I had to drive down to her school to get her. She knows that she isn't allowed to walk up to my school by herself.

To make matters worse, when you tell the parents their behavior on the trip, parents try to act as if they have shown their children how to behave when we know that they haven't.

Saturday and **Sunday.** I treated myself to a weekend at the Hershey Spa. I took one of my best friends with me. We both needed some "me" time. And that's exactly what I got. I did only five things all weekend long. I slept, ate, watched television, read a little, and got my treatments in between. It was lovely.

Sunday evening. I found out that Herbert has had my girls around another female already. Faith said that they spent the night over at her house. If the girls even mentioned one of my male friends who've I've known before him, he would have a fit. Hypocrite.

Day 130
Monday, March 26

My manicure didn't even last for twenty-four hours! What a crazy morning. I knew Ms. Brown was going be out, but I really didn't believe her. But Ms. Kaylor was out today also. So we had to split both classes, which meant that we all got four students. Then around eight thirty, Mr. Emanuel was assigned to Ms. Kaylor's room. We didn't have resource this morning, or for the rest of the week, because the first and second graders are testing this week. So that means that all the resource teachers are going to be assisting the teachers in their classrooms. I let the children watch *Happy Feet*, since they didn't have a resource. I had a lot of work to do. I needed to scrub their desks. They were so disgusting, I think that that is how I kept getting pinkeye last year. So this year, I try I be extra clean in the classroom. I needed to take down the work for March and start putting up the work and decorations for April.

I'll go back to the gym tonight. I am so excited, I need some downtime. Since I don't have a man to go home to every day, I go to the gym to work out any built-up frustration. TMI. Sorry about that. I'm a real person and have real feelings. It's cool, though. I'm not mad at all.

Day 131
Tuesday, March 27

I saw many obese children on the way to school today. It's a shame. The children could hardly walk and were out of breath. I don't understand. The parents are the ones that make the money and bring the food in the house.

I stayed after work trying to get the high-frequency words done. Somewhere near the end, it all got messed up, though. The first sixty words had the right number. I needed twenty cards for each word. So all together, I made and counted 1,196 words. But then I had another forty words that had different amounts of each. None of them had twenty-three in a given set. I had a headache by the time I finished for the day. I had a headache from the confusion with the mess I made for myself. I still didn't get to put them on rings. I was only able to separate all the index cards.

Day 132
Wednesday, March 28

I am so tired. Last night, I went to sleep at ten thirty, but I got up at four thirty this morning to bake the barbecued chicken I seasoned last night before I went to bed. Trinity is always hungry as soon as we get inside the house at six. So I need to have dinner ready or something for her to snack on as soon as I come in from work.

Anyway, it was another exciting day at Edgebrush Square Elementary School. First thing this morning, Kevmani's mother told me that she was moving back to North Carolina. I loved her dearly and her son too, but he drives me absolutely insane. He is like the ringleader of the class. I must admit that I wanted to scream and shout for joy when she told me he would be getting transferred. I'm not going to pretend as if I wasn't happy. I did jokingly ask her why she waited for him to give me a fit all year long and then wait to nearly the end of the year to leave. She basically told me that she felt strongly that he needed to be closer to his dad and being away from his father probably would cause him to start acting out in the first place. I understand. We are supposed to try to do what's best for our children, so I don't blame her at all for moving back down South.

When I went to pick up the children from lunch, it was hectic and noisy with the second graders down there. Ms. Jinx kindly got herself a chair and sat down. She looked like she was pissed and had enough of the noise and chaos. I don't even know why she was in there in the first place and I didn't have a chance to ask. It wasn't her lunch break. Oh yeah, that's right she came out of the classroom this year. She is supposed to be some kind of intervention teacher for the upper grades. So those staff members who do have homeroom classes have to do cafeteria duty. Poor thing. Of course, Kevmani was sitting at the bad tables. Rayshire cried the whole lunch period. She's been crying for the last month.

I told her to come on so I could walk her to the office, and she started screaming and hollering and trying to pull away from me. I took Rayshire up to the office anyway with all of her carrying on and what not. The social worker said they were going around to make a home visit. We found out later that Ms. Yizeman went and said nobody was home. I and Ms. Brown said that no one just answered the door. There is a difference. How do they know if the people were in there or not. You can't just try one time and then that's it. Every time Ms. Brown called from the school, the phone is answered. But when you go and visit then all of a sudden there is no response.

Kevmani was eventually sent to the assistant principal by someone in the cafeteria because he was looking up Reshae's skirt and kept talking about sex at lunchtime. He was just losing control. I think it's because he knows he is getting ready to leave soon anyway.

My class was with Ms. Jinx. When I came back, she was kind enough to walk them back to my classroom and read them a story. But before you can do anything after lunch, they all want to tell the bad things that everybody did at lunch time. Ms. Jinx said that every told on Kevmani. She said that Dimani was able to explain what sex was in great detail. Dimani said it was when a boy climbs on top of a girl and they do nasty stuff. I think that's too good of an explanation for a five year old.

Mrs. Scott sent me a note with Kevmani. She said that she called his mother and that he was getting a one day suspension. Not too long after that, Kevmani's mother snatched him up while we were in the middle of reading sight words. I don't know where she took him but I have a pretty good idea. When he came back he didn't have a happy look on his face either.

Mrs. Scott got cussed out after school because apparently, the man's child was hit by another student. Parents tell their children that if somebody hits you, hit them right back. It should be, if somebody hits you, tell the teacher. She tried to explain to him that that isn't the way things are done around here. You can't just have your child handling things with violence in school instead of telling first.

In any free time that I had today, I had to keep calling the gifted and talented organization for my daughter. I'm trying to get her into a summer program where she can take classes that are higher than her current seventh-grade level. The people said that since I make just a little too much money over their guidelines, I might not qualify for financial aid for her. I'm going to apply for it anyway!

My stomach was hurting today.

Day 133
Thursday, March 29

Wow! What a day. Somehow I ended up chasing two older students down the hall because they were fighting in the bathroom. One of them was my former third grade student Raquan. I've never seen him like that before. I thought he was going to seriously hurt the boy who bloodied his nose if he caught up with him. I eventually caught up with Raquan and sent him to the nurse to cleaned up and to report what happened. Then I went on my way.

I hung up flyers around the school since the kindergarten parents haven't supported their own children's end of the year trip to Six Flags. Mostly everyone around here likes to go to Six Flags! We had to open it to the entire school so we don't have to cancel it. Mrs. Scott gave me her number to give to Ms. Hone, and I left it on one of the flyers. So now, I got to go to all of the flyers and check, hoping no one took it. Ms. Hone is out today because her sister is having complications with her pregnancy.

Shamira's mom called to say that she was not to get on the bus and that she would pick her up at three o'clock. This is not a babysitting service. School gets out at 2:25!

Day 134
Friday, March 30

Stop sometimes and enjoy the sunshine!

It's lunchtime. I don't have lunch to eat. Ms. Brown went to get us a chicken box. I really don't want it because of all that grease. But I didn't have any breakfast either. I will be going to the market this weekend. No running to chase after kids today. I'm all dressed up ready to go to Whitney's ceremony today at three thirty. She's being accepted onto the national junior honor society so I have to be there because she'll be expecting to see my face in the audience as usual. I was still trying to figure out how to get Trinity. I don't know if I should take her or not. I think that I'll just wait to pick her up on our way to the celebration dinner. I don't know how long the ceremony is. So I'll just pick her up right before we all go out to dinner.

Anyway, at school parents are already trying to turn in money past the deadline. I don't understand why people think that you can just show up with a big massive group of people without paying for anything on time and in advance.

Today I also saw a big belly coming from under a little, teeny, tiny light pink shirt. The third grader was almost my size. I just don't understand why are children come to school looking a hot mess sometimes.

Dimani came to school on time, and three others came late. We decorated cut out construction paper eggs with high-frequency words first thing this morning. But the three that were late didn't get to make one because they weren't here. Ms. Brown said that some of her parents didn't understand the math homework either. I just kept saying that just replace the word *and* with *plus*. And replace the word *makes* with *equals*. I didn't know how else to explain that "2 and 3 makes 5." It is the same thing as 2 + 3 = 5. Lemonte got picked up late. I left before he did.

Saturday. Took Whitney to rehearsal, went to the gym, worked out on a new exercise machine. I don't know what the thing is but I liked it. Picked Whitney up, went to Sam's Club, put the stuff away and relaxed a little for the rest of the evening.

Sunday. Good day. I sang, Whitney got to dance, went over Ms. Kin's house (the new baby is adorable). I had a good time with the ladies. The rest of our team was there with the exception of Ms. Brown. Faith had a major tantrum while we were there, and she got a nice spanking for telling me no, screaming, and hollering as if she was crazy and falling out on the floor. Faith went to sleep in the truck and went right to bed when we got home. She didn't wake back up for the rest of the night.

NOT MY JOB !!

I am about sick of this!
I'm home life & YOU are the teacher

An

Directions: Read the poem below with your child. Have your child circle the words that have the –an pattern at the end of the word.

<u>Dan the Man</u>
<u>By Lisa Calicchia</u>

Dan is the man!
He can make a super tan fan,
Because Dan is the man!
He can fry eggs in a silver pan,
Because Dan is the man!
He can run faster than a colorful toucan,
Because Dan is the man!
He can drive a cool rainbow van,
Because Dan is the man!

I will teach my child street life☺
SCHOOL LIFE iS YOUR JOB (NOT) MiNE!!!

Teacher Objective: Reinforce introduce higher level skills that they will be see in the beginning of first grade next year.

This is the last quarter of the year. Now I want to reiterate one more time that we don't wait until a certain deadline to teach specific skills. They all kind of overlap. All of the objectives that we are supposed to. In quarter four, we're really trying to make sure students have mastered the skills they should have for the given grade level by giving them continuous practice to perfect those skills. We also provide instruction and practice for the new skills to get children familiar with some just some of the skills they will have taught to them in the next grade.

Parent/Guardian Objective: It is the parents job to continue to support their child and school.

Parents must continue to send their child to school on time every day. We need parents to understand that just because it's nearing the end of the school year, that does not mean that you don't have to send your child to school anymore..

Day 135
Monday, April 2

Sometimes you just got to laugh!

Well, I got a late start this morning. I was so tired and exhausted. My ribs are hurting from trying a new exercise from Saturday at the Y.
Well, we had Ms. Meiskolf's class because she had to take off from work to celebrate Passover. So we are supposed to have her children for the next four days. I don't think that it is going to work. I took the children to resource this morning. I was sitting at the computer this morning, trying to find pictures for the letter *J*. Ms. Johnston called

256

and told me that Jaron was on his way down. So I was a tad bit confused, discombobulated, speechless, or whatever other word you want to use. I just looked at the intercom as if it was crazy, as if the intercom was the person telling me that after almost two months of having the worst student I've ever had being gone, they decided to bring him to school today. I had no idea why he was coming back. I'm just glad that it is only four days this week. I'm trying to figure out my own personal problems, dilemmas and situations, and now I have to go backward with my class. I'm quite sure he didn't have a rebirth in the time that he was gone.

Rayshire's grandmother showed up today for the meeting with the social worker. Must I remind you that she is the little girl in Ms. Brown's class that cries every day just to go home and watch television? Ms. Brown asked me if I could watch her class while she goes to this meeting. Of course, the lady would come after we picked up the children from their resource classes. The meeting was supposed to take place while they were in their resource. That would have been much easier for the woman to show up on time for her appointment. So I had two and a half classes in my room on the carpet for about an hour. We started a new unit in reading today titled "Teamwork." The students and I discussed the concept so I could find out what they knew, which wasn't much. Anyway, I read *The Little Red Hen*. They understood the concept of teamwork after that. I think that it says somewhere in the Bible that if you don't work, you don't eat. It's something like that. Ms. Brown had a meeting with Rayshire's "ignorant" grandparent. Ms. Brown said that she was so embarrassed that she wanted to apologize to Ms. Yizeman on her behalf. I don't even know why we even have to bother to show up. Almost always parents go against what we say like we don't know what the hell we're talking about. I've learned over the last couple of years just to say little as possible because usually the parent totally disagrees with what is being said at the table. Instead

257

of being in denial and open to receiving help for their child, it's just a process I no longer care to be a part of. Special education isn't like it was twenty years ago. We no longer label children, prescribe medicine and stick them in a room away from their peers. Only the children with severe problems are handled in a way that would warrant the highest levels of assistance. And I mean severe problems like autistic or physically, mentally, or emotionally challenge to the extent that the child may need a one on one assistant or more than one adult in the classroom. Now what we do is keep the children in the classroom and bring whatever service they need to them. A lot of time services can be provided in the classroom. Some services like counseling and speech may be provided outside of the classroom maybe once or twice a week for thirty minutes in a separate office. It's all based on what the child needs. The last thing we want to recommend is medicine. If anything, the parents are the first one to mention hyperactivity and medicine.

Anyway, Jaron was playing with glue traps and kept messing with the students. He is totally out of the loop. As far as having routines, rules, and procedures of the classroom, he makes Kevmani and Nerimiah look like angels. I don't understand why they brought him back to school this late in the year.

While I was in the hall passing out the notices for the spring party this week to the other teachers, I caught my child Faith chasing and hitting Aniya. So I quickly caught up with both of them in the hallway and asked Faith why she was hitting Aniya. Faith tells me that Aniya hit her first. Now to be honest, the flesh side of me said to myself, *Good! She's defending herself.* But then I knew that wasn't the right way to feel while she was in school. So, I took them back to Ms. Ellis, trying to figure out why they were out of the room in the first place. The story goes that Faith was supposed to be collecting the papers since that is her job. Aniya felt like she wanted to pass papers. Faith told her "no" and that it was "her job" and then Aniya hit her and ran. Then Faith ran after her to hit her back. Bless their little four year old hearts. I did fuss at Faith and explain to her that she was to tell the teacher first if anyone hits her again. I also fussed at Aniya and told her not to put her hands on anyone else.

Around four o'clock, I got a really bad headache while I was hanging up the spring decorations outside of Ms. Ellis's door. This was my parental contribution since my child is in her class. The outside of Ms. Ellis's room looks better than mine. Her classroom is made up of the metal walls, which are magnetic and which I can use dry-erase markers on. She also has lockers right outside her room, so I can hang stuff on them also. Even though this is a short-holiday week, I still have a lot to do. We'll probably do different spring and Easter activities on Wednesday and Thursday.

I took Whitney to dance rehearsal. I want her to always be involved in something positive outside of school. I'm just trying to make sacrifices to ensure she just doesn't have school to do and that's it.

I went to choir rehearsal.

Day 136
Tuesday, April 3

You are no good to anyone if you don't take care of yourself first.

I didn't have a good morning at all. And before I could even get to work, I had to fuss at my eldest for the things she doesn't do at home. I honestly believe that she thinks that since she excels and does well in school, her lack of efforts at home is acceptable. My standard of expectation is that you do well in school because you are supposed to.

259

I'm not rewarding her monetarily or materialistically for doing what she is going to school for. So to make a long story short, instead of having her contribute to the family in a positive way right now, she is just making more work for me to do. Faith and Trinity are going to follow the behaviors that we model. I had the two little ones hanging up their coats and putting their shoes in the cubby when we get in the house. Now following my oldest knucklehead, the girls take their coats off and throw them on the table. They take their shoes off anywhere and leave them there. I have tripped so many times on things that are not in the right place. So for that and all of the other chores and her room that she doesn't keep up with, I told her she couldn't go on the skating trip this week. She has an educational trip to the Hippodrome Theatre today that she can go to. She will not be going on the skating trip just to have fun skating. That trip doesn't reward for behavior or academics, so she doesn't earn going on that one.

Then we are on our way to school, and I glance in the back to see that she doesn't have her seat belt on. I know it's a little cramped in the truck, but oh well. A little discomfort now will save you true pain in the future. And then on top of it, she doesn't get it. That was Whitney this morning.

And of course, I was running late again. My allergies and sinuses are acting up. I've had a real bad headache since last night. This morning, I was very overwhelmed with personal things going on. I have things that need to be done in the house, my girls' different personalities and needs, my court case in two weeks, and just other stuff. I was only a few minutes late. Once I had apologized to one of the parents and two students waiting for me, I tried to get settled into my routine. Ms. Laquetta brought in cupcakes and two bags of chips for our party tomorrow. She also told me that she did get the transfer and that this would be his last week.

The students ate breakfast, and I took them to their resource for the day, which is music. Mr. Parnette wasn't in there, so I walked a few classrooms down to find him. He's always around somewhere if you can't find him. I headed up to the office to sign and check my mailbox and walked back down to my class. On my way, I stopped in Ms. Hone's room to see if her sister Amy had her baby. The baby hadn't come yet, but she did have other news for me. Ms. Hone's car got stoned by one of her students, whom she suspected because of how they all left yesterday. She hadn't even had her brand-new truck for a month. She said that she was livid. So I waited for her while the school police came, which didn't take long. I was surprised that they came so fast. Probably because it was so early in the morning. The students usually need to warm up before they get into trouble. She needed a report to get her insurance to pay for the damages.

On the way to my room is my daughter Faith's pre-K class. As I approached her open door, I heard a cry, which sounded like my child's cry. Of course, I stopped in front of the door to see that I was right, and she was crying loudly and uncontrollably. I saw Ms. Ellis trying to get Faith to move from the little round table she was sitting at. But Faith refused to move. After about five minutes, I walked in to assist Ms. Ellis. Ms. Ellis proceeded to tell me that she just wanted Faith to move to a better-behaved table because that little girl was bothering her again. So Faith had to move because the other girl was making bad choices and not her. She didn't understand that and was giving Ms. Ellis a fit. So I went in and told her to get herself together, to calm down, and I was trying to let her know that it was okay. Then she got even worse when both of us moved her over to another table. She started falling out, screaming, and hollering as I've never seen before. So I picked her up to help her walk out of the classroom so Ms. Ellis could continue teaching. In the hallway, Faith was carrying on screaming. I was trying to get her to calm down, and she wasn't hearing it. So she wanted to keep carrying on, telling me no and so on. I also kept telling her that if she didn't get it together, I was going to spank her tail for having this tantrum. She kept on. I kindly walked her down to my room, closed the door, gave her three smacks on her bottom, and sat her in a chair until she calmed down. So on my way to pick up my children from resource, I took her back to class once she had gotten herself together. But ever since she came back from her visit with her father, Faith's behavior has been totally off.

I needed a hug! I called Magic Man, but he was busy in the Home Depot. He has definitely lost his magic, so now his name is just a name. I guess this is a season for him to go through his own stuff, and so he is unable to be supportive for me, so I'll just be supportive of him. Ms. Brown was on the phone while she was typing her lesson plan. I walked all the way up to Melissa—I knew I could get a hug from her. As soon as I saw her in a room that was full of children, I went right up to her and told her I was having a very overwhelmed moment. So Melissa jumped up when she saw my face because it isn't that often that I cry, especially at work. I usually carry my burdens with a smile as if nothing in the world is going on. But I was just overwhelmed. Dimani and Jaron came in late; my classroom was a mess because I didn't have the time do everything I needed to do. It was just too much. And then because of Faith's behavior, I was reminded of her father, which totally disgusted me. He doesn't call them or see them in between his visits. Any father or mother who does not interact with their children between visits is a person who just pays a bill. Just because you pay child support does not necessarily mean that you are helping to provide for your child. Providing for your child is calling them to tell them that you love them, asking how their day was in school. Visiting their school to just volunteer for an hour. So I was so angry with him because we hadn't had an official divorce, and he's already taking them around some other women, which means he really isn't devoting his time to them. You have four days with your children a

262

month, and you choose to share that time with someone else who isn't even a major part of their life. Anyway, I was overwhelmed, and it wasn't even nine yet.

Over all, I felt better after I cried and ate lunch. I didn't want to eat lunch, but I knew that I had to. While I was teaching my phonics lesson on initial sounds, I had to tilt my head down to look at the book. So Lemonte says, "Hey, Ms. Calicchia, what's that black stuff in your hair?" While I started feeling around my head to figure out what's in it, the other students told him that it was my hair. Once I figured out that he was talking about the new growth from my hair roots that was my natural hair color, I busted out laughing. Kids do say and ask the darndest things. So I pointed near my scalp, and they said, "Yeah, right there." I told Lemonte that there was nothing in my hair, and that it was just my real hair color. Then the children started going back and forth about how my hair isn't real. So I explained to them a simple process to cover gray hair, but it's all my real hair.

I had to do my normal fussing, but nothing major today. We continued working on the letter *F*. Rayshire was in the hallway all morning long, screaming and crying for a huge unknown reason. Ms. Brown took her back up to the nurse. I was glad that she did because that little girl was driving me and the students crazy. The remaining of Ms. Brown's students were quiet at first. Then they started getting restless. Ms. Brown took a long time to come back. So I had her class come over. I let our classes make spring cards. We couldn't use the word *Easter* because we don't know who celebrates the holiday. I honestly don't like doing the whole bunny-and-egg thing because it has nothing to do with the holiday. But I know how to keep my personal preferences and beliefs separate from what I'm supposed to do by law in the class. I told Ms. Brown that she's going to have to start giving me substitute-teacher pay.

When Rayshire returned, she came back talking about her uncle, who doesn't want to sleep with his wife, and that all these people get in bed with her. She was babbling about the same thing over and over. I and Ms. Brown just looked at each other. We assumed that's what she told the social worker. She did her work the rest of the afternoon though.

After I dropped the girls off at home, I went to Sam's Club for eggs for my house and doughnuts for my students who will bring in their applications tomorrow.

Day 137
Wednesday, April 4

Just because you are able to produce doesn't mean that you should.

Today got off to a little better start. I packed Whitney's extra clothes and belongings in her room last night. I came to the conclusion that she had too much stuff to keep up with. I picked out five uniforms for school, two weeks' worth of underwear, one pair of sneakers, shoes and dress shoes, two casual weekend outfits, and two dress outfits.

I got to work on time, which meant I was there fifteen minutes before the students arrived. I was especially proud of myself for beating Chalon and Aleesha to school. My two new students are on the ball. This morning, when the students came in, I asked for the applications for summer school. Once again, I brought in the doughnuts for breakfast for whoever turned theirs in this morning. Yuan was the only one who had his today. Nerimiah called out that his mother wouldn't fill out the application because she thinks that I would be his summer-school teacher. Ms. Joyner and Ms. Laquetta were in the room when he said it.

264

I was internally pissed off for about two hours about his mother's comment. It sounded like something ignorant that she would say too. If you want to keep your child out of summer school because you are too much of an arrogant, ignorant butthole to see that the teacher is trying to help your child and not to continue to baby and pacify him, then you obviously have some issues.

Jaron and Chalon didn't come to school today. I was wondering if she was all right because she usually doesn't miss school. Jaron, being in and out is normal. Dimani came in at lunchtime again. I just shook my head. The saying "better late than never" can be taken too far sometimes, and this is one of those times. Especially if that saying is lived by daily. As for the rest for the day, we all dyed eggs and I have dye all on my hands to prove it. We set up covered tables in the hallway to make an easier cleanup for us all. Ms. Kaylor, Ms. Brown and I took turns helping the children dye their eggs and then sending them down the hallway to wash their hands. It worked out pretty well. Finally, we had our party and a movie for the afternoon. Once the children got settled watching the movie I spent the rest of the afternoon cleaning all the crumbs off my floor and especially near Leandre's desk. The ants were all over the classroom floor this time.

Day 138
Thursday, April 5

There is light at the end of the tunnel.

Nerimiah and Jaron didn't come in today. That was just a great way to start my last day before spring break. Ms. Milliams came in to substitute for Ms. Meiskolf. That was fine with me, but we had her students all week, so one more day wouldn't have mattered. But it worked out as far as the pizza. We did get to teach math the way we wanted to

265

because there weren't too many children in one small room today. Their Easter activities had some skills on them like connecting the dots and counting by fives. The children aren't focused on a holiday week anyway, so they ended up watching a movie. I went out on my lunch break to get pizza for the children. Almost every one of the teachers who didn't have a party yesterday had one today. Ms. Brown watched my children in her room for a little while, while I volunteered in Faith's room. I stayed long enough to get the handle on their baskets made of milk cartons. They were real cute. I thought her teacher asked me to save my cartons to plant flowers in for Mother's Day or something. I didn't stay long because those four-year-olds were hyper and all over the place. Ms. Ellis said that that level was quiet for them. I did my time and got out of the way of their creativity. There were three other parents in there helping, so she had people to assist her. Today went by so fast. I passed out the projects and activities related to spring and Easter for them to take home. Lemonte asked me if they were going to another grade. I told him that they were just going to be out of school for a little while. And that they weren't going to another grade yet. Today was a pretty good day or I'm just very happy that I'm officially on break.

SPRING BREAK April 6–April 15

Everyone needs a vacation.

This week, we are on spring break. I took the girls to the beach for a couple of days. Even though the weather was chilly for the month of April, it's just nice to get away. I enjoyed seeing my girls waking up to see me there and not having to leave to go to work or to run an errand. Every morning when Trinity woke up, she just smiled as if she was the happiest two-year-old in the world. I knew that she was happy to spend quality time with her mommy. And I felt so much joy in my heart to see her happy just because we were together. That was the highlight of my break.

Day 139
Monday April 16

Everyone has a judgment day for something.

I had to go to court today. I kind of have mixed emotions. I'm content that I will no longer be legally connected to the evil spirit that has been weighing me down for the last five years. I'm just not happy about the process. As soon as the judge signs the papers next week, my divorce will be official. In my heart, I was divorced four years ago. Anyway, he told bold-faced lies on the witness stand. Even under oath, he lied, saying that he gets his kids every holiday in the odd years. He doesn't even like holidays or even believe in them. All he believes is that he is the man, which is just way off. I can't even respect him as a man right now. Any woman or man who uses their children as pawns as in a chess game, is worse than scum. I find it very difficult to say anything nice about him. He goes to work every day, and that's it. He was cussing in the court building, making fun of the judge by mispronouncing my name. He came in looking like a thug off the streets. He wanted Valentine's Day as a holiday. Valentine's Day isn't a holiday.

I can't talk about what happened at school today outside of what Ms. Brown told me. She kept my kids for the day so no one could complain on their first day back to work. Now even though today's entry isn't directly related to school, the following entry is reflective of some of the major problems in the world that shape society as we know it.

Wow! What a weekend. It's amazing how the things that happen in a little bit of time all around the world. I mean, it seems as if more and more people are losing their basic humanity day by day. I don't even know where to begin.

I heard of the man Don Imus, whom I had never heard of before. Today's shooting at Virginia Tech. There are people pouring chemicals on playground equipment and causing second- and third-degree burns on an infant. The war with more soldiers, and people dying. Parents are killing their children because of custody battles. The world is coming to an end.

For every person that does wrong, there is going to be judgment. Last week was the first time I have ever heard of Don Imus. I heard what he said about the Rutgers basketball team, and it was wrong. He apologized and was condemned, ostracized, humiliated, and fired. I really don't know too much about politics, but I believe that I know a little something about morals. But I have been really trying to figure out how come I haven't seen too many high-profile representatives (I'm not saying any names), groups, or organizations boycott all the remaining media and forms of entertainment that call women hoes, whores, b——es and black men niggas or niggers or whatever else there is to call them. And there are many other words that are derogatory toward any other man or woman, regardless of race. I don't get it. I don't care what color you are, no one should be called any derogatory word. Name-calling does hurt. And yet you have all these so-called artists making money off degrading people. I watched a little of the different news reports, and there seems to be a lot of evil in the world going on. We need to see the good news to inspire and encourage others to do better for themselves and their families.

Kevmani called me this evening. He just called to say hi, I guess. It was a nice surprise. I didn't think I would hear from him anymore. I had never heard back from a student who transferred somewhere out of the state. That was nice. Even though he drove me crazy every day, I do miss him. He has a good mom and was really smart.

Day 140
Tuesday, April 17

Sometimes, you just gotta jump into the swing of things.

I really did not feel like coming to work today. Listening to the radio this morning really got to me. My heart goes out to the parents, family, and friends of the shooting victims at Virginia Tech. I made sure that I prayed for protection for myself, my daughters, and all institutions of learning around the world. Then I headed off to school. You think you can take your child to school or send them off on their own and wouldn't think that these devastating tragedies would keep occurring. I have been also a little sad about the divorce. I'm happy that it's almost over, I'm just not pleased about the process. At first, I was so excited, and then it hit me later. I still have to go back on June 11 for the property issue. I cannot stress enough the importance of being careful about whom you have children with.

Today was a good day with my students. Early in the morning, I was out of breath, though. It is difficult the first few days after coming back from a long break. I was out of breath, and my throat was hurting before lunch. My throat and voice are strained because this is the most I've consecutively talked in over a week and a half. As soon as I started teaching, though, it got my mind off all the personal stuff and other bad news in the media. Everybody came to school. Jaron came in at about 9:20 a.m. Dimani came in at about 10:10 a.m., after I took the children to lunch. We worked on the short sound of *e* today. The kids were a little restless, which is understandable. I did take time to review all the classroom rules with the children. They did well with being able to tell me all the class rules and why they are important. We all have to get back onto our school day routines. They had to fidget and go to the bathroom all day long. They were tired and hungry too. At about one o'clock, they had had it for the day.

Day 141
Wednesday, April 18

Just shake it off.

It takes a lot to hold your tongue or walk away from a situation. However, it is worth it most times to let the fool be a fool. Because in the end, the fool looks stupid. I really appreciate the art of being an author and writing books, journals, articles, or whatever. I give them the utmost respect for doing what they do. It is hard staying focused and consistent on one subject when you have so much stress in your life. I think that the good thing is that since I'm a parent, then almost anything that I share backs up some of the points I stress in this book. When I'm going through trying times, I try to think of others around the world who are going through even worse times. I've been really trying to put my thoughts on the tragic events known and unknown. For all that we do hear in the media, there are even more where you are unable to cry out for help or to tell their story. Before I was even fully awake, my ex-husband was texting me a message a little over six in the morning. Is he serious? Who would disturb someone at six o'clock in the morning for something so trivial? A total idiot. He's going to be forty years old this year but acting like he's a fourteen-year-old. He has the audacity to tell me to tell my friend that he will be picking up Trinity at 12:00 p.m., and what is her address? I was immediately enraged. I truly understand why some people go off on the deep end. We went to court only two days ago, and already, he's trying to tell me what he is going to do. Now I tried letting him to be a real father by being responsible and taking Faith to her doctor's appointment on

Friday. It would be out of the norm for him because he takes them to Chuck E. Cheese's, Jeepers!, his sister's house in Delaware, and to the movies every weekend that he has them. I don't even think he is capable of getting stuck in the house in a snowstorm with those two. They are not bad, they are just normal two- and four-year-olds. If you don't really know any about little children, they are very inquisitive, mischievous, and extremely busy. Anyway, I already regret letting him take her. He uses the children as grounds for explaining that he can do what he wants to do with his children whenever he wants to. Her appointment is at one thirty. The earliest he needs to pick her up is one o' clock, but he just wants his legacy to be known for being a jerk right now I guess.

Now let's talk about my actual workday with the students. I only had six out of ten students this morning. Around nine thirty, I got a new student by the name of Quamainie. Before the parent left, I asked her if there was any important information that I needed to know. She told me that he was behind and that he didn't know much. She showed me his referral and told me that the school that he just came from was going to have to test him. Anyway, he did well today. He fit right in with rest of the children. I don't know how many times I have to tell you that their education starts the day the child is felt moving in the womb. Anyway, all the students had a good day except Jaron as usual. Shamira came in at around nine o'clock, right before we walked down the hall to take a bathroom break. Dimani came in at lunchtime. At lunchtime, as usual. I know her mother got a letter about her coming to school late every day. I guess it didn't matter because she still comes to school late for four days out of the week. Dimani would be so much farther along if she could just get to school on time. She misses the entire phonics lesson by the time he has gotten here.

When I went to pick up the students from lunch around ten fifty, Jaron was at the bottom of the steps. He wasn't even in the cafeteria. As soon as he saw me, he asked me if I could go get his lunch. When I asked him why he didn't eat, he said because the lady told him to get out of the line. I went over to Mrs. Yonson, and she told me what I already knew. He was being rude, disrespectful, argumentative, and cussing people out. Of course, I tried again to explain to him that that is not how we talk to people and that it is unacceptable. He said he understood, and I let him get his lunch to take back up to the class. One of Ms. Fields's students had green snot coming out of her nose while she was trying to tell what was wrong with her. The second graders were their loud and unruly selves. When we returned to the classroom, the other students returned to working with their letters and sounds workbook while Jaron was eating his food. That ended up being distracting for the rest of us. He put the frozen peach dessert all over his hamburger and ate it. I just shook my head. He said it was good though.

Jaron acted a complete fool starting around twelve thirty. He wouldn't come into Ms. Brown's room for math (no, I never got a math kit) because I put his name on the board. I had to put his name on the board because he kept messing with the other students and wouldn't keep his hands to himself.

While we were in Ms. Brown's class, he kept calling me Mommy. Even Ms. Brown got upset and fussed at him to call me the right name. So before he even came into math, he kept running down the hall. I wasn't chasing him either. So I called up to the office to let Ms. Landing know that he was running down in the hallway. I went in the room and started the drill with the rest of the two classes. I didn't, and don't, have time for any foolishness. While I was reviewing math skills with the students, Mr. Shiller walked in and said that he wanted to talk to whoever dropped him off. Mr.

Shiller said that he was never given permission to stay all day. Trying to have a good day with my students occupies my mind on the most troubling days. It didn't work today. And Jaron was stressing me out even more. I got a twitch over my left eyebrow during math. I didn't even know your eyebrow could twitch like that.

After math, I wanted the children to finish writing the high-frequency words. We were trying to cut out pictures that represent teamwork, and he only wanted to point to any picture of women who had any of their skin showing. Nerimiah finally got up and moved. I didn't even say anything for getting up without permission. All the other children were doing their work except him. Then it just got worse for the remaining hour and a half. He was running out of the room. After we finished math, he kept running to the lobby. When I walked the rest of my class down to get their belongings, he ran out of the lobby door. It was before two twenty-five, which meant I was still accountable for his tail. Ms. Siris was up there in the lobby too. We both went to the door to try to get him back in the building. It was cold outside too. Luckily, a parent caught him outside, knowing he didn't have any business being out there, and brought him back in. He ran out four more times. And four different adults kept trying to get him to come in. It was obvious that everyone knew him because all their words were the same. He gets it from his mother. But he wasn't listening to any of them either. And each time Ms. Siris and I would go get him, he would run away when I got closer. I wasn't running today. I'm not sorry about it either. I have my own stuff I need to run away from. Anyway, he finally ran all the way to the main gate, where Mr. Parnette was at his post. Mr. Parnette said, "Don't worry about that." He would watch him. By this time, it really was dismissal time. So I stayed inside for a little while to make sure my students were dismissed with the appropriate siblings or whoever picks them up. Afterwards, I wanted to see who was picking him up so I went over by the gate. I saw his uncle and told him how he acted a fool. Not only that, for the time that I was standing out there by the gate, Jaron was picking up big rocks and throwing them into a puddle of muddy water. I kept telling him to stop, and he wouldn't. He even splashed the dirty water at a parent as he walked by. That parent looked at him as if he wanted to spank the living daylights out of him. He turned around and looked at me and Mr. Parnette and kept on walking.

Day 142
Thursday, April 19

You can only do but so much.

All the students had a good day except you know who. I would have Kevmani back over Jaron anytime. I cannot help him the way that he needs to be helped. He needs counseling and treatment for emotional and social issues. There is only so much that I can do. With all of my professional training, education, and experience, it's not meeting his needs. He needs to brighten in his heart to have his mind together. Whatever is wrong with him that he doesn't know how to express is being channeled in the wrong way.

I don't feel good today at all. I have had a hell of a week just dealing with my own personal problems. Now it's the end of the school year, and I still have to deal with his foolishness. He has shown little to no improvement, and you would think that there would be a team of resources thrown at his feet. In all honesty, I don't think it would help anyway. His mother and family have to be willing in the first place to want to get the necessary treatment and services for him. We can't help anyone unless they want to help themselves. First, he is supposed to have somebody stay with him at all times. Secondly, they send him into the building, and then no one is to be found for the rest of the day. I'm trying to keep my professionalism about the situation, but I'm only human. People just don't understand how circumstances and different situations with children drive us and the rest of the world crazy. The sad part about all of this is that this is a behavior he learned at home. I sure as heck didn't have him in my care for the last five years. While I'm trying to teach, Jaron continues to mess with the other students, calls out, gets off his seat. He can't even work independently like all the other students. Even Leandre now sits a little more and has more controlled behavior. And Leandre is developmentally delayed. Jaron has no respect for female authority whatsoever. I think he needs a male counselor, therapist, and a male teacher. There are only five male staff members working in our school anyway, but he doesn't give them a problem.

Earlier this afternoon, Jaron ran out the building again today. The children had to go to the bathroom. So everyone lined up nicely, prepared to go into the hall, except Jaron. He wanted to run all out into the hallway. I asked him to get into the line, and he looked at me, backed up toward me, and mumbled no underneath his breath. Now I already told the students that I was feeling very sick and that I didn't feel well. All the children showed some sense of compassion except him, of course. Well, after he did that, after all the other stuff he did this morning, that was it for me. I wasn't getting ready to go into this long drawn-out battle with him today about doing what I tell him to do. So I told him to walk with me so I could take him to Mr. Shiller so he could get himself together. The next thing I knew, he ran out of the damn building again. What in the hell is going on in our village? I called the police too. I immediately called 911 and told them that the child ran out of the building, right after I called the office to let them know. I sure did. I wasn't going out that door running around. My track-and-field days are way past over. I'm not playing games with him, or anybody else for that matter. It is not my responsibility to chase a child around outside school premises. Jaron's mother called up here, high. Mother called asking for "Blake." Ms. Siris said she called all around the kindergarten class looking for a child that doesn't even go to this school. Jaron continued to act a fool anyway.

Ms. Fields was told about parents' abortion procedure. She came down and told me that mother said it right in front of her child. She's new to the city life so she's always surprised by the behavior of the parents and student here. There is no such thing as discretion anymore. Some will tell you their business in a heartbeat. Ms. Kin came in today. She brought us lunch since she said that she didn't have any food for us when we went to see her after she had the baby.

The behaviors of the students around the entire school are getting worse. It's as if five hundred children are having cabin fever at the same time. The weather was getting warmer, so the children are getting more and more agitated. Half of them don't feel like being bothered. And the other half are starting trouble with the other half that don't feel like being bothered. While walking through the halls, you can see or hear so many children arguing, fussing, and fighting over the most trivial things. It's the end of the school year, and you would think that children would ignore ignorant behavior instead of add fuel to the fire.

Day 143
Friday, April 20

Thank God it's Friday!

We celebrated Ms. Meiskolf's birthday today. When I saw Mr. Shiller earlier today, I told him that I wasn't going to be chasing after Jaron. If he goes out of the building, I'm going to call the police again. It is too late in the school year to be dealing with crazy behavior. Jaron came back to school with the same drama, except he stayed in the building.

Friday night. My sinuses are getting worse, but I can still function. I did say that I was going to hang out with Ms. Kaylor and Ms. Brown tonight. I just wanted to be out of the house. When I have too much time to think, I start thinking in the negative, and I didn't want to do that. I only hung out with Ms. Kaylor and her friends for a little while. Magic Man made me angry in a conversation we had while I was on my way. It's as if he doesn't want to be available until I'm unavailable. Anyway, I didn't feel like I fit in with the crowd that was at the party. I must be getting old before my time because I didn't want to listen to loud music. Besides, it's hard dancing on the dance floor when I tower over everyone else. I look like a giant towering over everyone and all they do is stare at me like they've never seen a six foot woman in person. We'll I guess I'm like six three with heels on. But still I feel like an out of place giant around a whole bunch of short people and there isn't one person my height or taller. I left the party because I wanted to go to the movies. I was heading toward the movies, and my cough got even worse just when I thought that my week couldn't get any worse. Then I had to deal with the ignorance of my ex-husband. He did a parent responsibility for a change and then instead of calling me with the information, he sent me four text messages. I believe that since I can deal with him, my one and only worst enemy right now, I can deal with anyone in the world. He is the worst kind of criminal. He's the kind of evil spirit that likes to eat at you slowly, saying things and doing things that would linger in your head if you let it. So I called because I was reading "stop breathing in her sleep" and "heart problems." And to make it worse, I was driving at that time. I was on my way over to my mom's house. So I called him and asked him what was going on. And he said that the doctor said that Faith might have sleep apnea, which is probably why she snores so much. I was waiting for him to question me about it, but I guess he was saving the interrogation for later.

Saturday. I watched movies all day. I go to the movies when I'm stressed. It's my favorite place to be when I'm upset. So I went to the $3 movie theater. That was it; that was my day. I watched *Perfect Stranger*, *Vacancy*, and finally *Daddy's Little Girls*. I went back home and went to bed.

Sunday. I went to church, went home, and went back to sleep. I had to see Lucifer's representative today when he dropped the girls. I swear I think I just married pure evil. He had the balls to say that he was disappointed in me for not picking up on what was wrong with Faith earlier. Lord Jesus! I try to do right, but all kinds of cuss words come from deep within my memory of my cussing sailor days when I talk to him. It took every bit of grace and dignity I had in me not to cuss him out. If Faith has been snoring since she was two weeks old, and I had it checked out then and every time she goes to the doctor for her checkups, then how would he know if he was never really around in the first place? I told him that I knew that he was going to think that he was some kind of hero. If you give somebody an inch, they take a mile. Then he took it a little farther and even said that if I want to continue to have uncontested custody of the girls then I need to stay on top of my job as a mother. I tell you, I just had to walk away from him before I end up going crazy on him. I walked away and ignored whatever else he was saying. I said thank you for the sleep apnea informational papers he gave me and walked away. I couldn't believe that he even formed his lips to say that. I was so glad that all three of the girls were in the car. I wasn't about to dignify his statement with a response. If those girls weren't in the truck, I think that the flesh would have gotten the best of me, and my mouth would have gone back to a sailor mouth for a few minutes. Ignorant! He's just plain ignorant.

Day 144
Monday, April 23

It pays to take a rest.

I have another sinus infection. My head was throbbing so terribly I woke up in the middle of the night in pain. I called the school and left a message that I wouldn't be in. My best friend Melissa took Whitney and Faith to school, and I dropped Trinity off at Trianne's. I went back home, ate a bowl of cream of wheat, took my medicine, and slept all the way up to two o'clock. Ms. Brown called me today to give me an update. It was the usual stuff but just a different day.

Day 145
Tuesday, April 24

Ms. Brown was pissed off because parents kept sending children to school sick. I was still out sick. But that's all she called to complain about. It wasn't really no point discussing my class because I know what's happening without even being there. Their behavior is probably worse because I'm not in school.

Day 146
Wednesday, April 25

Mr. Braswell was in my class today. Ms. Brown said that Jaron didn't give the male substitute any problems. I was able to make it out of bed today. I needed to go to South Avenue, school headquarters. My work ID was either lost or stolen, so I had to get another one. I only went to get it because the postal clerk told me that I needed two pieces of identification. I've never been anywhere in the school system where I needed to show my school ID for anything. While I was there, the guy Tony that was helping said that I needed to update my fingerprints, so I did that. I said no problem and just stayed a little longer to get that done. I heard a lot of parents don't volunteer in the school because they have to get fingerprinted. I think that they should have things and equipment at each school that can fingerprint everybody so there is no excuse why they can't volunteer in the school. We really don't need a lot of hindrances to keep parents and family members away from volunteering in the schools.

Day 147
Thursday, April 26

I got a full report today when I returned to school. Mr. Braswell said he enjoyed having my students and being in my classroom with all the materials that I have. He said that Jaron was trying to try him, but he put him in his place and he didn't give him any more problems. Of course, his grandmother gave him her number and left.

Day 148
Friday, April 27

I had a scheduled appointment this morning, so I didn't get to work until the time the students were dismissed. Ms. Kaylor said that they split my class and Ms. Brown's. I think the kindergarten team is taken advantage of as far as splitting the class. If one of us is out, they tell us to automatically split the class. Today is a half day anyway. I don't think these half days during the school year are going to work much longer. Most of the children are absent on these days. I think that they open up schools so children can have a positive experience for the day, food to eat, or just to make add up to the one hundred eighty days required for our school year. I think these half days are a waste of taxpayers' money—my money because I'm a taxpayer too! We had a teacher-parent social from eleven thirty to one o'clock. As usual, we didn't have a lot of parents show up. Parental involvement is so crucial to ruling the world. After the social, all the teachers were available to have report card conferences. I only had two parents show up during the whole time. I think that out of at least four hundred parents, only maybe twenty parents showed up for the social and maybe fifty all together for report card conferences. Ms. Brown wasn't in today, so I had her report cards. None of her parents showed up. I think Ms. Kaylor had two. She has a father that is very active in his daughter's life. Now I'm going to remind you that the children were dismissed early at eleven fifteen. Did you know that I had a dad come at two thirty To get their children's report card? It is the same few parents who show you the same concern throughout the school year. Guess what? I got my laptop, I got my laptop. My sister paid for it a month ago for a birthday present to me. It's a long story, but only six week to go, and I'm almost finish. I guess I'll have to write another book. And now I don't have any rodents and ants in my room.

Saturday. Spent the night over at my mom's, so we hung out over there all day long. I didn't do anything spectacular. My mom and I played Scrabble on my new laptop. That was fun. She was coming up with words I've never heard of, and the game accepted her answers. Anyway, I had fun hanging out with my mom, sister, and nephews. I ended up taking my nephews home with me. I don't like them all cramped in the apartment all the time. My ultimate goal is to get a fence around my yard and to get the swing set completed so they can come over more often and run off some energy. Whitney had Saturday school. Faith and Trinity enjoyed playing with their cousins, so it all worked out.

Sunday. I woke up and got all five kids up and out the door for church. My sister made it today too. So we all got a good word for the week. It was youth day, so we had some guest artist visiting. After church, my sister did my hair for me. I didn't get anything done at home. I really only had laundry to do. I was able to cornrow Faith's hair. Well, I did half at my mom's and the other half back at home. So I had a nice, drama-free weekend.

<h3 style="text-align:center">Day 149
Monday, April 30
Teacher Appreciation Week</h3>

We're have testing this week, which means that each teacher will take turns splitting their class to test another's. It's the last day in April. It's all downhill from here. Today was an overall good day. I felt so much better today. I had my energy back. I wasn't even coughing. The kids were happy to see me. Yuan and Jaron didn't come to school today. They may have thought I was still out and didn't want them to come to school unless I was there. I know for a fact that Yuan's parents would turn around and take him back home if I wasn't there. I was in and out last week, so they really didn't have time to see me. There was this kid with a gallon-sized bag of cookies and pretzels. They did not need all that for a snack. She really only needed about five cookies. It's going to be warm outside today. So that means this afternoon, we are going to see all the tattoos, cleavages, rollovers, and everything else that should remain covered even if it is hot outside. I call the rolls of skin rollovers. There is a respectful way for everyone to cover up. People just don't take pride in anything they wear anymore. People wear anything out of the house. I wonder if someone told them that they were hot. Nerimiah whined all day long. Every half hour, he was whining and complaining. First, his head was hurting, then he was tired and sleepy. After lunch, we took them out to the playground. There wasn't anything wrong with him for the twenty minutes he was playing. As soon as we were close to the classroom, he started complaining about his arm being warm. I was going to go crazy. I don't baby children. Especially little boys. There's a difference between giving children a daily dose of hugs and kisses compared to how many parents cater to their boys and girls too. Some mothers treat their sons as if they are the man of the house instead of a child. Whatever their son demands of them, they do. It would be a cold day in you know where before I ever cater to any child. These children need to be instructed and guided, along with discipline, in order for them to make it in the real world. Nobody in the real world gives you anything. A lot of parents are setting their children up for failure. It's not the school system, the community, or what's on television—it is them. Then you have some of the fathers who treat their daughters as if they are queens of the world or something. The inappropriate behaviors that children display aren't cute. Even when they are one-year-olds, it's not cute at all. And then when that toddler becomes a teenager, all of a sudden, when the teenager is disrespectful to their parents and other adults, it's a problem. Well, you let them tell you to shut up and get out of your face and let them hit you since they were two years old. It isn't all of a sudden. Usually, when a child's behavior is all of a sudden, then it's because of some event that has appeared devastating or tragic to the child such as death, divorce, or an accident, or someone has assaulted them.

Ms. Kaylor came into my room at about nine twenty. She was being called into a meeting for one of her students that originally belonged in Ms. Meiskolf's class. At that time, they didn't have a substitute for her. We are supposed

283

to have a substitute for meetings. Not split the class. It didn't matter to me any. No one doesn't seem to understand that our classes aren't even set for kindergarten students in the first place. We only have room for so many students. The remaining four teachers all had some students from Ms. Kin's class because Ms. Dons was out. I keep forgetting that she is the substitute for Ms. Kin. Which means at math time, Ms. Brown and I will have twenty-five children in her class that seats only fourteen. But if it's warm, we'll just have to walk back over to my room to finish the work. Kaylor is upset that Shean is supposed to be coming back to school. I'm still trying to figure out why Jaron and Leandre haven't been sent for treatments. Apparently, Shean, who is six years old, is diagnosed as being clinically depressed. He's been at some diagnostic center for the past two months. I don't understand how, if the mother is having problems with one child. Why do they continue to end up pregnant with more children? Things are really getting outrageous. I guess it would be wrong to say they should put a cap on the number of children people should have if they don't meet certain qualifications such as an education, job, or even just being at least eighteen years old. I guess that would be too much to ask, huh?

My room was a mess today. Stuff was all over the place. All my good pencils were gone. I had to go to Ms. Green to get some pencils. These kinds of pencils are the ones that are very difficult to break because they are so thick. Tomorrow, we all need to meet as a team to talk about what to do for the kindergarten closing exercises. We have only three students out of seventy who have paid their class dues. Last year's parental involvement was so much better. This year, we haven't much of anything close to parental support or involvement. Faith's teacher was out today. Her teacher's four-week-old grandson passed away over the weekend. Ms. Johnston was in with the class, so I wasn't worried.

At the end of the day, I always walk up to check my mailbox. Well, today I had to walk Lemonte up to the office because he hadn't been picked up yet again. It was twenty minutes after school had been dismissed, and he was still here. It was ironic that today, letters were sent home to parents and guardians about picking up their children on time. It basically said that if you don't pick up your children, school police is going to be called and that they would have to pick up their child from the nearest police station. Yes, it's that bad. People just don't understand the lack of respect that we get in the school systems. Those children either get dropped on the school property early or picked up when they get to finish their running around, hustle, fix, or nap.

While up in the office, Ms. Landing was being yelled at by the parent of the worst-behaved girl in the entire school. Now this mother looked as if she was about eight months pregnant. She was cussing Ms. Landing out at the top of her lungs. It was bad enough that she was acting a fool in front of her own child, but she was carrying on in front of the twenty little children who had yet to be picked up. There were so many teachers up there in that front office. Everybody was lingering around just in case something went down with this parent.

Day 150
Tuesday, May 1

This is one of those days when it is very obvious that we have to deal with crap from both sides of the fence. Well, a lot of little different things went on today. Most of them didn't even have to do with the parents and students. The students and I had a good day. Days like this remind me that we all have to work together. In an episode of *Run's House*, something Reverend Run said really stuck with me. He said that "teamwork means dreams work." He is absolutely right.

285

Less and less dreams of our children are going to come true if we don't get our country on one accord with our children. We are supposed to be working as a team. But now it seems as if too many people are out to get their own. They want to get what's best for them first. We have so many companies, businesses, corporations, etc., investing in the children of America and around the world, but here in the States, too many more parents are dropping the baton on their shift. We're supposed to pass the baton back and forth between the home and school until our children become leaders to continue to the next level of carrying the baton that invests back into the communities.

We started DIBELS testing this week. This is the last time we test their letter recognition, sounds, and how well they can use words in sentences. I'm very positive that most of the children have shown improvement since the beginning of the year. There was a huge commotion in the hallway outside of the cafeteria while picking up the pre-K and kindergarten students. Those second graders were down there running around the hallway, as usual. But today they were down there fighting. They were all on the floor. I blew my whistle, and they stopped on their own. I tell them every day that when I come down there, they are going to have to deal with me if they knock one of the smaller children down. We saw Mr. Shiller in the hallway on our way back to the classroom. We told him that the second graders are out of control. So we were shocked when he told us that he has done his time, and as far as he is concerned "as principal, I feel as though I shouldn't have to deal with cafeteria duty anymore. I did my time." So we were asked if we went to the assistant principal. We said no because he was the first one that we saw.

So we just went on our merry way to recess. One of Ms. Meiskolf's students peed outside while we were all on the playground today. There were five of us teachers out on the playground, and he didn't come to tell any of us that he had to go. The other children came to tell us, but I wasn't sure exactly who it was because he was up on a little hill about fifty feet from us. Yuan said that it was a little boy with a hoodie on. So I narrowed it down to one little boy, and it was him. He said that he didn't see any of us out there. It's probably something he does all the time. We told the rest of the boys that they better not even think about it. If you're not camping in the great outdoors, then only animals pee in the street. We didn't tell them that part.

Day 151
Wednesday, May 2

We still have more testing to get done today. There's testing, testing, and more testing. If the children don't have a basic grasp of the skills that have been taught to this point of the school year all year, then they definitely aren't going to learn it in the last couple of weeks of school. We definitely know who is able to go to the next level, who is going to do great, and who is going to struggle next year in the first grade.

Day 152
Thursday, May 3

Ms. Dons was out today. So that means two classes will be split. When I found out that we didn't have a substitute again for kindergarten, I immediately went to Mr. Shiller and told him that they would probably have to watch a movie because our classrooms are just not equipped to handle more than fourteen children. I taught my regular lesson for the day. When it was time for the children to work in their workbook, the other class had already completed that page. I just usually let them be a helper for somebody in my class. Ms. Fields didn't want to test until after lunch, which was fine with the rest of the team, so that meant that we all only had two extra students for the morning. In the afternoon, they remained for testing; we all got four more students.

Earlier this morning, the Junior Achievement lady called me and told me she would be in this afternoon. When she did arrive, she seemed as if she was half asleep or just really dry. She later told me that she was tired. I was sitting in the back, thinking that she better put some pep in her step before they do it for her. The Junior Achievement Program is when businesses volunteer to come into the classroom and teach five lessons about something related to the business world, primarily the use of money in the world. On the kindergarten level, they talk about trading and identifying money.

Day 153
Friday, May 4

I got off to a late start this morning. I was so tired last night from the lack of getting sleep at the sleep clinic on Wednesday. It's ironic to go to a sleep lab and don't get any sleep. I was fifteen minutes late for the students. They were in Ms. Brown's class. They were eating breakfast when I came in. She was already upset with her students because they had already started fussing, whining, and complaining about the breakfast. I would have liked to say that I had an uneventful morning. But I guess the Lord knew that this would be a boring journal if all this stuff didn't happen to me this year. And guess what, it would have happened if I didn't write it. Anyway, all the kindergarten teachers have been trying to get the details together for the kindergarten closing ceremony. Today was the final deadline for the children to turn in their class dues. Now their class dues include a graduation cap, tassel, a sash with the year on it, certificate of completion, magnetic photo frame, and other graduation novelties. We are going to order cupcakes and juice for

288

refreshments. Overall, this week has been an off week for us all because of the testing and all the drama on the side. But the sad part about all of this is that's it just normal typical day for us.

Dimani's mom wore the same outfit, underwear and all, two days in a row. Now we all have had days like that when you just get up and put what you had on yesterday. I think that it would have been less obvious if she didn't have on bright rainbow-striped underwear showing through her pants. It's kind of obvious when you wear a thin all-white sweat suit.

After the news I heard about my husband, who I thought was already my ex-husband, not signing the divorce papers, I wasn't going to go to the teacher appreciation dinner tonight. I went because I wasn't going to continue to let him ruin my life. It was really nice, and we had fun too. I got a Forrest Gump Award for running the biggest total of miles running after my students. Everyone in attendance got a hilarious award for something. I felt like a giant. After I put on my white sandals, I really towered over everyone, but I was used to being around them since they're like my extended family.

Ms. Strong, the Junior Achievement lady, came in again this afternoon. I really wasn't paying attention to what she was doing. I was trying to clean up stuff at the back of the class. I did have to tell Leandre to come sit in the back with me. He was too distracting for her.

Saturday. Today seemed like another day in hell. I woke up so happy this morning. My house is a mess, and I had a lot of housework to catch up on, but outside of that, I was totally unprepared for the information that I received in the mail. If it isn't one thing it's another. I called my friend Magic about ten times because I needed someone to vent to. Magic Man finally came over. I really don't get to see him that much and hang out with him as much as my other

289

friends, but he was there for me this weekend. He found out about one of the most degrading and humiliating experiences I had because this person that doesn't even deserve to have their name mentioned right now.

Sunday. Every day is a new day to start over. I got up this morning, and I tried all over again. I know that I have that one enemy in the world. And I know that when it is all said and done, I will be better for it.

Day 150
Monday, May 7

Sometimes you just must walk through the pain. Sometimes rest, refuge and peace are on the other side of "through"

I was very somber on my way to work today. I just don't know what to expect now. I've worked hard for thirteen years to be where I am today. And to lose it over a lie that my ex-husband told four years ago is just crazy. While I was sitting in the parking lot, I just kept thinking that Mr. Shiller is going to be at my classroom any minute to tell me to pack up my stuff and go. Then I started thinking about what the other teachers were going through right now at my school, and it could be worse. This weekend, I could have spent my savings purchasing a house to bury a forty-seven-day-old grandson with a ghetto family attending to start a fight, been in an abusive relationship, or working an extra job because teacher pay isn't enough. So I came in and just started my day as if nothing was wrong.

The first thing I did this morning was to go change the date of the graduation dues that I posted outside on the main entry doors. We said we would give parents one more chance to pay their child's classroom dues. Ms. Brown came over to tell me that one of her parents asked if Ms. Brown could pay the dues and she would pay her back later. Ms. Brown was like, "I don't think so." She, like the rest of the teachers, already spent enough money that she doesn't have.

Ms. Brown was as nice as that at the beginning of the year. She would pay for trip money here or there, in addition to all the buying that we do for holidays and different teaching lessons and occasions. But this year's group of parents are totally unappreciative of what we do in the classroom. Half of them came up here this year as if we owe them something outside of what we already do. Most teachers already go above and beyond the call of duty. I've never met a teacher who didn't buy something for their class. That doesn't even include holidays or parties. More often than not, we have to purchase our own supplementary materials to help us teach a lesson. We purchase hands-on and manipulative materials for the children to have things they can actually touch. The perfect example is that I didn't have a math kit this year. Luckily, I have bought a lot of things over the past eight years to help. But in the end, it really didn't help all that much because of the other things that I needed. And let's not talk about copying. Oh my goodness. I couldn't even begin to think about how much money teachers spend on copies and laminating. Everything has a budget, which means we only get so many allowed copying done for our classes. As of right now, early in the morning, I have only five out of eleven students who will have adorable graduation caps and sashes for the closing ceremony. I'm hoping the rest will turn theirs in by tomorrow. I don't want to hear any parent mouthing off about their child not fitting in. We gave them plenty of notices and plenty of time to get it in. We looked at the ordering information, and it takes at least three weeks to receive the items in the mail. So we definitely have to order the items by Wednesday to get everything back in time for the kindergarten closing ceremony.

As far as the day went, I had only half my class this morning. Reshae came in about thirty minutes late, so she completely missed breakfast. We were walking on our way up to the computer lab for their resource when she came in. At least the lady who walked her had Reshae's classroom dues. So that was good. Shamira and her mom showed up an hour and fifteen minutes late at nine o'clock. So she missed breakfast and computer time. And then there's Dimani, whose mom brought her in today while I was walking back to my classroom after I dropped the children off to lunch. So she missed everything this morning, as usual. I know that she got a letter from me because of the excessive lateness. I don't know what happened with the meeting because I wasn't told or included. I just found out because the mother said that she was going to try to make the meeting. Anyway, to me, apparently, nothing major happened because she still comes to school excessively late every day.

Leandre really got on my nerves today. Not because of my own personal dilemmas and feelings, but because he seems to be getting worse instead of better. He drools more, falls out of his seat more. He started hitting his classmates. He has learned how to write the letters *D* and *E* in his first name. He has stopped repeating everything we say and do. But outside of that, the noises and outbursts continue. I stopped by the support office this morning, but there wasn't anyone in there. So I stopped in Ms. Abrams's class to see if she could take him for a time-out, but she and her aides looked as if they already had enough for the day. It was an uneventful morning. Yuan was the only one to get into trouble today in the cafeteria. Somehow, he was playing with the sound equipment in the cafeteria and earned a time-out with Mrs. Scott. She sent him up not too long after I picked up the kids from lunch.

Faith came to my classroom this afternoon. She said her lips were bothering her. Ms. Rapor was in my room, helping as she always does. Since my truck is parked right outside my window, I ran outside the exit door right next to my room to go get her Chapstick. I'm going to have to get some small bottles of water to put in her lunch. The weather is starting to act like springtime, so I don't want her to get dehydrated.

I tried smiling today, but I just don't feel like it. People automatically know when there's something wrong with me. I'm too tall to hide even if I wanted to. Since I smile so much, as soon as I don't, people ask me what's wrong. I just told them that I'm tired.

Aaliyah's mom paid her dues today. So I have all the students who I'm moving on to first grade pay their dues. I had to send in a list of four students who really are prepared for first grade. Even though Nehemiah's mother won't write a letter for him to be retained, I wrote his name on the retention list. She said that since she was sending him to Sylvan this summer, she doesn't feel as though he needs to be retained. Well, I'm not going to go on what a parent thinks that they may do for the summer. Even if he does go to Sylvan Learning Center this summer, it won't help get the basic concepts that he should have learned all year long. Learning centers are not intended to supplement what they didn't get in school. Learning centers generally help in a specific area of need in a particular subject area. If I couldn't get him where he needed to be in one year, what makes her think that someone who doesn't know him could do it in two months? Don't get me wrong, Sylvan Learning Center and other places such as that are a great support. But that's what they are. They help reinforce what is done in school. They are called Sylvan Learning Centers. But of course, some people think that they know everything. I've had eight long years of college in different educational areas. This is what we do. We are with the children more waking hours than their own family. We know these children as if they are our own. I have never, and I will never, just pass a child on. As far as what the system's and administration's follow-up actions are, as far as the retention lists, that on them. If someone choses to pass a child on against what I have documented all year, then they are the ones who are going to have to stand behind that decision. Over the summer, a team will determine who is in most need to repeat a grade. As you get into third grade and higher, sometimes you have no choice but to move them on because of their age. I remember my last year teaching third grade. I had six students in the third grade who were supposed to be in the fifth. So three students were moved to the fifth, and the other three to the fourth in the next school year. So for me, my professional recommendation to pass a child or retain them has my name on it and I take it very seriously.

We had a faculty meeting today after school. We had to work on our cumulative folders again today. The state requires that each folder has a copy of a birth certificate, social security card, two proofs of address, and physical health records signed by a doctor. Mr. Shiller said that he was already reprimanded for some folders. So you know what that means. If he gets into trouble, we get into trouble. I don't know why we have to update the address because they move around so much in this area.

He gave out some nice insulated cups with lids on them. They were supposed to be in for the dinner on Friday. It was nice anyway because today is the first day of teacher appreciation week. I asked Mr. Shiller, was he going to take Before and After pictures with all the work that is going to be done to the building? He said that would be a good idea, and he would give me the digital camera and a list of all of the rooms that are going to be changed. He also said that we could start packing some stuff or throwing stuff away. I beat him to the punch because I packed my first box today on my lunch break.

Day 155
Tuesday, May 8

Today was a pretty good day. We turned over the last letter today. I think that I'll bring in a little treat for them. I've taught all the sounds, plus the long vowels. Dimani came in an hour early than her normal time, but still an hour late. Even though she missed music class this morning she was able to learn the sound and mechanics of the letter *V*. They had a little difficulty because some of them were confusing it with the letter *F* or *B*. I just gave them different examples and showed them once again how their mouth forms when they make the different sounds. Quamainie hasn't been to school for the last three days, and Jaron hasn't been here in fourteen days. Quamainie's previous school called to check on his attendance. When children are getting tested for possible services, they take attendance into consideration. A lot of children are behind, not because there is legitimate learning disability, but simply because of two things. The first problem is that the children haven't been exposed to the vocabulary and experiences , and secondly, if they do attend school, it's not on a regular basis.

At some point in the afternoon, Ms. Brown came over to tell me that she was going to the bathroom. We always do that so we can look out for the other class. It seemed as if she was right back in thirty seconds. She came right back, fussing about how the male parent, who sits on the red couch every day, didn't put the seat down. He walked out right before she was going in. Some days, he doesn't bother to put it up, and it's been urinated on. I always try to take a wad of soapy paper towel and wash the seat off. Even if I don't actually sit on it, the thought of urine right underneath you is not a pleasing thought. One of the women who lives with Aleesha's mother in the rehab building said that she would be picking her up. She also stated that the father is not to pick her up for any reason. I told her that I didn't even know what the man looked like. I asked, was everything okay? Apparently, she said that the father was trying to cause some kind of commotion yesterday on the way home. I just understand why some parents just can't let the relationship go. And I know from personal experience. It didn't work out, so let's make the best of being parents to our child. The other parent can't be mad because the other is moving along fine without them.

Day 156
Wednesday, May 9

I had fun today. We started a new unit about animals that live in and by the sea. Most of the children couldn't name more than sharks and fish that live in the water. I enjoy being able to actually teach new information that captures their attention. Since the children didn't have resource this morning, Ms. Brown and I had an art activity for them. So her class came over too. I set up twelve different foam stamps with different colors of paint. We let them use paint and sea-animal stamps to make a sea picture. While I had the paint out, I let them make their Mother's Day cards too.

Some parents were still trying to turn in class dues money. We reluctantly accepted it because we don't want anyone to feel left out. Ms. Kaylor didn't have a good day. Her student Shean was acting up today. He's been gone for about three months in some kind of facility. But he still isn't any better. It is very difficult to have students come in at the end of the year and throw off the rest of the class. The only thing I wasn't able to find was a picture of a jellyfish. I asked all the children what their favorite sea animals were after I read the two stories today. I made a list while they were telling me so I could find them on the computer later.

After school, I made each student a page of different pictures of their animals. I received a copy of the driver's license for Aleesha's dad in my mailbox. So now I make sure I keep that important information in the back of my head. We didn't practice today. It seemed as if time just flew by. I think that Ms. Fields had the Junior Achievement people in her room this afternoon. My Achievement First person called and said that she would be able to come in. I told her it was no big deal. I appreciated her calling, letting me know.

Day 157
Thursday, May 10

Today was a good day for me. Mr. Shiller came into my room first thing in the morning. The children were just finishing their sea-animals book. They were so excited and were telling him all kinds of information as they took their books outside in the hall to lay on the floor to dry. My room was a total disaster. I had stuff all on the carpet. My mind was so loaded with other stuff that I wasn't even upset. I just kept on working with the students. He even sat at my junky round table, which is supposed to be my worktable that I never really get to work at. He noticed my bland salad for lunch. I'm so glad that he saw the computer ink was being put to good and appropriate use. I showed him the students' sounds and letters book that they have been working on all year long. I think he understood that we really didn't have that much space in our room for the amount of stuff that we had. I love clip art. I just took the pictures that I printed out yesterday and gave them each their sheet and a pair of scissors. They did a good job cutting them out. I didn't give Leandre any. I didn't put all of his pictures out for him except one. One is all he can handle to cut out. I gave him a glue stick, and I turned to walk around to check the students' progress, and that quick, he turned up the glue so it was all the way out of the stick. I asked one of the ladies who work on the special education services if she knew why it was taking so long for him to be tested. Others were being told

297

that the system is backed up; there was no other reason. I'll ask her again tomorrow. Things would have gone a lot faster if the mother or somebody came up here advocated for him at least once a week.

Ms. Brown was appreciated today. Her new student gave her a teacher's mug with candy in it. You would never know if it was teacher appreciation week around here. I didn't even hear anything on the news about any teachers getting appreciated. It made me smile to see that someone appreciates their teacher. The children worked on another activity for their moms today. They took three colors of tissue paper and had to decorate a card that spelled *mom*. Nerimiah left a few minutes early. I told Mrs. Lacey that I would try to let him finish tomorrow. She had to go help get her daughter ready for the junior prom.

Mr. Benjamin was by himself, cleaning the building this evening, so I made sure that I swept and vacuumed my floor. So all he would have to do is just empty the trash can. He looks out for Faith and me, so I try to look out for him when I can. He's like a father figure while I'm at work. I got to clean my room. I hung up some works the students made—a little book about the sea animals that they have learned over the last two days. I've brought my progress reports home tonight. I have to turn them in tomorrow. I love the last quarter. You get to see the final outcome of that particular school year.

Day 158
Friday, May 11

I only had three children here for this morning's announcements. The weather is quite warm every day, and already, patterns are starting to change. I was supposed to preview the books at the book fair at eight forty-five, but I only had five students by then. So I waited until nine to go up, but then that was Ms. Kaylors's class time to look at the books. By that time, I had six, and then Dimani joined us at the front when we were actually on our way. Ms. Grazier was volunteering her resource time to show the kids around. My six students didn't mess up Ms. Kaylor's class turn, since my group was so small. Ms. Grazier asked me where were the rest of my students. I told that they were home I guess..

Saturday. I had a full day today. I got the girls up and had them start their chores. The little ones really just have to pick up their toys and playthings. Went to the mall with the girls. Whitney had to get the rest of the stuff for her trip to Boston tomorrow. I can't believe that they are leaving on Mother's Day. Not that everyone really likes celebrating that day. Faith and Trinity were a handful in the mall, as usual. I really don't like taking them with me to go shopping for anything. Then we went to a birthday party for one of Ms. Brown's students' sibling. I know it sounds confusing, isn't it? Then we went to a Mother's Day cookout for about two hours. I get confused myself sometimes with all the stuff I have to do sometimes.

Sunday. I woke up at about five forty-five. Of course, Whitney wouldn't get up. I told her that if she missed the bus, it would her fault. She heard me that time. After she got dressed, we then stopped by Dunkin' Donuts for breakfast.. The buses weren't there at seven as they were supposed to be. When the busses finally arrived we gave her all the hugs and kisses she needed and sent her on her way.

Day 159
Monday, May 14

As soon as I walked into my room, I smelled the barbecued chicken and broccoli I left in the classroom all weekend long. I was so upset with myself for leaving the food there. I hate wasting food. And that food I made last Thursday was good. I just took the container to the big trash can in the hallway and dumped the smelly, spoiled food. I went to the utility closet and rinsed the containers out in the utility sink. I only had two students for morning announcements. By the time I took the children to computer class, I only had five. Leandre, Aleesha, Chalon, Lemonte, and Yuan. That's it. I wish I could go ask every parent what is the problem with getting up and bringing their child to school every day. If there is nothing physically preventing one from getting out of the bed, then a child should be in school every day.

While I was waiting to take the children up to computer, Mrs. Scott called down to my room and asked me to come up to talk about the incident that happened on Friday with the second graders. So I took the children up to the computer lab for their resource time. It looked as if I had a special-education class by having so few students. Since there were so many children and adults in the meeting, we were all in the teachers' lounge, which isn't very big. So when I went in, Mrs. Scott instructed me to tell the ladies what I witnessed on Friday. I didn't have anywhere to sit, so I just stood at the end of the long rectangular table. So as soon as I started to explain what happened, the parent sitting immediately to my right looked at me talking about "who are you?" while looking me up and down. Now in my head, I was thinking, *Here we go*. We got a ghetto-fabulous, nasty-for-no-reason, "my child don't do no wrong, what the hell you got to say 'bout my child" attitude. I took a deep breath and smiled. I politely told her my name, occupation, and how long I've been teaching at the school. The whole time I was trying to talk, she just looked me up and down from the side of her eyes. When I finished explaining what had happened, she went into everything else but what her child did that was wrong. There used to be a time when the teacher's word meant something; now it's our word against a mischievous child's and the in denial parent.

Afterwards, I saw the other parents that were in the meeting in the hallway on my way back. I went up to them and thanked them for acting as decent, respectable parents; then she had the audacity to say that she didn't even care. That really got me heated up on the inside because I'm a parent, and my child is in this school. If she didn't care that her daughter kept hitting, mugging, and bumping into children, then she was asking for trouble. The other parents were very nice and listened to everything that was being said. If their child was wrong about something, then they were reprimanded. Not this young lady. She's lucky we didn't get a roomful of parents like her. Our parents don't mind having to fight at the drop of a hat. I went to the staff development room to volunteer for the book fair. There were four of us in there. I straightened up some books along with the speech lady. Mrs. Siris collected the money. Ms. Grazier was orchestrating something. We all volunteered whatever time we had. I also rearranged some pencils, pens, erasers, and other novelties for the children to see.

I picked up the kids from Ms. Menwick's computer lab. Walked down back to the room. I taught the lesson to five children too. It's the end of the year, and there's no guarantee that the children will continue to have good attendance for the rest of the year. We had fun, the five of us. I had to keep talking to Lemonte and Aleesha because they kept playing and acting silly. We also played a sounds game using a game mat. I altered the game so that they all would be winners. They didn't even pick up on it. They were just happy to be doing something fun and new. I took the children to lunch. I took a nap in my classroom. I just laid my head down on my table and went to sleep for forty-five minutes. I didn't have any breakfast or lunch today, so I think I was drained of energy. I felt good this morning, but I would have eaten by then. I found some applesauce and crackers in my closet. I try to keep little snacks in my closet on occasions that I don't have food to eat. Anyway, I took a little nap. Ms. Brown had already left to get the kids. We took the kids out to the playground. It wasn't until we lined the children up that I saw that Dimani came to school. It was after eleven o'clock. They should have just kept her home. Now I have six. Ms. Kaylor asked me, could I keep Shean shortly after lunch? I thank God he doesn't give me any problems. He comes in and does the work. I think that the pace in which I moved was slow enough for him. I didn't have the children work in their workbooks. Instead, we worked on our sounds and letters book. We practiced for the closing ceremony.

We had a quick meeting after school with Mr. Shiller. We have to turn in paperwork tomorrow that was due today or last week. More paperwork wasted. I think that taxpayers would be highly upset if they see the amount of unnecessary paperwork we have to do. We have to do these checklists for each student three times a year. First, we have to bubble the hard copy and then enter the information on the computer. We do double work for nothing, and then we're wasting triplicate paperwork.

Day 160
Tuesday, May 15

Theo was at my door before I got there. He had a note from his mother explaining that his little brother, Yuan, wasn't going to be in school today because his asthma was acting up. I'm going to tell her, if his asthma ever got worse, where he has to stay for days, then here is a program called Blue Chip, which will assign him a tutor that comes to get his work and takes it back home to him and helps him with the skills. Quamainie never came back to school. At lunch, when I went to check my mailbox, Ms. Landing said that the other school called again for him today. I told Mrs. Hopkins,

302

the attendance monitor, and she said that the mother called and said that both her children didn't come to school today because they had a slight temperature. I said okay, but what does that have to do with the last three weeks? I just don't even try to understand anymore. While I was up there talking to her about Quamainie, Mrs. Hopkins told me that Dimani's parent would have to go to court because she has missed fifty-four days. I know that in some of those days, she came in late and didn't check in at the office. If the child is late, they are supposed to check in the office and get a late pass or make sure that they are acknowledged as being late so someone can change the absent symbol to a late symbol.

Reshae came to school today. She voluntarily said that she didn't come to school yesterday because she had to go to a cookout at her cousin's house. Nerimiah came to school today and started whining and complaining as soon as he got there. I told him that I didn't want to hear it. His mother came into the classroom to pay the remaining balance for the Six Flags trip. She would have told me of one of his many ailments that he has from week to week. He got into trouble at lunchtime for punching and hitting Nyaa in the cafeteria. Then he got into more trouble for lying about it. And then to make matters worse, he kept talking back to all of us. So he didn't get to play at all outside today. I filled out my paperwork for Mr. Shiller. It took only five minutes. Shean came to my class again today, but this time, he didn't make it for the rest of the day. He didn't want to do the reading work, just circling words that end with –an, and he started talking like a baby, moving the chair around the room, calling out. So I told him that his break with me was over and he could go back to Ms. Kaylor's class, but when I went to hold his hand, he started having a tantrum and falling out on the floor. I let his hand go and went across the hall to Ms. Brown so she could watch my class while I went to get Mr. Shiller. I walked myself all the way to the front office and knocked on Mr. Shiller's door. This little boy had no business coming back to school with such severe problems.

Little three-year-olds were playing on the school's playground on the top of the hill. I saw them as I was walking back to my class from taking the children to lunch. I noticed them because they were about eight tiny, little toddlers playing with a huge branch that had fallen off the nearby tree. The branch was as long as the four of them. I was scared that one of them was going to get hurt. They just kept trying to lift the branch. Then I noticed that I didn't see any adults with them. So I immediately backed up and went out into the breezeway. I couldn't get to the children because the gate was chained. So I just talked to them through the gate and told them to put the branch down before they got hurt. I asked them where their teacher was, but they didn't know what I was talking about. I scanned the rest of the field, and then I saw a lady, about one hundred and fifty feet from where we were, on top of the hill. I couldn't see that there were four more because the playground was obstructing the view. I only saw the lady because I'm tall. So I stepped to the left to see that there were four women, all the way at the end of the field by the fence, sitting underneath the tree with even more toddlers. I was pissed, excuse my French. These children were totally unsupervised while they were yapping their mouths away. We eventually went out to the playground and they were still out there. We thought that they would have left since they saw all of coming out to play. The ladies didn't have any activities for the children to play with. Our students were playing with the toddlers, lifting them and everything. We told them to stop because we didn't want to hear anyone's mouth if one of the toddlers got hurt.

Arcus Handal was acting a fool again in Ms. Gelette's fifth-grade class. She's a sweet, patient lady because he's one of the children that calms down and responds only to the school police. We have an epidemic of not having enough strong men in the school system. Children respond differently to men when they have nothing but women all around them at home and at school. That's another whole book in and of itself. She said her pressure is all up. He's ramping and raging in the hallway. Hitting children for no reason at all.

The children practiced and did a great job. During practice, Mrs. Hopkins walked all the way down to tell me that I had to write a letter for her to take to district court about Dimani's lateness and tardiness. Nerimiah's mother looked really pissed off while rereading his progress report. I put in there that he should not go to first grade, and that I felt that he needed to be retained. I don't care if he gets tutoring every day in the summer. It is not going to prepare him to be ready for first grade. She didn't even come out of the exit door where I was standing. I just knew that she was going to come say something to me. But she didn't; she just used another exit.

Day 161
Wednesday, May 16

Yuan came back to school today. I gave all the students a bright pink sticker that reminds them that picture day is tomorrow. One of my parents called from the hospital to make sure her son had turned in his homework. Now that's what I'm talking about. I'm going to declare today as Thank You for Doing Your Best as a Parent Day. Thank you all for those of you who send your child to school on time. Thank you for answering your phone when we call. Thank you for sending your child to school with their uniform on. Thank you for sending your child to school dressed as a child and not like a prostitute or pimp. Thank you for making your child do all of his homework. Thank you for listening to your child when she tries to talk to you. Thank you for not sitting on the couch all day watching television. Thank you, parents, for looking into a job or a class while your child is in school.

Thank you, Grandmom and Grandpop, for brining your grandchildren to school. Thank you, big brother, for the supplies you send to school. Thank you, big sister, for coming into the classroom and helping me file papers. Thank you, Uncle, for making copies for me at your job. Thank you, Father, for helping with our project at school. Thank you, guardian, for asking how I was doing today. Thank you, Aunt, for asking me how your child is progressing or not progressing. Thank you for asking me what you can do to help your child. Thank you for washing off the tables in the cafeteria. Thank you for chaperoning field trips. Thank you for walking the halls, ensuring the safety of our school. Thank you for talking the drug dealers into staying away from our school. Thank you for all that you do. It means the world to me, and it truly makes a difference in the life of your child. Thank you!

Day 162
Thursday, May 17

About five minutes after I got into my classroom, a picture lady came in and asked if I was in charge of the pictures today. I said, "No, Mrs. Scott is in charge of pictures." And she said, "Well, she's the one that sent me to you." That meant that I was delegated the responsibility to make sure that all six kindergarten classes and the two pre-k classes got their pictures taken.

By the middle of the day, it was brought to my attention by the parent who sits on the red couch every day that his son didn't get his picture taken. I had to apologize to my coworker because Ms. Abrams's special-education class wasn't included. It wasn't on purpose, but I didn't know that I was supposed to be responsible for making sure nine different classes got the information they need last week. I did hang up the posters last week as soon as I got them so anyone who was in the portable knew that picture day was today, and any one teacher or parent could have asked anyone in the portables about cap and gown pictures. Poor Lemonte didn't come to school today. Skamira's mom stayed up there almost all day long. Most of the people going on the end-of-year field trip didn't pay their balance. Picture day lasted almost the whole day. Pre-K was done right before lunch. I had to run out on my lunch break to see if I could find some more bright streamers since I couldn't find the colors that I wanted for our jellyfish. I found some colors but still didn't get to make them because of picture day. Ms. Johnston said she saw two little pre-K children grinding each other under the tree outside. Shean acted a complete mess this afternoon. Ms. Fields and Ms. Kaylor both had to take him up to the office. He carried on in a terrible fit so bad that he needed to teachers to handle him. Ms. Meiskolf had to leave early today, so she split her class. I got two of her students. We made whales today out of brown paper lunch bags, a blue crayon, wiggle eyes, and black construction paper. Their whales are so adorable. I'm going to hang them up tomorrow while they are out.

Professional Development
Friday, May 18

We had professional development today, so the students were out. We had a meeting about the cumulative folders again. Apparently, many principals are going to get fired or demoted if their school's records aren't up to par. So we have gone over our folders time and time again. We had letters that we had to give to parents to try to get the needed documentation, but to no avail. Not one of my seven children turned in any of their needed documents. We have sent home notices to parents several times asking for information. We can't make the parents bring the documentation in. Here we go again—the school takes the burden of parents' responsibilities. Something has to change immediately. I pray for the day where couples have to get a license to have children. They can lose social service benefits, tax breaks, or something for not taking parenting classes. It's bad enough that we have the government in everything as it is now. But something has got to give. Our school's staff always have to come up with incentives for the parents to do this and the students to do that. Why not just send in the required paperwork you need to send in when we ask or it?

We ordered the novelties, caps, sashes, and other items for the closing ceremony today. That wasn't so challenging since all we had to do was add up the number of students whose parents paid their class dues.

Day 163
Monday, May 21

I received a copy of a newspaper article in my mailbox, talking about how teachers need a pay increase because the cost of everything such as gas, food, and taxes have gone up except our pay. This is the time of the year when teachers start making plans and preparations for summer work. Some openings are announced in April for teachers to submit applications and resumes. But there is no guarantee that a teacher will get a position, especially in a public school. In most elementary schools, summer school is not mandatory. So summer-school enrollment is low. If children don't enroll, then teachers have no jobs for the summer. I know some teachers don't even receive at least one summer-school application back. How can you turn up free instruction? Especially in the summertime. It is difficult for me to find reasonable summer camps. I wish I could put all three of my girls in camp for free, and they would be having fun as well as receiving daily instruction. I don't know what is wrong with parents these days. No one wants to be inconvenienced, but it is definitely all right for them to inconvenience others.

The teachers around the school are so excited. Every day, we all are counting down the days until the last day of school. Children all across the system began to be a little more challenging to deal with. A lot of them get that "I can do whatever I want to 'cause I'm not coming back to this class/school next year" mentality. I don't think that they understand that they can still get into serious trouble even at the end of the year. They seem to think that nothing can be done to them because the school year is almost over. They just get wilder and wilder as the end of the year approaches. We all get anxious about some children just taking it to another whole level. Some can make the last twenty days seem like one hundred.

America would be bankrupt if teachers got paid overtime.

Day 164
Tuesday, May 22

I tried making it at work all day today, but my body was aching all over. I was able to get into work and get the students started. Eventually, I had to call up the office and tell them I couldn't make it the whole day. When the substitute came in, I went home and left until my girls were dropped off by my girlfriend. I don't know what in the world happen to me. I tell you it's this building and the mice feces and other germs in the air!

Day 165
Wednesday, May 23

I came to work today even though I wasn't supposed to. Faith had a field trip today, and I didn't want to disappoint her. I toughed it out and stayed even while I was absolutely miserable.

Day 166
Thursday, May 24

Ms. Fields brought me a student's homework paper with a shocking note on it. It basically said that she is tired of the homework that the child is getting because it's her job to teach her son about schoolwork, and it's her job to teach him about street life. And I could end the book on that note. The ignorance of our American people is what is making America what it is today. It is the parents job to always be a parent. If it's not the parent or guardian's job to ensure that homework gets done, then who does the job belong to.

I do feel just a little better. I don't know if was a little virus or not.

Day 167
Friday, May 25

I feel so much better today. I'm weak, but I feel way better than I did earlier this week.

Saturday. I stayed in the house today. I had to walk the appraiser around my house. I didn't like how he was looking at everything. He was supposed to appraise it for how much it's worth now. Not how much could it be worth if I fix it all up? There is a big difference. I felt like he was just trying to set me up. I didn't care what anybody said, I felt this whole divorce thing is a conspiracy. I didn't want anything but my freedom and my girls. Once again, I was in a bad mood and didn't want to do anything, especially not any schoolwork.

Sunday. I went to Philly with my sister, Faith, and Trinity. I had fun being out of the house. I get tired of doing the same old thing in and out every single day. I'm waiting for the day when I have the finances to hire some help once or twice a week. I'm waiting for the day when I can take real vacations whenever I feel like it. I need to start working on fourth-quarter grades, but I just didn't feel like it.

Monday, May 28
Memorial Day

I worked outside in the shed and yards all day long. I had so much negative energy and feelings that I needed to work off. I called my sister earlier today and asked her if she would bring my two nephews over so they could help me in the yard. They're only eight and nine and wimped out after the first fifteen minutes after they started working. After Tate and Gregory got their very long break, they helped me stuff twenty bags with vines, weeds, and dirt. Afterward, we all went back to my pop's house and had some cookout food.

Day 168
Tuesday, May 29

Today was a pretty relaxed day as far as instruction. Everyone was still in sleepy mode after the long weekend. Everyone wanted to lay their heads down on the desks. All morning long, it was quiet, but the children weren't lively enough to even want to engage in learning. I understand. All of the staff looked as if they were ready to go back to bed. Everyone pretty much enjoyed their weekend but still wasn't quite off their relaxing schedule for the last three days.

For reading this morning, the children colored different sea animals for their book that they are going to make. The children liked this unit too because they see animals that aren't part of their everyday life. The last

311

chapter in math is counting to one hundred in different ways. This is more of a review since all the kindergarten teachers have been teaching the children to count to one hundred since the first day of school anyway. All day was pretty much a review for them. I didn't want to work them in full force right off the break. They needed to get their little brains active again.

After school, I was able to pack six clear plastic containers. I went back to Walmart to purchase eight more. I wanted to take all my good stuff home so they don't get stolen—I mean, misplaced—over the summer. I took the materials that someone would steal such as construction paper, writing paper, and glue. Materials are precious commodities around here. I still have a huge amount to pack. I'm definitely trying to leave on the last day and not have to come back.

Day 169
Wednesday, May 30

Today is a good day. The spiritual vitamin this morning was to "trust the process." I made a conscious decision to trust the process that I'm going through right now. I just got to go with the flow of things. I'm on a roller coaster that I can't get off. I have this terrible habit of worrying. I need to work on just being calm in the midst of storms and rocky roads.

Eternity's mother put pink eye shadow on her today. I knew the child didn't put it on because it would have looked a hot mess. I don't understand how in her mind she doesn't see how a child wearing makeup is totally inappropriate for a five-year-old. I don't think any young lady under the age of eighteen should have makeup on unless it's for a prom, pageant, or some special occasion. Even then, it shouldn't be that obvious as if it was painted on with a paintbrush. And definitely no child in middle school or elementary school should be wearing any eye shadow, lipstick, or anything else. A little lip gloss, Vaseline, or Chapstick for dry lips will do.

At recess time, five of us were talking about the different jobs we could get this summer. The job suggestions ranged from working at strip clubs to hacking. It was an interesting, hilarious, and enlightening conversation. I couldn't work at a strip club if I wanted to. My knees are too bad to do anything other than walking and working out a little in the gym. Mr. Raswell was the substitute for Ms. Dons, who is subbing for Ms. Kin until this Friday. Anyway, he said he used to hack as a side job to supplement his pay. He was telling us about all the good places to pick up people who need a ride. He also gave us plenty of hacking tips about what to look out for. When we came back in, Ms. Brown gave out the popsicles that she brought for them on her lunch break. I guess she got them while she was buying containers to pack her stuff in. It's supposed to be in the nineties this week. I'm sure going to miss the air conditioner next year if I'm going back into the main building.

Day 170
Thursday, May 31

All hell almost broke loose in here today. The problem of the day was that the high and mighty at North Avenue said that we can't go on our end-of-year field trip next week. All of us went into a panic today. All we had to do was think about telling the parents about the trip being cancelled, and we were frantic after that. A lot of parents and family members rearranged their work schedules to go on this trip. Apparently, someone was injured at an amusement park because of their own carelessness, and the remaining schools going to an amusement park for a trip cannot go. We all went to Mrs. Green, the superwoman of fix-it-all at our school. She is very fair and compassionate and always listens

313

to our concerns and issues. Sometimes more overboard than others, but she is there for us all. Well, that's my opinion from what I've observed and experienced. Anyway, we knew she could make some phone calls. We were praying hard that she could make some successful phone calls. The greatest argument that we had was that we collected the money and sent the money for tickets already. We weren't going to get the money back. And we paid a deposit for the buses as well. We also required that each child be chaperoned by their own parent or adult family member. None of us was going to be responsible for keeping any student with us. I think that that was what was able to convince the bigwigs to change their minds. I understand safety and all, but I don't think the rest of the population should be punished because of one person's actions. Today was a very high-stress day. It was nerve-racking.

Day 171
Friday, June 1

We had a half day today. It was a pretty easy day. Ms. Brown was off today, so Mr. Braswell was subbing for her class. He and I combined classes because there wasn't much for them to do anyway. I found out that I was teaching summer school today. I was surprised because I didn't apply. At least I don't remember filling out an application. I have to fill out so much paperwork in a school year anyway. I couldn't tell you what in the world I completed off the top of my head. But I said, "Thank you, Lord!" and called it a day. That also meant that Ms. Brown wouldn't be working because there would be only one kindergarten teacher working for this summer. I felt so bad about Ms. Brown because I know that she depends on working summer school every year. I've always needed money in the summer; it's just a waste of time to have to pay for babysitting because that would just about cancel any pay that I get. This year I

314

have to do what I have to do. Maybe I can work out a deal with Trianne since Trinity wouldn't be there all day. Mr. Shiller also told me that he wants me to teach second grade next year. I told him that I didn't want to and that I wanted to stay in kindergarten. I really don't need any more extra and unnecessary transitions right now in my life. If Mr. Shiller only knew just a tenth of all the hell I'm going through right now, he wouldn't even consider me. My heart wouldn't even be in it 100 percent as it should be. He told me that he would make me team leader and give me the top class. He's told me that so many times before I don't believe him. I don't want to be team leader either. That's just more responsibility and headaches with the same pay. Too many get caught up in titles, but not me. Now if he says that I would get a couple of dollars more, a stipend or something, then that would get my attention.

Day 172
Monday, June 4

What a day!

Today Mr. Shiller told me that he was putting me back in third grade. I felt like saying, "The hell you are! You go back and teach third grade." I'm trying to figure out how in the hell do I go from third grade to kindergarten, then back to third grade. Those are significant jumps. I was already upset of the second-grade move because of all the money, time, energy, and effort I put into kindergarten materials I've invested in over the last two years. But to send me back to the third grade is just worse. He should have just left me in the third grade. I've taught three different grades so far, and every single time, I'm told that I'm the so-called chosen one because I can handle it. Well, maybe I don't want to handle it. Maybe I don't feel like handling it right now. Then I have to listen to that inner voice that says, *The Lord won't put more on me than I can bare.* Yeah, okay. I think that it is just unfair that I keep being asked to move to different grades. Some teachers may move once in a couple of years. But twice in two years. That's insanity! Then people wonder why there is such a high turnover rate for teachers. I think I will put in for a transfer. It's definitely time for me to do something else. I just don't see retiring in a system that has so much going on that just continues to bring teachers down instead of build us up.

Day 173
Tuesday, June 5

The crisis today is that we don't have enough caps, tassels, and sashes for the students on Thursday. Parents would be having a fit if they paid for their child to get something and they didn't receive it. We'll have to sit down and figure out how the count went wrong. The Six Flags tickets came in. Ms. Brown and I stayed after school to separate and write all the names on the tickets. We wanted to be ready and organized when parents started to pick up their tickets. Even though parents know that they are responsible once they get them in their hand, we know there is going to be at least one parent who does something wrong.

Day 174
Wednesday, June 6

My kindergarten team and I decorated the gym after school. We practiced most of the day. Mr. Handler was kind enough to let us set up in the gym. He and some fifth-grade students set up all the chairs for tomorrow. I'm glad it was nice outside because he was able to take his remaining classes outside for instruction. Otherwise, people would have been mad for being inconvenienced because of our

316

ceremonies. No one likes it when a resource is cancelled. It's busy and hectic.

About twenty minutes after school was dismissed, the fire bell went off. I was thinking that there must still be some students left in the school playing, so I just continued with my paperwork. A few minutes after the alarm rang, I began to smell smoke. I thought it was my mind playing tricks on me, so I continued filling out my paperwork. It turned out that there really was a fire. Some kids who had nothing else to do set some leaves on fire next to the building near one of the entry ways. I tell you in all these years there has never been a real fire here at the school, so nobody paid any attention to the alarm. It was the smell of smoke in the building that starting convincing to move out of the building.

Day 175
Thursday, June 7

It was a wonderful, successful day. The day was almost perfect. The gym was packed with parents, families, and friends. There were too many people for the size of the gym. Outside of about twenty parents and families who wouldn't sit down so other people could see, it was a nice program. I was surprised that all the students left afterward. Usually, there are several pre-K and kindergarten students left after the ceremony. There isn't any rule that says that they have to stay or go. Most families go out somewhere to celebrate their little one's first year of success. Someone stole two of my children's graduation bears out of my box. I would just have to go out and purchase two more bears on my own. The parents just don't want to wait after the ceremony to get their child's paperwork and goodies. It took the rest of the afternoon to clean the gym. The fifth-grade boys put all the chairs away. I had brought a change of clothes so I could clean up.

317

Day 176
Friday, June 8

Six Flags; what a day. Overall, it was a good day after we got the parents and families out of our way. Parents brought coolers, and we told them they couldn't bring them in the first place. People got on the buses, who said that they were driving. We had to make them get off the bus. And before we could leave the parking lot at eight o'clock in the morning, they were already throwing trash out of the windows and onto the school grounds. So I and my mouth kindly went onto the second bus and asked them to remember that we are on a school trip and that all of us are representing the school regardless of whether they are students or staff. My speech of encouragement was a little longer, but it was basically saying, please don't be ignorant and embarrass yourself and our school.

Once we arrived at the park and gain entrance, a parent cam right over and said that they lost their meal tickets for lunch. We told the parents and families that we were not responsible for anything once the signed for their tickets. I told him that there wasn't anything that we could do. I just told him to meet us over at the pavilion at one o clock and maybe we could tell the people that he and his family was with us. We all went on our way. he was able to eat lunch without a problem.

Saturday. I rested and napped all day long! Today was the Spring Fling but I didn't make it this year because I was still tired from Thursday and Friday.

Sunday. I went to church and rested all day long.

Day 177
Monday, June 11

I was at work only for a half hour today. I heard that no other kindergarten students came, except about five. I didn't have any students that came in today. I was at the doctor's with Faith earlier. I came to school for the parent appreciation lunch and then went to court. To make a very long story short, I didn't really care for the outcome. One of the devil's imps was awarded $30,000, minus $3,500 for half of what he paid in closing costs. I cried and cried and cried. It doesn't seem fair at all. Sometimes it seems as if the enemy always wins. But when I look at the bright side and put one aspect into perspective and say that I have full custody of my girls, then that is the greatest outcome for me. I know my girls won't have candy at ten o'clock in the morning when they are with me. I know that they will have constructive, wholesome, and productive days. I can try my damnedest to raise them to be intelligent young ladies of God. I can see them every morning when we wake up. I can watch them grow. I'm just happy the marriage is over. Dealing with him in any kind of way isn't over because that's just the way things are with him. We will still have to communicate about something. This chapter is over. Even though it doesn't seem as if the decision is fair, we kind of cancel each other as far as marital property. I have a nice amount of child support for the girls, so I'm cool. He might get his lump sum in 180 days, but I'll get half of his pension money in a couple of years. I don't even want it. I still don't say this is the end of it. God never fails!

Day 178
Tuesday, June 12

There were no students for me today. I was cleaning and packing all day in my room. Our school is going to be a K-8 school, so I have to pack all of my stuff anyway. I'm very pissed off about changing grades, but there's really nothing I can do about it right now. I could quit, put in a transfer, go to another county, or fill out for another position. That wouldn't do any good for the beginning of next year, though. I had so much stuff and junk to pack. Today I took a load of stuff home to put in my shed. I already have enough junk packed in my basement and shed to have a whole classroom at home. Ms. Kin had three students, and Ms. Fields had one. The rest of the K teachers didn't have any students either. I heard that only about six pre-K children came all together.

Day 179
Wednesday, June 13

No kids for me today. I cleaned my room and completed my cumulative folders. I put in their report cards, progress reports, and readiness checklist and wrote in all the necessary information on the folder and other documents. Today I took all my plants home. One of them won't be back next year because it is too big and too heavy now. It's that plant that looks as if it has elephant ears at the top of tall thick green stems. I have my two spider plants that I have had from nine years ago when they were still babies. I have three hanging baskets of those vines. I don't know what the technical terms are for these things. I just have a lot of plants. I keep them in my room to liven things up a bit. Once I got those plants in my truck, I didn't have room for anything else.

Day 180
Thursday, June 14

I truly thank God it's Thursday. Today is our last day of school! Did you read it right? It's our last day of school. I made it to another year. No students today so I continued to clean my room. I cleaned and packed, cleaned and packed. That's all I did today. Since the things that stay here are going to be put in the gym with everyone else's things, I went to the Home Depot and bought some red duct tape to put around all my boxes and to put on all of my classroom furniture. I wrote my name on every single piece too. After I packed a box, I put red tape on it; then I set it in one of the two stacks in the middle of the floor. One stack of the boxes was to be taken home, and the other was to stay in the room until the movers come. We are supposed to have them moved into one section of the room. We usually have to move our own things to our next room. I think that there were so many teachers moving to different grades and different rooms; we were told we would have movers. I'm almost finished. I just want to walk out of here today and go home to start my weekend. Magic Man came to take a load of boxes to my house in his pickup truck. That was great help. I was surprised he actually showed up, but thankful.

My students' cumulative folders are done. Their final report cards are in their folder, along with all the pertinent information needed for their teacher next year. My classroom is clean. I didn't go through the entire check-out process either. We have a bright golden-colored paper with about fifteen different things we are supposed to have checked out by different people. It sounds easy, but it isn't. Usually, the people we need to check our rooms and the different things we need are either unavailable, or they are checking someone else's room. I just turned in my room key and left my self-addressed stamped envelope for my last paycheck. Usually, we have to turn in our roll book and get that signed off. Then someone has to come in to check if we have all of our reading stuff turned in. Then we have to turn in all our math materials to the support teacher in charge of math. I didn't have a math kit this year, so that didn't even apply to me. I did the important stuff and left. I'm finished for the year!

Well, as we all say on the last day of school, "Have a great summer!"

Part II
My Proposals: The Calicchia Legislations

All of the following proposals are what they're called, proposals. I didn't want to take up the remainder of the book with my thoughts and ideas in full detail for each one. So I just gave a little synopsis of each one to give an idea of what I would like to be laws or laws that need to be refined. However, anyone, any official, government agency, celebrity, superstar, colleague, the person next door, Mr. President, athlete, or anyone else who would like to help me, please feel free to contact me. I'm quite sure I can be Googled.

1. I believe that every expectant parent should take prenatal classes. I'm not talking about your regular prenatal visits with your doctor. I'm talking about prenatal classes with teachers, dieticians, social workers, and so on. They need to get an overall understanding of how difficult it is to raise a child. Usually information for parents is one sided and doesn't come from many different point of views. Being a parent is the most important job in the world that we don't get training for. It is rewarding, but a parent doesn't get to choose when those moments are or how frequent. I know because I have three. I feel as if I got a degree for each one of my children, and it's still a challenge. I wouldn't change it for the world, but parenting is an ongoing and evolving process. You can't raise your kids exactly the same way you were raised. Sometimes you can hold on to some of the good old-fashioned ways, but you also have to be able to evolve in order to keep up with what the children are currently experiencing.

2. If you were abused or neglected, the way you treat your child is also determined by what went on in your own

childhood. You don't want to pass on your problems, fears, and negative emotions because of what you experienced. Even before someone makes a decision to have children, they may need to be assessed to determine if they need counseling.

3. After the children are born, then for some high-risk parents, there needs to be better monitoring and more accountability. There are too many grown children. I'm talking thirty-year-olds that are still making bad choices, and their choices are affecting their children's lives. Too many grandparents are enabling their own children instead of telling their child to get off their tail and get themselves together. It's not always drugs and alcohol abuse. A lot of times, a parent is off track because of laziness or poor decision making. They make all these bad choices, and their family members are the ones that keep bailing them out. The grandparents, aunts, uncles, sisters, brothers, and the rest of the family are all taking care of the minor children instead of their own parents.

4. I propose three levels of parental monitoring or, shall I say support. I really don't have it all worked out but I do have the basic frame established. The lowest level would be the low-risk category. A parent would be classified as a low-risk parent if they don't have any obvious negative indicators that would suggest that they would have a more-than-usual time raising their child. These are parents who don't appear that they would possibly neglect or abuse their child. And I say low risk because we've all heard of picture-perfect families, and the mother or father just snapped and killed their children and family, and even themselves. For example, a parent who is stable, meaning they have a steady job or career and safe place to live, they've graduated from high school and maybe have had some higher education, or

even a degree, and they are at least twenty-five years old and have taken prenatal classes.

The next level would be moderate risk. This level would be for parents who have at less positive indicators. So parents who have a home but don't have the income and education to support a child

The high-risk level would be those parents who have many negative indicators at one time. They may have an addiction; are poor, young, and immature; have no income, are living with someone else or in an unstable, volatile environment, etc.

5. The more problems that complicate a child's life means that there should be more support given to help the family. This way, there would be some kind of system in place to make sure that all parents get basic information, and then depending on what level you are on, that would determine the amount of support and information that needs to be given to the parent on a regular basis.

6. I would like to see a mandate of parents and guardians taking ninety-hour courses for childhood education. It is difficult being a parent, and it becomes even more difficult as different scenarios and events further complicate the parenting role. There should be some clear-cut guidelines, and parents should know what they can and cannot do as far as the law is concerned. Make parents have their children in by a decent hour or get fined.

7. I would like to see stiffer parental convictions on parents who introduce their children to any and all sexual acts, drugs, violence, partying, and any other criminal offenses. Parents can serve their time working in schools instead of in prison, unless they are violent or are pedophiles themselves. Parents can patrol the community when their child violates curfew. Parents can take AA and NA meetings

when they introduce their child to drugs and alcohol after they serve their given time from the judge or jury.

8. One percent education tax. The way I figure it is that every person should help with the schools by paying a one percent ax. I think that if everyone was to pay one percent to a national education fund, then that money could go towards fixing up each school in America. It could go towards many things that are needed in the school systems in America

9. All school board members, CEOs, and other nonteaching officials who want to make decisions and haven't been in the classroom in years, never will be, must teach in a title in one school for one week out of the year.

10. I believe that children starting in the fifth grade need to begin to have classroom instruction on sex and related issues. I've talked to a lot of teenagers who have said that no one has ever talked to them about anything. And I don't mean taking a one-hour class on a Saturday either. They need to know the physical, mental, emotional, social, and financial responsibilities of having sex and/or raising a child. There should be puberty classes, sex education, and financial education taught beginning in elementary school.

Part III
A Side Note from Teachers

I have been approach by many colleagues to included just a small insight on the unreported rising cases of violence against teachers and school staff.

This was written on behalf of many colleagues. In order to protect all of those who approached me, I just chose to write in first person.

Apparently, several teachers were allegedly beaten up in their classroom. Now that there is media attention on it around the nation, maybe people will understand what we are up against in the schools. No, it's not every day that teachers are beaten up. But every day, teachers and school staff are hit, assaulted, verbally abused, and definitely disrespected. Every day in a school somewhere, a teacher or staff member is breaking up a fight and getting injured that way. We can't say two words to a child without having a war break out in the classroom. We treat the children with respect, but we don't receive it in return. It's as if they want us to treat them how they are treated at home to get any respect from them. But as soon as we cuss them out or hit them, then our jobs are on the line. I don't understand why we have to continue to be stuck in this bureaucratic crap. It seems as if a lot of parents are talking about how bad public schools are, and those are the very same ones whose children are acting like a jackass every day, interrupting the learning of others. If a student is repeatedly aggressive, verbally abusive, or spreads damaging rumors, then there should be immediate disciplinary action taking place. If there are certain protocols and procedures in place that are not working, then the system should immediately find new ones that work. I am getting sick and tired of the child with the repeat behavior coming back to the classroom the next day without the parent even coming up here for a conference. I'm sick of it. And when the sorry-excuse–making parent comes up here to give some more sorry and lame excuses as to why their child has no respect and home training, I have to sit down and listen to their bull crap with all professionalism. It appears to be the child's word against ours in the sight of the parents. And a lot of parents and families know their child is causing all kinds of problems but don't want us to deal with it. They just want to fuss at the child, take them home, and let them go outside and play. I heard a parent say that right after she talked to her child's teacher and promised she was going take privileges away from the child, she didn't do it. She said, out of her own mouth, that she had no intention of doing anything. She said she was saying it so the teacher would feel better. There are no real consequences that these children suffer that will affect them. Until the parents and guardians get their crap together within their homes, then it's just going to continue to get worse. There are a lot of children that display behaviors that resemble the behaviors we see out in the communities. And if the parents don't get their children under control while they are young, then we will continue to see an increase in violence and shootings and gangs and so on. I just want to pack my stuff and go home. I'm sick of this crap. We have to be professional, we have to be levelheaded, we have to do the right thing, we have to have class and respect, we have to not talk in the hallway. No, I don't want anyone talking about my child's personal home information, but if the whole school knows the child is bad as hell, then talking about the child in closed doors about them hitting others and yelling and having a tantrum isn't going to change anything. That's another thing too. We have to hold our anger and frustration in. We can't just walk up to an administrator and just start expressing ourselves. I want the person to feel what I'm feeling about the situation. If I have to wait and calm down, then the offense of the child is not as vivid as when it just happened, it's as if, "what's the point?" We don't have an outlet other than going back to our room and crying or looking really stupid for even bothering to take the child up to the office. The principal's hands are tied with too many other children even more offensive and aggressive. Maybe if some people felt a little shame, guilt, remorse, and embarrassment, then maybe that would be a motivator to seek help and/or do the right thing. If a child hits another student or a teacher, it appears to be no big deal. Why does it take a teacher or student being assaulted on the Internet to cause outrage and disgust of behavior? We are expected to follow everything by the book while some of these children get off scot-free.

Part IV
Follow-up After 2099 Publishing
One-Two Years Later

The summer after I completed the book. I went on my first cruise. It was okay. My company was sick, so it wasn't as much fun as it could have been.

When school started, I was given a second grade class. I had two boys who had behavior from hell. One hit me, and the other had some social and emotional issues I wasn't professionally trained for. I called the school police and pressed charges but there wasn't anyone to follow through with it so nothing happened to the one who assaulted me. The remainder of the boys argued and fussed every day. The girls were good but lazy and had no stamina to work. Out of sixteen students, ten of them were repeating the second grade. (The mom of a student in this very class is the reason why I changed the title of this book once to, *I Want to Teach Not Raise Your Kids*). The first year after completing the book, I moved four classrooms down the hall. Did I still have an air conditioner in my room? Yes, however I had to empty two buckets of water every day that it was on, but I had air.

The school system restructured the entire building again, so people had to move all over the place. Following that restructuring in the second year, I am now teaching kindergarten again back in the main building. I'm in the original room that I started in eight years ago when I was teaching third grade. I have twenty four children and a wonderful assistant. The dynamics are still basically the same. I have little heat and no air conditioner.

I still hear from Ms. Laquetta and Kevmani throughout the year. He's doing great and she had another baby boy. They are still living down south.

There are only five students of that original class that are still here at the school. They are Dimani, Lemonte, Re'shae, Quamainie, Chalon. All but one, Quamainie, is in the first grade. He had to repeat Kindergarten because he did not come to school until the end of the year.

As far as my personal life, it is still challenging being a single parent. I'm kind of terrified of being in a relationship again. I just don't have the patience, time, energy, money nor effort to invest in someone who refuses to make a life commitment to me. It's a very scary thing to meet a good man but who still doesn't have his stuff together.

I love my girls, no matter what. They are still the most beautiful girls in the world to me. Whitney is in high school and doing alright at this time, Faith is in the first grade doing excellent, and Trinity is still adorable but feisty, and I tried to get her into preschool. They wouldn't let her in though because her birthday is after September 30. She'll be in preschool next year.

Magic Man and I tried being more than friends. He said that it wouldn't work out for him. I got the old "it's not you it's me" line. Oh well, his loss!

My sister had a another beautiful baby boy who has such a sweet disposition.

I'm still in the middle of retraining my eating habits and getting my weight under control. My knees are still jacked up. Today as I was teaching, one of the students called out, "Eew! Your arm is wriggly!" He was talking about the fat under my triceps that was hanging down. The kids have no manners at all.

I found the loved one I was looking for in April of 2008. I met him July and I haven't since returned. I just wanted him to know that I forgave him and that was it. I really have no desire to have relationship with him. I am at peace about that situation.

Herbert had to do another tour overseas. Temporarily, he's back and a good dad to the girls. He eventually became much nicer to me since the divorce. I wonder if its because I remember he had an entire different account I forgot about. Some turn of events happened, and I didn't have to sell my house like he wanted or pay him anything. I didn't want anything from him but to be free from the verbal and mental abuse. Maybe one day we can be cordual again, but I seriously know in my heart I can't and don't want to be friends if he doesn't change his selfish and narcissistic ways

I still go to the most powerful church on the planet with the best pastor, choir and church family and Minister of Music.

Barack Obama was elected the first Black president of the United States.

Five Years Later

I don't know where any of the children are that I wrote about in my book. Once the students or teachers leave the school community, it's not that often you hear back from the children. Once in a blue moon you will be blessed to run into a student you taught many years ago and the remember you. I remember them though. I have all my years of class photos and most rosters to match the faces.

My daughters are awesome and becoming fine young ladies. They are all smart and have their own talents. Life as a mom hasn't been perfect, and they give me a run for money, but I couldn't ask for more loving and compassionate daughters. Whitney will be graduating and out on her soon earning or learning. Whitney turned out to love music and singing. Niana is my middle child that keeps me praying the most. She's very athletic and plays all kinds of sports. Now my baby girl is unique because she doesn't like people, don't want to hang out with people and don't even talk to her teachers. She's smart and can do the work but she's and introvert and is just fine being to herself. She's my little scientist. She likes projects and she likes to dance.

I've traveled more, been on two cruises and I love them. I'm in a better space now with who I am and the women I have become. I'm at peace with all of the after-divorce escapades. People are who they are. The other party isn't even worth mentioning. He is who he is, and karma will pay him a visit one day.

Six Years Later

The most significant thing that happened is that we lost Pop to lung cancer November 30, 2015. ALL cancer sucks. Rest in Heaven Pop! I Love you!

Six-Ten Years Later

I still love my girls, no matter what. Obviously I'm biased, and they are still the most beautiful young ladies in the world to me. Whitney is in her mid-twenties now, working in the banking industry and is doing good at this time. Faith is in the 12 grade getting ready to graduate and go to college. Trinity is still adorable but still an introvert. She is now in high school as a 9th grader and still isn't a people person but loves dancing and working on all kinds of projects.

As my youngest two girls grew older, found their own voices and were able to respectively share their opinion as I taught them, it became a problem for someone I have no respect for, Herbert. As far as Herbert (now called the devil) is concerned, unfortunately, he's a negative factor in the girls life and even isn't worthy of being mentioned. Being a "great" dad only lasted a couple of months and then sporadically saw them as he saw fit over the last ten years and hasn't seen them in almost two because they voiced their concerns with his behavior.

As far as how my career has progressed, my first city schools' principal of all my years working at the school retired. So, from 2012-2014, my new principal pulled me out of the classroom and I worked as a mentor teacher on the administrative team. My first year out was emotional as I navigated how to work with the teachers, staff, parents, students and community members. That elementary school will always have a place in my heart because we were truly a school family! In 2015, that principal was promoted and moved on and in came the worst principal I ever had. I thought I was going to retire at this one school, but God had other plans. I applied for a next level position as an Educational Associate- Dean of Curriculum and Instruction, got the position and went to another great city school with awesome kids and school community. I'm currently still there and it will soon be my fifth year. I look forward to my next position as an official Assistant Principal and in about five years or so, a school Principal.

Today, April 13, 2020

My two teens have been home with me for the last four weeks. Schools are closed and millions of parents around the world abruptly had to homeschool their children. Around March of 2020 for most schools in America, were last to join the world in closing schools and introduce virtual learning. Most people, 80-90% depending what part of the world you are in, are home because businesses are closed due to the coronavirus, Covid-19. (On this day of this republishing manuscript, April 13, 2020, "Covid" does not exist in the editing portion of this app)

For the sequel to this book stay tuned. It will be out after this pandemic is over!

In the meantime, I want us all to appreciate every moment of life we have!

My condolences to all the families around the world who has lost a loved one or more to this Covid-19. My heart goes out to you and your family.

To all of you who have recovered and continue to recover, I wish you complete healing and recovery!

To all of those who haven't been sick or hasn't displayed any symptoms, please stay home for those who are on the front line, the weak and the most vulnerable!

I want us all to send many thanks, prayers and well wishes to the countless number of people who have lost their jobs or businesses, in a countess number of sectors and industries. To the restaurants, small business owners/employees, barber shops, hair salons, nail techs, sporting venue workers, temporary employees, mall employees and so many more, I'm praying for you!

"THANK YOU!", to those who continue to move our nation and world while the rest of us are staying at home being safe. To the heroes on the frontline during this world crisis THANK YOU! To the nurses, doctors, the housekeepers and custodians of the hospitals, community living workers, everyone that works in any health care related facility, truck drivers, groceries store clerks and stockers, sanitations workers, postal and delivery workers, the police on all levels, firefighters, EMTs, and so many countless others on the front line, "THANK YOU!"

Thank you and bless you to all of you have stayed home and taken quarantines seriously, created moments of laughter, joy and inspiration, cooked with your family, played games inside and outside, appreciated teachers and schools for the work that they were doing when school was in session.

Thank you and God bless you to everyone who has donated, time, money, food, shelter to the homeless and healthcare workers

Thank you and God bless you to all of the business who have stopped making their original products to make masks of all types, hand sanitizers for hospitals and health care workers, ventilators and anything else needed on the frontline

Thank you and God bless you to all the leaders of faith. I love Jesus and I still lift up all of those who leading their people in faith through on-line services, prayer calls, on line sessions, safe food distributions and raising money to help those under their leadership in need.

Thank you and God bless you to all of those in a leadership capacity, no matter the profession, who are leading with integrity in decency and in order doing right by those who need your guidance during this difficult time.

To all of those using social media for the better good to share encouragement, laughter, family fun and challenges, inspirations, free resources and apps, individual and unified concerts, music, virtual parties and happy hours,

To those who work in media forms, the news on tv, radio, newspapers, on line, etc who had integrity to share the truth.

Thank you and God bless you to all the companies that work with educators and made your products free to children, families, educators and school districts.

To all my colleagues all around the world that worked a school but who is now not just working at home. We are working at home and trying to maintain our sanity, learn technology forums and keep with your own children, families and pets during a pandemic. Thank you to those who have spent countless hours in google classrooms, meets, virtual/audio calls and collaborate to stay connected to children and their families. To the staff working at on the next steps, planning, curriculum, collaborating with other districts and community members to lead us with the least amount of chaos as possible. To everyone and anyone who has visited homes, delivered food to children and families, came out your comfort zones on cameras, made and passed out packets, raised money for schools and communities

To my own daughter Niana, ALL Classes of 2020, seniors in high school and colleges or those in trade schools, who have yet to know that feeling of walking across the stage of accomplishment, the best is yet to come. I know this has not been easy because I've been doing my best to help my senior and her emotions to navigate through this unprecedented time in history. Carry that accomplishment with you and walk tall and proud! Please know that your invested years, hard work and efforts of reaching this monumental moment in life is not in vain! You still have something so vital that cannot be taken away from you, your education. You set out to do what you wanted to do, and you did it! I salute and celebrate you!

To anyone who may feel I have forgotten you, you are not forgotten because I pray for everyone in this world to see better and brighter days on the other side of this pandemic. There have been so many countless heroes who have shown love, humor, memes, dance videos, positive challenges, positivity, virtual hugs, listening ears, shoulders to cry on, tissues to wipe tears, forgiveness of debts, compassion, courage, love, humility, so much more and hope!

Remember, every moment is a new moment to start over! So, keep spreading hope! We will get through this!

9 781647 491154